To: Holly

From: Mommie

(Christmas 1996)

"With Love"

The Value in the Valley

a Black Woman's Guide through Life's Dilemmas

Iyanla Vanzant

Simon & Schuster

New York
London
Toronto
Sydney
Tokyo
Singapore

SIMON & SCHUSTER
Rockefeller Center
1230 Avenue of the Americas
New York, NY 10020

SIMON & SCHUSTER and colophon are registered trademarks
of Simon & Schuster Inc.

Designed by Hyun Joo Kim

Manufactured in the United States of America

9   10

Library of Congress Cataloging-in-Publication Data
Vanzant, Iyanla.
Value in the valley : a black woman's guide through life's dilemmas
/Iyanla Vanzant.
p.   cm.
Includes bibliographical references.
1. Afro-American women—Life skills guides. 2. Afro-American
women—Psychology. 3. Self-esteem in women—United States.
I. Title.
E185.86.Z39   1995   95-6428
646.7'0082—dc20   CIP

ISBN 0-684-80287-2

This book is dedicated to all African-
American women who are imprisoned;
those behind bars as well as those
imprisoned by fear, hate, anger, shame,
guilt, oppressive domination and outdated
stereotypical roles and expectations.

To All the Valley Dwellers, let the motto be:
When you're down and out, lift up your head and shout,
I'M OUTA HERE!

Acknowledgments

My deepest thanks go to:

GEMMIA VANZANT, my daughter, whose incredible ability to stay grounded, centered, and supportive is the food which helps to nourish my spirit; and whose uncensored, constructive criticism keeps me in touch with reality;

NISA VANZANT, my final offspring, who keeps reminding me that I'm not special, wonderful, or marvelous, I'm just "Ma";

"YU," my other half, who never misses an opportunity to give me the opportunity to see what I *really* look like;

DAWN MARIE DANIELS, my editor, whose genuine love, support, and tolerance never ceases to amaze me;

DENISE STINSON, my agent, who pulled me out of a valley I had absolutely no business being in;

CARL COOPER, ESQ., my former law professor and present legal counsel, whose loving support and guidance keeps my foot out of my mouth and my butt out of the valley;

ERICA JACKSON, my assistant, a mountain climber par excellence;

"MAMA" MUSINAH BERRY DAWAD, who is always so willing to take care of the details, leaving me free to figure out some more details;

MICHELLE VENTOR, my sister-friend, who put the clothes on this naked idea;

MARGE BATTLE, for her strength, persistence and tenacity, which allows her to eat the mountain one bite at a time and teach me how to do it without getting indigestion;

MARIA CAROTHERS, TRISH WEIR, the AAWC staff and all of the sisters who attended the 1990 San Diego Conference and made this concept something worth writing about;

RALPH STEVENSON, my brother-friend, whose love has pulled me out of many ditches, valleys, and dungeons;

LINDA SMITH, TONY WALKER, ATTICUS WALKER, LUANNE BENNETT, SARAH DARLING, LIONEL the "Indian" and the rest of the staff at WINDY HILLS VILLA, JAMAICA, W.I., for providing me with a safe haven; and for waiting on me hand and foot while I was in the final stages of labor with this book;

BROTHER CHARLES "CHUMA" WHITE, for taking such good care of me during my labor in Denver, Colorado, when I was about to deliver this book;

All of my "SISTAHS" out there who have ever held my hand, looked me in the eye, and said, "Thank you";

And of course, THE DIVINE CREATOR, FATHER MOTHER GOD, who always knows exactly what I need, exactly when I need it.

For several years, I worked as a spiritual life counselor, assisting people from all walks of life regarding their challenges, issues, and problems, which very often had spiritual implications. Like any other doctor, minister, or counselor, I have always maintained the strictest level of confidentiality regarding the information others have shared with me. The stories used in this work are examples drawn from my experiences. However, the names, professions, and all other identifying information has been changed to protect the privacy of those who have shared their most intimate selves with me. Any similarity between the examples cited in this book and living individuals is purely coincidental.

Many of the examples are outgrowths of my own personal experiences, things I have either witnessed or participated in to some degree. As a priestess and student of many spiritual disciplines, I have heard many stories and been involved in many situations which demonstrate the working of spiritual laws throughout life. Again, the stories presented here are examples of the working of spiritual laws and not the divulgence of private and confidential information.

I have heard many quotes, read many books, and heard thousands of testimonies which attest to the existence of a spiritual universe. As with any other body of knowledge, spiritual research, theory, and personal experience is shared among teachers, students, practitioners, and onlookers. Eventually, this information takes the shape and form of a body of contemporary wisdom. This information or knowledge is then shared openly, freely, lovingly, among all. Many of the theories quoted in this work are not original ideas; however, my experience of them is original. I share them with you as knowledge, information I have received during my eighteen years of study in the fields of spirituality and empowerment. Those sources I know and remember, I have cited. Those I can no longer identify, I have shared with you based on my experience with them. If I have quoted anyone without proper citation, I apologize. If I have misquoted or altered the quotation of anyone, the alteration is a reflection of my experience, not an attempt to reinterpret your work.

Contents

INTRODUCTION | 13

1. THE ANATOMY OF THE VALLEY | 22

2. THE VALLEY OF LIGHT | 59

3. THE VALLEY OF UNDERSTANDING | 84

4. THE VALLEY OF COURAGE | 116

5. THE VALLEY OF KNOWLEDGE AND WISDOM | 144

6. THE VALLEY OF O.P.P. | 167

7. THE VALLEY OF COMEUPPANCE | 193

8. THE VALLEY OF PURPOSE AND INTENT | 217

9. THE VALLEY OF NONRESISTANCE | 248

10. THE VALLEY OF SUCCESS | 271

11. THE VALLEY OF LOVE | 295

12. ALL THE WAY OUT | 314

Author's Note

Throughout this project, I have used the term "Black women" to describe those whom I know to be descendants of Africans living in North America, the Caribbean, and Latin America; otherwise known as African-American women. I have used this term purely for the ease of writing and not to in any way disavow the history of Africans in this country. In my personal life, I use and prefer to be known as an African-American woman simply because of the inferences of the word "black." At its root is the word "lack," meaning not whole or complete.

As a Yoruba priestess and metaphysician, I know words are things which create conditions. I also recognize one of the major issues facing African-American women today is the feeling that we "lack" something. The *something*, we believe, may be good looks, or ability, or any number of human qualities. These feelings of lack so permeate our mind, body, and spirit, we have, in many cases, lost faith in our worthiness. Nothing could be further from the truth. In the words of our brother Hugh Masekela, as far as the African woman is concerned, "Nothing more need be added. The only thing left to do is, to do."

We are the daughters of the Mother of Creation. The secret of life is etched into the genetic composition of our DNA. We are the doors of life. All that lives has come through the portal of the woman. The fact that we are human "beings" says we lack nothing essential for our survival. I therefore ask your pardon in my use of the word "black" for the purpose of this work. It is in no way meant to support notions of unworthiness or to disrespect our ancestral origin.

I also ask that you pay particular attention to the Meditations with the Mother, which appear at the beginning of each chapter. These words were presented to me during early morning meditations at the ocean in Montego Bay, Jamaica. Following my morning prayer, I would experience the presence of a haze which descended over me as I was instructed to write. Many times, the words would bring me to tears. Always, they stirred a feeling of protection and revelation. The haze, identified only as "the Mother," asked that I relate these words to "the daughters" just as they were given. They have been edited only for grammatical correctness.

Introduction ❧

❧

BLACK WOMEN DO SO MUCH WORK *IN* WE DO NOT WANT TO WORK *ON* LIFE. WITH THE DISHES, THE laundry, the children, the men, the job, the money issues and other family problems, it is a bit much to ask that we "work" to make our lives better. We do not mind working toward that new home or car, to keep the bill collectors off our butts, or to put the children through school. These things we do not consider "work." They are a part of our responsibility as women. As far as the rest of life goes, what we want is to stride through, enjoying the good times and avoiding any, if not all, of the difficulties we have come to know as part of our lot. We are very simply tired of trying, hoping, struggling, and working.

It is difficult for the average Black woman to accept that life is more than hopping from one mountaintop experience to another. Although it may be perfectly obvious, somehow we forget there is a valley between every mountain. If women know only peak experiences, we become great striders, with high profiles, but eventually we become lousy workers. We must learn to work *on* life since that is what will be required of us as daughters, sisters, wives, and mothers. We must know how to do the work it takes to get out of those dark experiences called "valleys."

Valleys are purposeful. They open our eyes, strengthen our

minds, teach us faith, strength, and patience. These are all essential mountain-climbing skills. Valleys come in many shapes, sizes, and disguises. There are many times we may fall into a valley without knowing how or understanding why. There are also those occasions when we have no idea that we are in a valley. Unfortunately, many Black women have become so accustomed to hard times and bad situations we think that is all life has to offer. In order for a woman to wake up and get the message of a difficult experience, she must realize there is always value in the valley.

Valleys remind us of all the things we "shoulda," "coulda," "woulda" done had there been more time or had we had just a few more hands and feet. The valleys with which all of us are familiar are the pitfalls we experience when we least expect them. Somewhere deep inside we know we are having the experience in order to learn a lesson. There is something we missed "the last time" we were in this or a similar situation. Momma will remind you, "I told you so!" Friends shake their heads knowingly, grateful that it is not them "this time." You—well, you are down for the count, trying to figure out how the hell this happened! Again!

A valley can be a job you hate but need in order to feed the family. It could be inadequate finances with growing basic needs. The valley could be wealth with a diseased body. Or health and wealth with toxic, abusive, and disruptive relationships. There are times when the valley is a person you love who cannot get it together. Very few Black women have escaped the valley of loving a man who turns out to be a demon for the dungeon!

For other Black women, the valley is a child who goes astray in spite of all of your teaching and preaching. The valley can be depression, confusion, loneliness, or a high level of "pissosity." The valley can be an addiction, an attitude, an obsession, or all of the above. The valley is usually dark and bleak. It always feels ugly. Yet no matter how dark and bleak the valley seems to be for you or someone you know and love, there is always value. The key is in remembering that no matter how low you fall, you can always get up.

If we think of life as a twenty-four-hour day, we know to expect twelve hours of light and twelve hours of darkness. The darkness is what we will call the valley experience. Many of us, afraid of the dark, panic when the lights go out. It is difficult to see and we do not know what is going on. Black women instinctively need to know everything, down to the most minute detail. Unfortunately for many of us, the things we know and grab onto in the dark are the very things which throw us, headfirst, into the valley. However, if we know what to do and how to do it, those dark hours of a valley experience will prove to be the most valuable times of our lives.

In the valley, we change because we are forced to grow, to stretch, to reach beyond the limits we place on ourselves and allow others to place upon us. We cannot see through the darkness of the valley, so we are forced to trust our intuitive knowing, our ancestral link. In the valley, we develop faith and strength, the stuff our grandmothers were made of. We realize that something has gone terribly wrong. The "something" is, more often than not, that we have been doing "our thing"—the same thing we do repeatedly which gets us into trouble. In the best possible scenario, a valley experience forces us to do something new. We are forced by life to do "a new thing."

In the valley, we are not in control. Good! Black women love to be in control. We want to know what is coming, how it is coming, when it is coming, and whether it will wiggle or jiggle when it arrives. Believe it or not, it is usually our attempts to control events and people which lead us right into the valley. Surrender, trust, and patience are some of the valuable character traits we know we need and are forced to develop in one or more of our valley experiences.

Black women seem to have an insatiable appetite for *helping* and *saving* people. Of course, we cannot control them, we cannot save them. Many of us cannot control our mouth long enough to save ourselves from a bag of Lay's potato chips—we cannot eat just one, but we want to save the world. That is how we missed the lessons the valleys are designed to teach. Had we been paying attention to Grandma instead of passing notes to the boys, we would not have missed the lesson, "Mind your business and leave other people alone!"

Being in the valley is like being in the womb. It is a dark solitude in which you are bounced around without your permission.
It seems so dark and frightening you may not realize that you are
actually being protected, nurtured, and provided with all you
need. Like a fetus, you must stay in the darkness, the womb, the
valley, until the precise moment you are ready to come forth. The
valley is a time of preparation. When you are ready, you move
forward.

Often, the preparation for that forward movement is hard. It is
painful. And it is frightening. You are squeezed and prodded until
you are in just the right position. As you are guided into alignment with the forces around you, you begin to relax. When you
do, you move ahead, easily and effortlessly. That is what most
Black women want: easy, effortless movement in and through our
lives. It is most unfortunate that we usually get in the way of the
very thing we want.

My experiences have taught me how purposeful valleys can
be. The pain and trauma which brought me that insight came at a
time when I thought it was more than I could bear. Today, I will
be the first to admit that the lessons I learned in the valleys will
last throughout my lifetime. Once I got the hang of it, I realized
valleys helped me to cultivate the qualities and attributes I
needed but continued to resist. The valleys provided me with the
time and the opportunity to look at my most resistant, uncooper-
ative self. I thought I was perfect. "One way. My way!" Since I was
right, I believed everyone else was out of their mind. As a result,
I spent the better part of my adult life going from one valley to
another. I wanted my life to change, but I was not willing to
change. The valleys taught me that change of life requires change
of mind. When I resisted change I nearly lost my mind.

I spent many years in the valleys of Courage and Understanding. I had a permanent address in the Valley of Other People's
Problems, Perspectives, and Purposes. I served on the board of
directors in the Valley of Knowledge and Wisdom. One day, I
found myself in the Valley of Light. Through the dark experiences
of that valley, I learned nonresistance was the only way I could

recover my mind and change my life. I also discovered that facing the truth about myself was the only way out of the valley.

The Valley of Light taught me I could no longer deny what I was doing in my own life, to myself. I had made a mess of things and it was bound to get worse. There was no way I could continue to dress up the stories I was telling myself about myself and everyone else. I was forced to look at "me," explore my feelings, and admit what I thought were some pretty god-awful things about me. I resisted the process because I thought it would be so painful and awful I would not survive. I could not admit to what I thought was the truth about me. I certainly did not want anyone else to figure it out. I attempted to fix things that had gone awry in order to hide other things because I believed *I was bad*. Finally, one day, I fell headfirst into the deepest valley of all, the Valley of Love. Once there, I had to look at myself and my life. There was nothing else for me to do.

The Valley of Love meant the end of a relationship I knew was not good for me; being fired from a job I actually hated; my car being seized for unpaid parking tickets; my son being accidentally shot; an eviction notice being hung on my apartment door; and a boil on my behind. The left cheek of my behind. The feminine side. The side of intuition. Intuitively, we all know the truth; we simply hate to admit it. In the valley, I learned that the only thing that really mattered was what I believed about myself. The other people in my life, the events and circumstances, were merely a reflection of my accumulated thoughts and feelings. Up to that point, I had believed I was ugly, stupid, and incapable of taking care of myself, and that most people were out to get me. In the valley, I came face to face with the truth.

With everything and everyone I thought important gone, I was forced to focus on me. That is what valleys do, they force us to do what we resist. When I thought about the things I had said and done—and not said and not done—it became clear who was out to get me. I had been attacking the problems in my life and getting my butt kicked royally. I was attempting to fix the people and problems when I was the principal player in disrepair.

I was settling for less than I wanted and telling myself it was all right, knowing it was not all right. I was buying friendship and acceptance because I believed *I was not all right.* In the Valley of Love I came face to face with all of it when I realized that throughout the entire process, I had been blaming everyone else for what I was doing to me.

In the Valley of Truth, I learned I was no different from anyone else. I was a human being having a temporary human experience, which I was taking far too seriously. I was not at war with the world or life. No one was out to get me. Other people in the world were so busy having their own experience they did not have the time or inclination to worry about me. I learned it would be impossible for me to have a good relationship with anyone else until I had a good relationship with myself. I did not like me. I was not honest with myself. I did not want to be alone with me, so why would anyone else? Truth + Love = Freedom × Power. I had to find my sense of personal freedom and power. In order to do that, I would have to face the truth about me and love me anyway.

One day, in the midst of my self-discovery, I saw a sign which read:

> **THE ONLY MISTAKE I EVER MADE WAS**
> **WHEN I THOUGHT I WAS WRONG**
> **AND I WAS MISTAKEN.**

You mean I am not wrong? I am not messed up? I am not a hopeless failure? Do you mean to tell me that my biggest issue in life is that I am having a series of temporary human experiences? I am supposed to know each day is a new day, an opportunity to do something new? Do you expect me to believe that I don't need to know what to do about everything, all of the time? You mean as a human being, the only thing I need to know is that there really is a higher power and bad things happen anyway? Somewhere deep inside, a voice said, "That's right!" Well, I started laughing. I laughed at myself. I laughed at life. I laughed all the way up the mountain, down into the valley, and up the mountain again. There are times when I still laugh at my humanness. Hopefully, after the experience of this book, you will develop an understanding of the valleys that will enable you to laugh with me.

When you see yourself in the various valleys (and believe me, you will see yourself or some version of you), tell the truth! Do not make up one of your excuses for doing what you do to create drama or reinforce your fear. Acknowledge yourself and decide what, if anything, you are going to do about you. Do not beat up on yourself with "shoulds" or "should nots." Do not criticize yourself. Do not judge yourself. Understand that we all do what we do based on who we are and the information we have at that time. The information is usually based on our past experiences, perceptions, and fear-motivated behaviors. Whatever the information, whatever our perceptions, we will get what we need to learn in order to do better. That is the universal law.

If you are in a valley now, or have been in the same valley repeatedly, you are not alone. There are thousands of people in the same valley, at the same time you are. Once you realize this you can slap your knee and laugh at yourself. My guess is that if the laughter of all the people in all the valleys goes up at the same time, the energy will create a mighty rumble. If we are lucky, the rumbling will create a shift. The shift is bound to create a breakthrough. If Mother Nature is not too annoyed with us, the breakthrough will carve out a piece of life we can name "the Valley of Fun"!

IYANLA, MARCH 1993

MEDITATION
WITH THE
MOTHER

Those who wait to seek God at the eleventh hour,
usually die at ten-thirty.

O daughters, how long will you walk upon my back, eat of the
fruits of my life, return to me at the end of your toiling, and still
fail to recognize and honor me? How long will you ask that I sup-
port your steps, open your paths, provide your sustenance, before
you take time to remember me? A mother is long-suffering and pa-
tient. Yet she wants to know that her suffering and patience will
pay off.

You daughters have not yet realized the connection you have
with me, the responsibility you have for me, or the commitment
you must have to me. I am not just a passing fancy to a few who
have created images and told stories about me from the days long
gone. I am the essence, the cause, the fiber of your being; alive in
the marrow of your bones. I am your soul, your heart, your womb.
I am your purpose and only through me will your life be purpose-
ful. I am the Earth, yes! I am your spark of creativity, yes! I am
love, yes! But most important of all, my dear daughters, I am the
light in your eyes; the inspiration in your hearts; the connection to
the divine, noble presence in your being.

Come to me, daughters, let us conjure together the stream of
light, love, and healing this world longs for but shuns by its resis-
tance to honoring "the Mother." I am in the valley of your mind, the
deep, dark place you fear to tread and which men have told you is
dangerously meaningless. Come to me, daughters. Do not fear! I
await you with a healing balm. A joyous song. A powerful prayer.
Think, dear daughters, how blessed you shall be when you can
hear your Mother pray again.

The Anatomy of the Valley   1

IT WAS NOT *UNUSUAL* FOR THE TELE-
PHONE TO RING AT EIGHT-THIRTY IN THE MORNING. AND IT WAS ONLY
slightly unusual for *her* to be calling *him* there. Although she
worked for him, it was evident by her tone of voice that this call
was about something more than business. Two hours into *their*
conversation, *she* wanted to speak to *Ann.* The moment the conversation began, Ann knew she was headed for a valley. She
could not, however, figure out which one. By the time *all three of
them* were on the telephone, it was clear: Ann was being cut up
into tiny little pieces. Those pieces were being strewn across all
the valleys at once.

"There is value in the valley," is what Black women must remember when we find ourselves in those tight spots, dark places,
uncomfortable situations, we think make our lives so miserable.
Whether we accidentally fall into a valley or are shoved in head-
first, the question we must ask ourselves is, "What is the lesson
here?" What is the lesson to be learned from those situations we
do not like or want to be in? The first thing we must do is realize
that difficulties in life are always educational. Art may be easier
than history. Gym is usually more fun than math. There is, however, something valuable to be gained from every subject and sit-

uation we face if we want to graduate to a higher level of living. Of course, in every class, there is also the issue of passing or failing.

Ann listened intently as the woman on the other end of the telephone recounted the sordid details of her two-year relationship with Ann's mate of one year. With her head in the Valley of Understanding and both feet in the Valley of Courage, Ann had a sinking feeling in the pit of her stomach that she was on the brink of failure. With a steady hand and unblinking eyes, holding the telephone away from her ear, she quietly demanded of him, "How could you do this to me?" Wrong move! It put her heart in the Valley of O.P.P. and her hands in the Valley of Comeuppance. As fear of failure welled up in her mind, promising to overtake her, Ann had to fight back the tears. *He* was lying across the bed with his head in his hands. Each time he looked up, it was as if he were seeing a ghost. A big Black ghost. A ghost with one hand on her hip and a frying pan in the other. Ann took a deep breath and braced herself to spend the rest of her days in the dunce corner.

Those dark conditions and difficult situations are like valleys because we get there when we lose our footing. We fall down only to find ourselves alone in a physically, mentally, or emotionally uncomfortable place. Valleys look dark and feel dangerous because there never seems to be anyone around who can help you get up. A fall into a valley means you are in some kind of pain. Throbbing head, broken heart, fractured ego, you are trying to figure out what happened; how you got into this mess and how you can get out of it, fast. The pain intensifies as you remember the details of your plight. You imagine all of the possible, plausible, and horrible outcomes. Now you panic. Actually, you feel frantic as you mentally construct your ultimate and looming destruction. It is pure drama, and as Black women, we do it so well.

When we are confronted by a situation we know we must face but would rather not, we shift into high-gear fear—fear of failure, rejection, the unknown, and the ultimate fear, the fear of being wrong. No one wants to be wrong. For Black women, many of whom believe they have been overlooked, misrepresented, and objectified by major portions of the population, the fear of being wrong sends the brain into overload. Black women will go to any lengths to avoid being wrong. The fear of being wrong forces us to shut down. We shut our eyes, ears, and ultimately, our hearts. If the situation is critical, very important, or dear to us, we may be frightened enough to shut our mouths. A Black woman in fear, with a numb heart and a shut mouth, is a woman in pain.

He finally spoke to *her:* "I told you it was over!"

"No, you didn't! You told me we would work it out! Then you kissed me and we made love!"

Ann was able to part her lips: "You kissed her?"

There was total silence. They had all stopped breathing.

"You kissed her! Now just a hog-slopping minute! Are you telling me that you are sleeping with this woman after you told me you weren't?"

Ear-piercing silence. Somehow, in all the drama, Ann had missed the fact that *they* were *still* seeing each other. This was quickly changing from a valley to a dungeon. The dungeon of clarity. Then *she* spoke:

"Why don't you answer her?"

"Are you sleeping with this woman?" Ann had shifted out of fear into indignation.

Meekly he answered, "Yes."

That was the final push. Ann fell flat on her face into the Valley of Knowledge and Wisdom.

It is hard to think when you are in pain. As you frantically anticipate your destruction, which is sure to result when you confront your greatest fear, pain seeps into every fiber of your being. The fear of making a mistake, of being wrong, descends over you like a cloud. We are not talking here about the kind of pain Midol, Anacin, or extra-strength Excedrin can relieve. We are talking about the pain of having your entire existence threatened. The pain of having what you want, need, and love, invalidated or taken away. You picked the wrong one, again. You did not do it right, again. You are in trouble, again. As a result, your head hurts. Your heart is bleeding. You want to think, but the pain is overwhelming. Sound familiar? I thought so!

When We Think We Are Wrong!

When Black women are wrong, we are not only wrong in and of ourselves, we are wrong for our mothers and our greatest grandmother. It is a genetic wrongness which aches down to the bone. The wrongness of Black women has been studied by physiologists, analyzed by psychologists, proven plausible by genealogists, even become the topic of debate at senatorial hearings. A wrong Black woman might as well be a dead one. The mind is dead. The heart is dying. If something is not done quickly to reconcile the feelings of wrongness, the spirit will die. But wait! Isn't being wrong one of the best ways to get your face on television? Never mind that—we cannot, will not, go down without a fight! On the way to dying, we have to be angry and hateful because we are wrong and have failed. We strike out at, speak out against, those things and people who "made us" wrong, helped us fail. It is all so wonderfully dramatic. For many angry, wrong Black women, failure means your lifeless body must be ceremonially laid to rest in the Valley of Nonresistance, which gives you exactly the excuse you need to buy that new dress.

Ann decided on the spot, "I will not fail! I am not going to be wrong! I will not fail this test!" In her best monotone, Ann explained she had had no idea that *he* was still *intimately involved* with *her*. Ann had to admit she knew the woman worked in one of his businesses. She also knew they shared an apartment when he was in that state. Ann knew he kept a few of his clothes in that apartment. Ann also knew that he lived, conducted most of his business and spent the majority of his time in another state. Ann knew because she called him there and visited him there. To the best of Ann's knowledge he was in the same state with *her* one day a month. *She* politely informed Ann that *he came home* at least two days every month.

"What kind of relationship is that?"

A good one, *she* thought. "He had promised me . . ."

"Well, look," Ann said, "I'm outa here. You've got this! You can finish your conversation with him while he gets ready to get out of my house."

When you find yourself in a valley, the best approach is to surrender control. This does not mean you are giving up hopelessly, admitting defeat in anticipation of destruction. That is drama. Surrender is another story altogether. Surrender means you do not fight or struggle against whatever you are facing. It simply means, sit down, shut up, and listen! Be still until your mind is clear and you truly understand where you are, how you got there, and most important, how you can get out without struggle. Difficult situations such as valleys help us grow because they nudge us into a position where we must confront the things we need to know but hate to admit about ourselves.

The valleys also help us understand how we create the greatest, most damaging thrust of the downward plunge into bad situations. In those rare instances when we do not create our own trouble, our dramatic response to trouble creates more difficulty than the actual situation. Every Black woman knows at least one drama queen. These are sisters, friends, mothers, who are forever clutching their bosoms as they declare how horrible, awful, terrible, whatever it is, is. In response to their hysteria, we go into action doing whatever it is we do. In most cases, it is our consistent, conditioned responses to challenges and difficulties, based on past experiences, which send us directly into a valley experience.

In the valley, we are confronted by all of our past experiences, perceptions, and judgments of ourselves and others. The valley is the place we have stored thoughts and feelings, a sort of garbage dump we must wade through in order to move beyond the fear and limitation we now face. We Black women may tell ourselves that when something is over, it is over. Yet there is a part of us which loves to hold on to tidbits of information, believing they might be useful at some point in the future. Experiences which have caused us pain, fear, anger, or disappointment become our greatest enemies when we hold on to them. If we use these historical tidbits as the barometer by which we gauge the present situations in our lives, the stench of the garbage eventually seeps through. Our senses are altered. We respond to what "was" rather than what "is." When this happens, it means there is something we have not learned. We must go back to school. The valley is school.

Ann hung up the telephone. It was then that she realized, "I'm not crying! I'm not numb! I may be a bit rattled, but I'm not dead! I was lied to and betrayed, but I'm not dead! I was wrong about someone I truly love, and I'm not dead. I didn't fail the test!" Ann went into the room with him, stared at him briefly, and shook her head in amazement. She repeated her desire for him to leave. She had a brief moment of faltering. She wanted to know "why." She realized, however, that to know why and not understand it would probably kill her. She decided that "why" didn't matter.

It started as a murmur in the deepest recesses of her brain. As it grew louder, the words became audible: "I can do this! I *can* do this! Yes! I CAN do this!" He was putting on his shoes. Ann verbalized the mantra: "I can do this!" She got a facecloth from the linen closet, took it into the bathroom, doused it in cold water, and placed it on the back of her neck. "I can do this!" He was standing up. Ann could feel his confusion, pain, fear. "I can do this!" Ann left the room. He left the house. Ann wasn't dead, but what she didn't know at the time was that she was in a very deep, dark valley. As his car pulled away from the house, Ann chanted: "I CAN DO THIS!"

At every single moment, we are given the opportunity to choose our future. What we do today will determine what we face next week, next month, or next year. It is at the moment of a particular occurrence that we are called upon to make a choice: Will I do it the way I've always done it, or will I do it a different way? Our ability to choose is based on what we believe about ourselves, the world, and life. If you believe in garbage, you may choose to stay where you are. If you believe in change, goodness, and growth, you will put your butt on the line and choose a new way. The garbage we believe in, the things we fear, and our need to be right form the skeletal framework in the anatomy of a valley.

What Is a Valley?

In order to avoid confusion, the confusion which is bound to well up in your mind as you try to figure out what valley you may or may not have visited, this brief definition is offered. A valley is a life situation designed to teach a character trait or spiritual virtue which has been undeveloped or underdeveloped during the course of your life. These traits and virtues are things we know we "should" practice, but forget or resist incorporating into our lives. Patience, trust, faith, courage, wisdom, honesty—each of these in some way corresponds to a natural law or universal principle which governs the orderly flow of life, whether or not we recognize it. The universe we call "life" is actually a spiritual process governed by spiritual laws we are expected to embrace and live by. In fact, each of us is charged at birth with the responsibility of doing so in order to realize emotional growth and spiritual evolution. Unfortunately, we do not realize this very integral fact until much later in life.

Evolution is not an easy task when we view it from a human perspective. As human beings, we are trained to resist that which is difficult and to all but ignore that which is spiritual. We abandon the life-fulfilling process of spiritual evolution for intellectual pursuits. We want to be smart and right, not enlightened and evolved. We are encouraged to develop personality, not spirituality. Although we do not recognize it, we have the opportunity to develop personality through the practice of spiritual traits and virtues. Unfortunately, the pressures of the world tempt us to reject spiritual strength at the first opportunity to get to the top of the personality heap.

The valleys help to bring the true purpose and meaning of life back into focus. Life is learning, growing, giving, sharing, and loving ourselves into a state of unconditional, peaceful acceptance. Your spirit needs peace and love, not a BMW and a VCR! Valleys are situations designed by life in response to our thoughts, emotions, and behaviors, which are the true indicators of our spiritual needs. Valleys force us to examine what we are doing, why we are doing it, and to decide whether we choose to satisfy the needs of personality or to pursue the evolution of the spirit. The pressure we experience during these growth opportunities in life is what we will call "the valley."

The Valleys Defined

What makes the Black woman's learning experience unique with regard to the experiences of all others? What separates what people learn and how they learn from their experiences in life is how they respond to the experiences. All human beings must develop the same traits, embrace the same virtues, and learn the same lessons. What is unique to a particular group of people, based on race, ethnicity, or gender, is their orientation to the experience of life. What do we expect? What do we want? How can we merge our desires and expectations into a cohesive framework?

Our experience as Black women is unique because of our orientation to the life process. More than half of us believe that everything that goes wrong is our fault. It is our fault because something is wrong with us. The thing that is wrong with us may be tied to our being female. It is often the result of our being Black. Even when we realize and recognize that life's events are not our fault, we still think it is our responsibility to fix whatever or whoever is wrong. Most important of all, Black women are not unique insofar as we are not educated about the universal laws which govern life. This lack of education does, however, affect us differently because we are the daughters, sisters, mothers, wives, friends, workers, and underlings to whom most everyone turns to fix the wrongs.

Our ignorance regarding the universal laws and spiritual principles keeps us on a treadmill of trying to figure out what is wrong, hoping we can fix it, trying to show others we can, and struggling to save and protect ourselves in the process. Our conditioned responses to being on the treadmill—trying to get off, struggling not to fall off, fighting to keep from being pushed off, and figuring out how we got there in the first place—take us further away from the spiritual essence of life and the peaceful acceptance of who and what we are. Because women are the mothers, teachers, and supportive foundation of the rest of the human community, it is important that we have the knowledge so that we can teach and share it with others. Because Black women have been so much, to so many, for so long, it is imperative that we get what it takes—because we need a rest!

THE VALLEY OF LIGHT

There are ten valleys which Black women commonly fall into based on their orientation to life and their everyday human experiences. The most common experience, called the Valley of Light, teaches us the lesson of stillness, a state of solitude and silence which forces us to take a look at ourselves. As we look within, we develop the ability to lovingly reflect on ourselves, our lives, and those around us.

Ignorance is a form of darkness. When we are ignorant about our true nature and identity, as well as the divine rights granted to us based on who we are, we are living in darkness. Black women are more prone to stay in the "darkness" of what others have told us about ourselves than any other group. These external forces tell us what they want us to think, to know, in order to ensure they get what they want from us. Because it is the nature of a woman to serve, our internal instinct is to do what is expected of us. Because Black women have been in a position of servitude for so long, we resist the urge to question or challenge what we are told. However, when the time comes for us to question or challenge, and to know the truth about ourselves, we must be cast into the light. Light creates a self-reflection, which is the character trait we develop in this valley. Reflection alone is not a trait. The ability to reflect on self is.

The Valley of Light represents those experiences which force us to question who we are, to acknowledge what we want, and to decide what we are willing to do about who we are and what we want. The Valley of Light is our opportunity to withdraw from the activity of our lives and the people in them, to reflect on what we have been doing, identify the unproductive behavior we have adopted, and figure out what we will choose for ourselves in the

future. From the darkness and ignorance which surround the experiences that take us to this valley, we emerge with a new
awareness, prompted by a renewed belief in and love of self.

The Enlightenment Process

The Valley of Light is the "mother" of all valleys. Our ability to
master the lessons of these experiences will determine our ability
to emerge from all other valleys. In the Valley of Light, we are introduced to our God self and reintroduced to the process required for spiritual enlightenment. Your God self is your spirit,
that part of you that is connected to the life and power source of
the universe. It is the breath expanding in your lungs. The blood
running through your veins. Your God knows exactly what to do
and how to get it done. This is the part of you that is forever enlightened and desires to shine in the world. Your God self knows
every aspect of the enlightenment process. In the silence of this
valley, it will emerge in your conscious mind. The enlightenment
process in the Valley of Light is the same process used to get the
lesson in every valley.

The first phase is *detachment*. This is the development of the
conscious ability to see yourself and others. In order to see yourself in the light, you must be able to detach, to pull back from the
world and be still. The next stage is *discernment*. More than an
ability to see, discernment is being able to understand what you
are looking at and how it relates to you. This is a process of dis-
section, cutting open what you have in your life in order to examine it. With that done, understanding seeps in, enabling you to
throw away what is not needed. Once you can see and understand, you reach the next phase, *enlightenment*. With your new
vision and understanding, how should you proceed? What is the
character trait you need to develop or virtue you need to practice
in order to maintain your new state of consciousness? You know
because you can see and understand. The next level of the
process requires doing. It is called *integration*. This is the active
part of the enlightenment process. You must now take the information you have and integrate it into your life. Because you have
consciously decided to discard the old, the useless, in the dis-

cernment process, you have the opportunity and ability to do something new. As you do, you reach the fifth and final stage of the enlightenment process, *evolution*. By integrating the information which has been revealed to you, and by practicing the trait or virtue you now know you must develop or embrace, you can proceed in your life making better choices and wiser decisions.

The enlightenment we gain through the experiences which take us to the Valley of Light, cause us to reflect on ourselves, and ultimately results in self-mastery. Self-mastery and mastery of the enlightenment process are what will be required in order to grasp the lessons of all valleys. The character trait needed, or the virtue to be practiced, is determined by your individual level of development, and will change according to the universal law that governs a given valley. The experience you have and the lesson you will learn is in direct correlation to the virtue or trait you need to embrace at the time of the experience. Say, for example, you mastered patience or honesty to a certain degree; a later, more profound experience can help you foster an even greater mastery and understanding of it.

How well you learn your lesson is determined by your ability to master yourself through developing a character trait or by practicing a spiritual virtue—your level of mastery determines whether the valley experience is positive or negative. When your responses to any given situation are based on fear or nonproductive habits, a trip to the valley will be negative. When you are willing to move beyond habit and confront what you fear, a valley experience will be positive. You are honing your knowledge of the principles of the universe and the laws of nature. It is your level of mastery and knowledge of the principles and laws which actually determine whether the experience is a ditch, a valley, a dungeon, or Spiritual Special Education.

The lessons of the Valley of Light experiences teach us the power of silence and solitude and the value of self-reflection. Your experiences in this valley will promote your development of the virtue of awareness. Through the light of your reflection and awareness, you find the ability to love yourself. With awareness and self-love tucked in your bra, you realize no matter how low you fall in any valley, if you understand yourself and what you have done to create your valley experience, you are equipped to climb the mountain again. This is the purpose of the next level of experiences, called the Valley of Understanding.

THE VALLEY OF UNDERSTANDING

All of us have had experiences where we believe someone has done us wrong. We have felt betrayed, abandoned, or rejected by someone we loved, trusted, and probably went out of our way to help. When we find ourselves in the midst of this type of experience, undoubtedly we will say, "I don't understand how or why they did this to me!" Of course you don't understand! You are in the Valley of Understanding. Here we are provided an opportunity to strengthen our vision of how we see ourselves and others. This valley helps us understand those aspects of our own nature which must be confronted, accepted, and mastered.

The lesson of this valley is acceptance, learning to see ourselves, other people, and situations as they are, not as we want them to be or fear they might turn out to be. We do not always listen to what is said. We hear it and tell ourselves it means something else. We do not always pay attention to what is going on. We see what we want to see, hear what we want to hear. It is a hazard of not being aware, not being able to accept what really is, and living in fear. It is due to our lack of understanding that the stench of past garbage pollutes our hearts and minds today. The experiences of this valley help us to see how our garbage gets played out through the actions of other people. In the Valley of Understanding, we get a glimpse of all the lessons we will be required to learn in all of the valleys. Here we are tested. We are tested to determine our level of self-understanding.

The universe brings to us other people who show us who and what we are. If we do not understand what is really going on or recognize the lessons we must learn, we mistake our own issues as the shortcomings of others. This valley brings us to the realization that the people in our lives and the situations which confront us are somehow a reflection of our own human nature. The Law of Human Nature which governs this valley helps us to accept what we see without judgment. Nonjudgment is the virtue we must develop in order to gain a deeper understanding of our own nature. The experiences of the Valley of Understanding prepare us for and lead us to the next valley, the Valley of Courage.

THE VALLEY OF COURAGE

For Black women, fear is a major thrust into a valley experience. So many of us, although totally unaware of it, live in a constant state of fear. Fear of failure, rejection, the unknown, being alone, and not being in control. These fears actually emerge as our personality, the bad habits we embrace, and the excuses we give ourselves to stay in self-denial. Fear enables us to convince ourselves that the poor or failing quality of our lives is caused by something or someone outside of ourselves. The truth is, most Black women are riddled with fear. We are afraid "in" the world. Afraid "of" our men. Afraid "for" our children. Most of all, we are afraid of our own power.

Black women are not taught the true meaning of the virtue of courage. We are taught responsibility, accountability, and dependability. We are taught to be neat, clean, and as quiet as possible. Courage, we are taught, is a "guy" thing. For years, I allowed myself remain in bad relationships, meaningless jobs, and mental and emotional confusion by telling myself "they" would not allow me to move beyond where I was. As I grew in spiritual consciousness, I realized that I stayed where I was so long because I was afraid to go anywhere else.

The Valley of Courage is named for the character trait it teaches. In order to have courage, we must develop the ability to surrender. This is the trait we master in this valley. We must surrender our secrets: our secret fears and secret thoughts about ourselves and the world. As we surrender, we begin to trust the universe called life. We learn to trust the spirit within. We begin to examine what we really believe about ourselves, our lives, and the people we have attracted into our experience. The Law of Belief which governs this valley enables us to see that it is not life we fear, rather our beliefs about life create our fears. When we master our fears, we become courageous and trusting. With courage and trust, no valley is too deep, no challenge too difficult to confront.

The Valley of Knowledge and Wisdom

From the Valley of Courage, we usually take a trip through the Valley of Knowledge and Wisdom. We all know everything we need to know. The knowledge we need to face most of life's experiences is imprinted on our genes. It was passed on to us by our grandmothers, reinforced through and by our mothers. Our challenge is to develop the wisdom required to put what we know to good use, which is often made difficult because Granny and Momma did not come right out and tell us what they knew. Oh no! That would have made it too easy! Instead, the knowledge and wisdom is couched in old wives' tales, euphemisms, and innuendo.

We all remember being told, "Never say never." Then there is the classic warning, "Stop saying what you can't do!" How could we forget "Stand up straight. Hold your head up when someone is talking to you!" And no grandmother would be worth her weight in salt had she not told you, at least fifty times a year, to "Mind your own business!" There is knowledge hidden in the midst of the sassy gems. Momma knew it. Granny knew it. However, in the midst of the hysteria of your puberty, followed by the hormonal imbalance of your adolescence, which flowed right into the transformative migration of your adulthood, they forgot to tell you what they really meant. Now your job is to find out and use it wisely.

You will know you are in this valley when you are faced with a situation which you can't seem to get out of or around. When everyone you talk to tells you something different and none of it makes sense. Your memory tries to fail you as Granny's face cascades before you. She is waving that finger at you. Momma's voice is ringing in your ears reminding you of all the things you never listened to. You struggle against admitting that their mumbling, ranting, and raving are finally beginning to make sense. The issue now becomes, are you going to be obedient, this time? Will you exercise your freedom to choose? To speak? To act? To stand tall and hold your head high? Do you believe you have the power to trust what you "know" and act on it? The Law of Obedience is at work here. Obedience is a virtue we must grow in if we are to act wisely.

When you are in the Valley of Knowledge and Wisdom, you are down for the full count. The drama is not working and no one wants to hear your story. This is really an optimum learning environment. There is absolutely no one for you to talk to and you are forced to figure out what to do. The lesson of this valley is to sit down, shut up, and listen to the quiet voice within which knows exactly what is best for you in the face of any situation. If you can practice a little discipline, you are sure to get it done. Discipline is the trait we develop in this valley. Yet discipline alone will not save you. You must have faith, which is the lesson this valley teaches. If you have faith that your listening will pay off, you will be disciplined. If you are disciplined, you must be obedient. When you are obedient, suddenly, miraculously, you realize you know exactly what to do and how to do it. The problem is trying to stay focused on what you know and not get caught up in O.P.P.

THE VALLEY OF O.P.P.

A friend's teenage daughter was moping around the house with such fervor that she left a cloud of dismay as she passed through the room.

"What's the matter with you?" her mother demanded.

"Naaathinnn" was the response she dragged out over thirty seconds.

"So why do you look like that? Why are you spreading negative energy throughout the house?"

"I want to go out, that's all!"

"Go where?"

"Skating!"

"So go skating!"

"I can't! Cathy's on punishment and she can't go!"

"Well, what does that have to do with you?"

"Cathy is my best friend. I can't go without her! I won't have any fun!"

"So stay home and suffer! But do it in your room!"

How many of us stay where we are, physically, mentally, and emotionally, suffering in silence, because we dare not move beyond our circle of family, friends, or loved ones? There are many. It is an affliction which plagues the average Black woman. It is called O.P.P.: Other People's Problems, Perspectives, and Purposes. It is a valley which for many becomes a life-threatening dungeon.

The Valley of O.P.P. is the situation in which you find yourself when your life is going well, you have all you could possibly dream of, and everything is going your way, but you cannot enjoy it because you are bogged down with "O.P.P." It is when you put your life, your goals, and your dreams on hold in order to help someone else create their life. They may fail and blame you, which means you are stuck in guilt. Or they may succeed and forget you, in which case you are stuck in anger. O.P.P. is about people pleasing. The lesson of this valley is freedom. Freedom comes when we have mastered the inner strength and ability to say, "This is not my issue!" Strength is the trait we must master in order to embrace the virtue of honesty. You must be honest enough to say what you will do, won't do; can do, cannot do. Most of all, the Valley of O.P.P. teaches us there comes a time when we must say "No!" and not feel guilty. It all corresponds to the Law of Sacrifice which governs this valley and motivates us to ask ourselves, to whom and for what are we sacrificing our divine right of freedom? Most of us do not realize we are free to think, do, and move on our own. We do not realize this because we are not on purpose.

THE VALLEY OF PURPOSE AND INTENT

We love to flit around doing a little of this and a little of that. Running here and going there. Starting this and finishing something else, while there are things we should start and don't, things we should finish but cannot. We are too busy flitting with no real purpose. In the most severe flitting cases, we get very little done for others and even less done for ourselves. But we look and feel very busy. Life has a cure for flitting and flitters. It is called the Valley of Purpose and Intent.

The experiences which take us into this valley are designed to force us to question what we are doing and the purpose of it all. The lesson of this valley is alignment. We each have a purpose, you know. Each of us has come to life at this time to do a specific thing. Unfortunately, we spend far too much time flitting around, which prevents us from developing clarity about what exactly our purpose is. Clarity is the virtue we develop in this valley. When you have clarity, commitment is an easy task. This valley is designed to foster the development of the character trait of commitment.

In the Valley of Purpose and Intent, we are afforded the opportunity to get really clear about our purpose in life and to make a commitment to pursue that purpose. You know you are in this valley when no matter what you try to do, it does not work. When your best-laid plans go awry. When no matter what you say, people do not hear you, do not listen to you, and just do not seem to care about you. This is also the valley we end up in when we have a lot of irons in the fire. If we are not on purpose, the winds of change are sure to blow hard, making sure the fire under the irons—which probably serve no purpose—will not stay lit. But isn't life like that? Just when we think we've got it all together, something else will come up to prove us wrong. When the winds blow and things come up, rest assured, you are in the Valley of Comeuppance.

THE VALLEY OF COMEUPPANCE

Everyone ends up in this valley sooner or later because we are all held accountable for everything we think, everything we say, and everything we do. It is the Law of Cause and Effect in operation. This valley has a double lesson: responsibility and forgiveness. As Black women, we must take responsibility for our lives. We are powerful, even when we do not mean to be. Our thoughts create. Our words create. Our actions have a rippling ef-

fect on everything and everyone with whom we come into contact. We cannot afford to wag our tongues mindlessly or direct
our thoughts with vengeance. It is dangerous! Not only to the
people we direct it towards, but to ourselves, when it comes up
in our lives.

When we lose something we treasure, when we are denied
something we deserve, or when we are slandered in some way,
the issue is not, "Look what they are doing to me now!" The issue
is, who have you wished harm on lately? Who have you spoken ill
of lately? Is there a confidence you have betrayed in the past, let
us say, ten or twenty years? We want to blame somebody else
again. The universe will not hear of it! The universal Law of Cause
and Effect is teaching us a lesson. The lesson is, everything happens twice, first on the inside, then on the outside. In other
words, whatever is going on in your life has its roots in what is
going on in your mind and in what is coming out of your mouth.
It will all come up for you to see.

The lesson we must learn and the trait we must embrace to
free ourselves from the experiences of the Valley of Comeuppance is forgiveness. We must forgive others for what they have
done and what we think they have done to us. We must also forgive ourselves for the things we have done to ourselves and others. If we do not forgive, the barnacles of the past hang on to our
minds and hearts. These barnacles cause us to say and do things
which have no place in the sisterhood of oneness. Eventually we
may change, but if we have not given, accepted, or asked for forgiveness, the universe owes us a turn. The theory is, "What goes
around, comes around." And it doesn't have to come from the
same place you gave. The virtue to be mastered is consciousness.
Be conscious of what you are thinking, saying, and doing. When
you are conscious and consciously forgiving, you will be able to
overcome whatever comes up. That is, unless you are one of
those who continues to resist the lessons. Not to worry! Life has
something for you too. You are a prime candidate for the Valley
of Nonresistance.

THE VALLEY OF NONRESISTANCE

Picture this, if you will. You have just found the most stunning dress you have ever seen in your life. You can just picture the heads turning as you walk into your uncle's cousin's daughter's wedding in this dress. There was only one left in the store and it was your size. The dress makes you look five pounds thinner and five years younger. This is a baaaad dress! You must have it! Now here's the problem. The dress is very lovely, but the color is off. Too off for brown shoes or beige shoes. Black shoes will dress it down, white shoes will kill it. Not to worry! One of your shoe haunts is bound to have something that will match or at least come close.

This is your lucky day! The very first place you try has the shoe that matches the dress exactly! Now Murphy steps in. The display model is a six. The one other pair available is a seven and a half. You need an eight! However, you *can* get your foot in a seven and a half. It is tight but bearable. The salesperson offers to stretch it for you. You graciously accept by saying you are going to buy panty hose and will return in fifteen minutes. You come back. Try the shoe on for the sixth, no, seventh time. Miraculously it feels fine. You walk around. No problem. You try a few dance steps. No pain. Knowing perfectly well the dangers of putting your size eight foot into a size seven and a half shoe, you whip out your Visa card and lay down eighty dollars for a pair of shoes which could very well cripple you. A pair of shoes that are bound to end up collecting dust in the bottom of the closet. To cure Black women of their compulsive urge to do what we know we should not do, the university of life has created the Valley of Nonresistance.

This valley is about much more than our tendency to put a square peg in a round hole. This valley responds to our inability to recognize what is square and who is round. This valley goes beyond the Black woman's inability to see or accept people and things as they are. The Valley of Nonresistance, which bears the nickname of "Have It Your Way," is the only classroom which effectively teaches us we cannot fix things, change people, or make something anything that it is not. This is a valley of potential Spiritual Special Ed, designed to assist those of us who want to make things happen, who insist they must happen, not in the simplest or most advantageous way, but in the way we want them to turn out—the way they always do when we fail to use common sense, ignore the intuitive urging from our hearts, accept what we know is less than what we want, and squeeze ourselves into places we have no business being. These things happen in a manner which makes us painfully aware that "our way" may not be "the way."

The Valley of Nonresistance is governed by the Law of Nonresistance. The lesson we learn in this valley is cooperation. The trait we must embrace is humility. The virtue we develop is balance, knowing when to do, what to do, and how much to do in any given circumstance. The greatest value of this valley, over the course of a woman's lifetime, is that the lessons she learns here are bound to limit the number of pairs of shoes she buys and cannot wear. Think how sad that will make Visa! Think how happy that will make your feet!

THE VALLEY OF SUCCESS

Some of us will never forget that beautiful pair of shoes that did not fit. We carry the pain of it in our hearts and minds, repeating the story over and over, trying to convince others that things never seem to go our way. We cannot and do not admit that we are giving our lives away to other people, so we make up a story. "Well, I guess it's just not my time." "No, that's okay, you take it. I can wait." These are just samples of the *personal lies* we tell ourselves to cover the core belief, "I really don't deserve it." The Valley of Success, which is nicknamed "I Didn't Really Want It Anyway!," is the way the universe cures us of telling personal lies.

Black women are not taught how to ask for what they want. We do not want to bother other people. We do not think what we want is important. An even greater number of us rarely expect to get the things we ask for. We may believe we ask for too much, or that we really cannot have more than we already possess. In this valley, we learn through the Law of Success that life gives us exactly what we expect. If we go through life expecting a thimbleful, that is exactly what we will get from life. The trait we develop in this valley is expansion. We must expand our expectations in life. The lesson we learn in this valley is patience. Expansion doesn't happen overnight. It takes time and we must be patient with ourselves and life. We must have patience in our worthiness to receive. We must have faith in the process of life by knowing it will deliver all that we are ready and willing to receive. Here, we free ourselves from the claws of the green-eyed monster and the fangs of self-denial. The Valley of Success is life's way of pushing you to your greatness.

THE VALLEY OF LOVE

The dungeon of all valleys is the Valley of Love. We have all been in this valley at one time. This is when the bottom drops out! Your eyes are swollen. Your head is spinning. Your heart is broken and your lover is gone! In the Valley of Love, the lessons of all the other valleys come into play. The Valley of Understanding reminds us of all the warning signs we did not see or failed to heed. The Valley of Knowledge and Wisdom reminds us of all the things we wanted to say and wanted to do, but did not have the courage or wisdom to say or do. The Valley of Purpose and Intent kicks in, reminding us that we were never quite sure of where the relationship was going or what we expected from it. Even when we were clear and expected the best, the Valley of Success reminds us of the number of times we changed our minds.

The Valley of Love is the real garbage collector. All of your fears are exposed and revealed. They come up for the sole purpose of teaching us that the relationship we have is only the mirror reflection of the relationship we are having with ourselves. Whatever that is, whatever that looks like, will be revealed in the Valley of Love.

If you have broken any universal laws, you will face your judge and jury in the Valley of Love. The jury is yourself. The judge is your mind. If you are deficient in any character trait, the Valley of Love is your booster shot. If you have forgotten to, failed to, or chosen not to practice any one or all of the virtues of life, the ramifications of your actions will come up in the Valley of Love. Here we learn that the purpose of relationships is not to make ourselves feel good. Relationships help us heal. This applies not only to our intimate or love relationships, but to all our relationships.

When our relationships are based on total self-acceptance, we can accept others as they are, love them just as they are, without trying to fix them or expecting them to fix us. In order for our relationships to facilitate healing, we must practice unconditional love of ourselves, family members, friends, and mates. Unconditional love allows us to love someone without expectation, judgment, fear, or the need to be in their face all the time. It enables us to live and love, rather than living just to find someone to love in the hope that they will make us feel lovable.

The Valley of Love is ruled by all the universal principles. Cause and effect, belief, awareness, courage, sacrifice, nonresistance, faith, trust—you name it, you will need it during the experiences which take you to this valley. The stellar principle and guiding light of this valley is the Law of Love. Very simply put, God is love. God is the spirit within who knows what we need even before we ask. That spirit of love wants only the highest and the best for us. It does not require that we demean or deny ourselves in any way for the sake of its name, love. Since many of us have not been taught who we are or what love is, we think we are missing something, we think there is something else we need. In the Valley of Love, we get exactly what we need to find the love we already have within.

So You've Fallen and Think You Can't Get Up!

We are perfect, even in our imperfection. There is, however, always room for improvement. Valley experiences bring us to conscious awareness of exactly what it is that we need to improve. Valleys help us recognize, develop, and utilize the spiritual quality or character trait needed to foster spiritual growth and self-improvement. We think bad situations come up in our lives because we are bad, or have done something bad. It simply is not so. We must grow into our greatness. Until we are equipped to do so, until we recognize that we are able to do so, we will find ourselves dealing with the same situations and people who create the same negative feelings we say we no longer want to experience. In other words, until we make a change, have a shift in consciousness, we will stay in the valley.

Your anticipation of greatness and goodness is what makes the valleys so valuable. They help us to recognize that whatever comes up in our lives is in direct correlation to what we need to know and learn in order to evolve. Valleys keep us from being in places we have no business being in by forcing us to realize we can do better. We must do better! Change is the first step toward betterment. If we get the lesson and make the change, we will do better! As long as we think we are cute enough and smart enough, we will not see any room for improvement. Even if we are surrounded by unproductive people and limiting situations, we can do better if we get the lesson and understand the role we play. As long as we resist the lesson, for any reason, we stay in the valley, whining, complaining, blaming, not growing or changing.

This brings us to the good news and the bad news about valleys. The good news is, once you get the lesson, develop the trait, embrace the virtue, and make the shift, you will rise up out of the valley. You will have revelations which bring clarity and a deeper understanding of things which once haunted you. When this occurs, those old situations and people will either make the shift with you or they will move out of your life. If you really get the lesson, if you are really willing to change and grow, you will be required to release the old and make room for the new. That in and of itself is a lesson. Don't worry—the valley will prepare you to accept it.

The bad news is, once you make it out of a valley, it does not mean you are free. There are other valleys with other lessons, other areas you need to strengthen and improve. You will be tested. You must be able to demonstrate what you have learned. You must exhibit through new thought patterns, attitudes, and behaviors, that you really got the lessons of the valleys you have passed through. Unfortunately, on your second, third, and fourth trip to the valleys, the signs are not so easy to recognize. "The bigger they are, the harder they fall," is a fitting description of the valley phenomena. The more you know, the more you are required to know and practice in your day-to-day living.

A Little Valley Is a Ditch!

The universe of life is really merciful. If and when we are willing to learn, we will receive our lessons lovingly and gently. There are those times when what could be a deep valley turns out to be just a little ditch. This means we are down, but we can see our way up. We have stumbled, but our face has not hit the ground. A friend of mine always reminds me, "To stumble does not mean you fall. Sometimes it means you move ahead a little faster." Stumbling into a ditch does not render you helpless. There is something for you to grab or hold on to. Hopefully, it is something you have heard, seen, or learned from a past lesson.

A ditch is life's way of reminding you there is something you know but are not using. You need a wake-up call so that you will not repeat the same mistakes. A ditch lets you know you are headed for a valley. It is life's way of pointing out the warning signs. You will see things you cannot ignore. Hear things that will jolt your memory. If you have mastered yourself and the enlightenment process, you will know there are real dangers which lie ahead. You must be very careful. You will be required to make some hard decisions. Most important, you must be able to act on what you know. If you cannot or do not recognize the signs, employ the process, a ditch will very quickly turn into a valley.

A ditch is like a toothache. When the tooth starts to hurt, you can take some aspirin to make the pain go away, or you can go to the dentist, get the thing x-rayed, and find out what is really going on. Ignoring or numbing the pain may give an infection or a serious problem the opportunity to become worse. Going to the dentist may cost you a little more in time, energy, and money, but you will get to the root of the problem. We may stumble into another ditch when we profess we have learned our lesson. We go around affirming and believing we have truly learned our lesson. "It will never happen to me again!" "I will never do that again!"

Grandma tried to warn you about saying never! To test your level of mastery, the universe may send to you an identical or similar situation clothed in different garments. The people will be different. The circumstances will be different. The temptation will be great. The core or underlying issue will be the same.

When you are being tested, you have pangs of familiar feelings. You may even comment on them. "Something doesn't feel right about this!" "I'm not sure what to do yet!" Other people involved will try to assure you there is nothing to worry about. They will encourage you to abandon your own discernment process. Rest assured, you are in a ditch. Spirit will not lie to you. When things are right in your spirit, you will be at peace. No peace, no spirit! It may be time for you to pull back and watch. Gather more information before you move ahead. At any cost, when you are in doubt, pray! If you have truly learned your lesson, you will recognize your pattern and retreat. The ditch has broken your fall! You are not dead! However, if you allow yourself to be convinced that it will be "different this time," or if you think, "This cannot happen to me again," you will persist. If you move against the warnings, chances are you will end up in the same valley for the same reason as before: You missed the lesson.

Some of Us Need Spiritual Special Ed!

Unfortunately, there are those Black women who repeatedly miss the lesson, stumble through the ditch, and fall head first into the valley. These are the women who will never admit to themselves or anyone else that there is even the slightest possibility that they have made a mistake, poor choice, or unwise decision. These women are simply never wrong. They continue to do things their way, over and over again, getting exactly the same results. They refuse to admit, "My way is not working." They do not get the point—the point being that if they really knew what to do, they would have already done it. The point is, they want to be right at any cost. The need to be right, coupled with the fear of being wrong, eventually renders these women spiritually retarded and makes them prime candidates for Spiritual Special Ed.

I met a woman who insisted on having relationships with men who were born in the month of June, under the zodiac sign Gemini. She was convinced the men born under this sign were the only men who could satisfy her emotional and sexual needs. Her mantra was "I just can't help myself! I love Gemini men!" When she found herself dating a man who was not born under this sign, she would find something incredibly wrong with him as an excuse to dump him. This woman would search around, ignoring perfectly wonderful and interested suitors, until she found a Gemini.

Her first Gemini lover was married. After promising to leave his wife and two children for two years, he eventually moved to another city. The second Gemini, the perfect Gemini man, literally left her at the altar. The third one fathered her two children during their first three years together and refused to marry her. Instead, he married her sister's best friend. The wedding was held in her sister's house. At the age of thirty-five, she met a man who was born on the cusp of Gemini and Cancer. She was reluctant, but decided to go for it. He cleaned out her bank account after they had been living together for nine months.

At the end of each romance, she would cry and bemoan her fate: "Why can't I find a good man and have a good relationship?" She decided there were no good men at all. She resigned herself to accepting whatever she got and making the best of it. Friends and family told her to be patient. Her prayer was to find a good Gemini man who could make her happy and help raise her children. I told her she might want to consider a Leo man, a Scorpio, or anything other than a Gemini. Since she was really into astrology and believed Gemini was her most compatible sign, she dismissed my idea as being completely absurd. She knew there was the "right Gemini" out there and she would keep trying until she found him.

When you are in Spiritual Special Ed, other people laugh at you. They listen to your story and shake their heads. You think they are agreeing with you. The moment your back is turned, they point at you, telling other people how you just don't get it. You keep drooling on yourself, spewing the same dribble which gets you into so much trouble. People want to help you. They ask you questions which you find very annoying. You think to yourself, "What is the matter with them? Why don't they understand that I am right? I am going to prove to them that I am right if it is the last thing I do!" Trying to prove to yourself and the world that you are right eventually renders you spiritually retarded, a candidate for Spiritual Special Ed, unable to move from point *A* to point *B*.

When you are spiritually retarded, you argue for and hold on to the very things which limit your ability to grow. You whine and complain because you are unwilling to do the remedial work. People around you get tired of hearing your story. They speak openly behind your back: "Well, you know how she is! She doesn't listen!" When you are spiritually retarded, you cannot hear and do not listen. You are busy affirming the party line, "I am going to do this if it kills me!" If you continue in your way, resisting the lesson, insisting you are right, struggling to have your way, you will eventually die, mentally, emotionally, and spiritually. Constant struggle and conflict can kill your will to live. But life will not give you up without a fight! Life needs you, your gifts, talents, and energy. Life therefore has given us Spiritual Special Ed as a life preserver; if you hang in there long enough, you will get the lesson!

No valley is an absolute fun place to be. The objective is for you to realize you are having a learning experience, recognize what it is, realize how you got into the situation, and be willing to make the required changes to move beyond where you are. Spiritual Special Ed is not a valley in and of itself. It is the result of the attitude and energy you bring to the learning experience. Your willingness to learn or resistance to learning will determine the condition of the valley in which you find yourself. When you are in a valley with resistance and resentment, chances are you need remediation. When you are willing to take responsibility for what you have done or not done, learning from the challenges, obstacles, and difficulties you face, you will grow. You are an easy learner. In your case, the valley is merely downtime—time to reflect, regroup, and heal.

In Every Lesson There Is a Blessing!

As the Reverend Michael Beckwith of the AGAPE Church of Religious Science says:

> *When you are in a valley, a difficult experience, do not fight it. Your job is to figure out, "If this situation were to remain the same for the rest of my life, what quality would I need to develop to have peace? Do I need patience? Faith? Tolerance? Or some deeper understanding of who I am?"*

If you can remember this, you will realize that every valley experience is an opportunity for you to take one step closer to your greatness.

Peace is a universal principle by which we all must learn to live. The valleys help us grow the character traits and embrace the spiritual virtues we need to find peace within ourselves and life. Whatever the situation in which we find ourselves, we can find the answer through peace, a peace-filled mind and a peaceful heart. Peace is the most advantageous learning environment. In it, we can hear ourselves think and feel what is going on within the universe of our being. In peace, the healing process begins. We realize our experiences, no matter how dark they may be, are merely lessons to guide us. Trouble comes to pass, not to stay! Valleys may seem like troubled times and troubling experiences. In reality, they are transitory conditions you must pass through on your way to peace. It is your attitude, your consciousness, which transforms a temporary valley experience into Spiritual Special Ed.

Spiritual Special Ed is for the stubborn, the hardheaded, downright obstinate Black women who actually have a great deal to do in life, a special gift to offer. Yet they refuse to surrender to the guidance of their own spirit. They hold on to "their way." They cannot trust spirit because S/He may not do it right. These women, of whom I am sure you know at least one, only learn one way—painfully. For many Black women, painfully is the only way we will accept the lesson. Fine! Have it your way! The universe responds to us by giving us exactly what we ask for and need.

Pain gets your attention. Pain forces you to focus. When you are in pain, you pay attention to what is going on in you and around you. Spiritual Special Ed experiences are painful. They are the universe's way of saying, "Look! Something is not working! Stop and pay attention!" You stop, not because you want to, but because the pain forces you to realize you have no other choice. There are those Black women who have become conditioned to living in the midst of a dull ache. Others have steeled themselves to the point that they can survive in excruciating pain. These women *wish* they knew what was wrong. They *try* to make things better. They *hope* things will turn around. Wishing, hoping, and trying means you are not *doing* what it takes to alter the situation. A Special Ed experience will show you exactly what you must do to excavate the source of the infection that is causing the pain.

Spirit Never Strikes Without a Warning!

The lady Gemini-lover eventually spent three years in the Valley of Light: silence, solitude, and for her, celibacy. Choosing not to be depressed and lonely because she was alone, she used the time to get clear about her true feelings and what she really wanted in her life. She decided a loving, committed relationship with a supportive, loving mate was more important than astrological compatibility. She spent the downtime preparing herself for that experience by finding new things to do that she eventually hoped to share with her mate. She also spent quality time with her children, family, and friends. She went back to school to complete her first college degree. She bought a new wardrobe which helped to change her self-image.

One day, it all seemed to pay off. She met a truly gorgeous man on the elevator. He helped her carry a heavy box. They began to date. She refused to ask him his birth sign. She liked him, he seemed to like her, but there was something strange about him. She could not quite put her finger on it, so she detached, just a bit. He gave her his office and beeper number. No home phone. According to him, he was rarely home. "I'm a workaholic," he said. Still, there were other things he said and did which were vaguely familiar to her. She began to pray for clarity. He was clearly more loving, supportive, and generous than any of the others, but there was no peace in her heart about the relationship. Finally she asked him, "What is your astrological sign?" He was born under the sign of Cancer, but his moon, his emotional outlook, was in the sign of Gemini. Remember discernment? Figure out what was going on. She was in a ditch and she knew it. The lady began to back up. Within two weeks she discovered that not only was he married, but he had another girlfriend.

When we find ourselves in the same valley repeatedly as a result of our conditioned responses, we must stop and do a new thing. The situation may look different. The route we take there may be altogether different. The lesson we must learn does not change. Get honest! Pay attention! Change what you do to create a change for yourself! If we use valley experiences as reflective tools, we gain clarity. When we put forth the effort required to gain an understanding of our underlying motives, we can turn any valley into a ditch. The lesson for the Gemini-lover was not about astrology. It was about her belief that there were no good men. For most of her life, she had expected to be treated badly by men. Expectations equal results! Furthermore, she had convinced herself that she had to accept whatever she got in life. "If you hold out a thimble . . ." The fact that she thought a Gemini could give her what she wanted was her conditioned response. Fortunately, this friend was willing to grow. It took two more years in the Valley of Light. Anything worth having is worth waiting for! Eventually she married a Scorpio.

The same lesson, applied to a different area of our lives, will take us to a different valley. Dishonesty in relationships, for example, will send us to the Valley of Love, while dishonesty in business will send us to the Valley of Comeuppance. The different valley experiences provide us with the opportunity to develop and practice the traits and virtues we need in the different aspects of our lives. Since we all believe we have reasonable excuses for doing the things we do, we believe we should be spared on the "little" things. When it comes to valley experiences, however, the degree of the infraction does not spare you a trip. But it will determine how quickly you get the point and the length of your stay.

Valley experiences are not one-size-fits-all. They are custom-designed. What could be a small infraction for one person could result in a long valley experience for her, while others seem to get away with murder. The key is what you need to learn and your willingness to learn it. Some are held accountable for behavior patterns. Others for thoughts and desires. Some people are held accountable for what we call personality. Others for what can genuinely be called learned behavior. Regardless of the degree or level of responsibility, doing the same thing, ending up in the same situation, repeatedly, without any indication of a willingness to change, is spiritual retardation. Special education is required.

You Have to Figure Out What Valley You Are In!

You can determine what valley you have fallen into once you identify the lesson you are learning or the virtue you must practice to eliminate the pain of the experience. There are several ways to figure this out, based on the complexity of the experience you have. The first way is to sincerely ask yourself, "What is the lesson here?" If you ask earnestly, with a desire and intent to know, you will enter the Valley of Light. At just the right moment, the answer will pop into your mind or be revealed to you in some other undeniable way. This is the simplest way, and therefore, the path of most resistance. Black women rarely do what is simple and easy. It is an outgrowth of our addiction to drama. If it ain't hard, it ain't Black! Furthermore, we have been taught not to trust ourselves. How, then, could we possibly believe that the correct or appropriate response would spring forth from our own minds? So we move on to the next, more difficult method. We ask *why.*

If you ask why enough times, of the right people, you are

bound to stumble upon the lesson. What makes this a slightly more difficult method is you are bound to talk to a number of people who, because of their own lesson, cannot help you at all. Another percentage of the people you speak to will tell you what they think you want to hear. If you are lucky, there will be in the mix the person or people with the honesty and wisdom to tell you the absolute truth about yourself in a loving and passionate way. What they will tell you will be so simple, you won't believe it. You will instead spend lots of time and energy trying to figure out which of the other people have given you the best answer.

Eventually, you will find yourself in such pain and confusion that you will take the easy way out. You will go back to the simple answer. You will think about it. It will present some very provocative thoughts and ideas. If you can resist the urge to beat up on yourself, you will be able to identify the lesson, embrace the virtue, and honor the universal law governing your situation. The lesson will usually be something you already knew. Either it crossed your mind before—you were warned about it, or you had a dream about it—or you have lived through it before. Spirit never strikes without a warning. We see the signs. Unfortunately, we allow ourselves to call the warnings something else. Your lesson will be something you must do or stop doing if you want to change your experience.

Packing for the Journey

Are you ready to take the trip, to explore, examine, and hopefully gain a conquering understanding of your deepest, darkest, most painful experiences? If you are ready, you will need a few supplies, things you must know and remember in order to reach your destination successfully. First of all, remember: A valley is an experience. It is temporary, transitory, moving through your life in order to help you grow. Life's objective in providing us with these experiences is self-mastery. As you master yourself, you master the conditions of your life.

Life wants the best for you. Life wants you to be happy. Life supports you in moving toward your happiness by providing you with very simple principles to follow. Life calls the principles universal or natural laws. They are the very things your mother tried to tell you, but you did not listen. Now, as an adult, life is holding you responsible for governing your life in accordance with its laws. These are the character traits you must develop, the virtues or principles you must practice and apply to every area of your life. When life becomes aware that you are not practicing a certain principle or that you are resisting the development of a particular character trait, it tests you. It allows you to make the choice. Will you take the high road, follow the law, or will you go on your merry way and continue to make a mess of things? The tests we face in life are called valleys.

You can successfully emerge from any experience if you understand the process, if you have a formula to apply. You have a formula. Be sure to apply it to all valley experiences. Detach, discern, enlighten, integrate, evolve. Be still! Figure out what is *really* going on. Accept the truth as it is revealed to you and make a decision. Integrate what you know into what you do. Do whatever is right for you to move beyond where you are. Remember, the peace must be within. Do not be overly concerned with what is going on without!

If you do not like tests, you will not pay attention to what you are doing and what you are creating in your life. You will stumble around in darkness, stubbing your toes and pulling very heavy, burdensome experiences into your life. If you are in the dark, it is difficult to see. You may even think someone else is pushing or pulling you. Perhaps you believe they are trying to stop you from moving freely in life. If you think someone is after you, bothering you, trying to stop you, you'll probably be very pissed off. When you are tested, you will blame someone else for your own lack of preparation, but life knows the truth! Life knows that you are in need of special help, special assistance. Life loves you so much that it sends you just what you need.

If you find yourself in Spiritual Special Ed, a very painful experience you have been in before, check your attitude! Follow the process, examine yourself, and bring yourself to a peaceful state of mind about whatever you are going through. If you can do that without blame or guilt, chances are you will graduate with the rest of your class.

Lights! Cameras! Action! The spotlight is on you. As we move through the valleys together, look at yourself. Identify your issues, patterns, challenges. Apply the process to you. Be sure you know what to do and what you have done. Identify what worked and what did not work. Check yourself! Always check in on your attitude. Examine what you are thinking and feeling. If you feel any resistance welling up in your heart and mind, if you are judging, criticizing, calling anyone you see in these pages stupid or dumb, stop! Go back to the beginning! There is something you may have missed. What you see in others is a reflection of you!

If you are in a valley now, be sure to heed the warning signs as you see them. It is quite possible you can turn a valley into a ditch. Above all else, be sure you celebrate the progress you have made. Honor your growth! Laugh at where you were by acknowledging where you are now. Remember, you are not alone. There are thousands of us taking the journey with you and the Mother is leading the way. Just to be on the safe side, use the following road map of the valleys as a study guide so you will always be able to recognize where you are and what you need to do about it. I will be waiting for you at the top of the mountain with an ice-cold nonalcoholic piña colada.

The Valley Roadmap and Study Guide

VALLEY OF	LAW OF	LIFE LESSON	CHARACTER TRAIT	VIRTUE
LIGHT	Self Knowledge	Stillness	Reflection	Awareness
UNDERSTANDING*	Human Nature	Acceptance	Spiritual Vision	Non Judgment
COURAGE	Belief	Trust	Surrender	Courage
KNOWLEDGE AND WISDOM	Obedience	Faith	Discipline	Instinct
O.P.P.*	Sacrifice	Freedom	Strength	Honesty
COMEUPPANCE	Cause and Effect	Responsibility	Forgiveness	Consciousness
PURPOSE AND INTENT	Compensation	Alignment	Commitment	Clarity
NON-RESISTANCE	Non Resistance	Cooperation	Humility	Balance
SUCCESS	Attraction	Patience	Expansion	Self Value and Worth
LOVE	All	All	Dependent on your needs	Unconditional Love

*-Potential Special Ed

MEDITATION
WITH THE
MOTHER

The night is far spent, the day is at hand: let us
therefore cast off the works of darkness and let us
put on the armor of light.

—ROMANS 13:12

O my daughters! You have been taught such lies! I wish I could say
they were mistakes. I cannot! You have been taken off course by lies
and my heart is burdened and bludgeoned by your apparent in-
ability to heal or help yourselves. You have been taught that you
are nothing, useless, without a man and the things men appropri-
ate to you or for you. The truth is, men and their things convert you
into useless nothings! I am not condemning nor dismissing men or
your sacred unions with them. I am revealing to you that "I," not
"they," make you whole. When you honor my energy, the "Mother"
energy, the Divine energy in your soul, your union with men be-
comes functional, not fictional!

It is fiction to believe that a man can make you whole or com-
plete. You were made "completely whole" in the beginning when
the Father and I joined to form the cyclic activity called life. We
were joined at the hip and the heart to recreate ourselves for our
pleasure and longevity. Now today, our daughters have been
taught to believe they are worthless without the sons, when in fact
the sons would have no existence without the daughters. They
alone cannot recreate themselves.

It is a good thing that you give yourselves to the sons. However,
you must be certain that the son you give yourself to is a "good"
son. In your quest for men and things, you may forget what this re-
quires. I am with you at these times. These are the times I send you
to the temple of solitude to reconnect with me. I find need to nur-
ture your heart, nurse your wounds, and resurrect your intuitive
knowing power.

But you, my daughters, resist! You use electronic devices to drown out my words and dim your senses. You live in your heads, trying to figure out what to do, rather than in your hearts, where I instruct you. When you live in your head, you cannot feel the surge of life growing inside of you. You cannot connect with the divine ability to create your world and recreate yourself. You live in your head because you have been taught to dishonor your heart. To feel is not honorable in your world. To feel is a showing of weakness. To feel is to be vulnerable. Yet to feel is the only way to cultivate your connection to the spirit of the Father and Mother alive within you.

When you, my daughters, behave in the manner of men, you disconnect yourself from me. You begin to think. You think you are right. You think you are wrong. You think he loves you. You think he does not. In solitude, if you would become still, come to me—I will tell you all you need to know. It will be functional and real, not fictional and temporarily satisfying.

Trust me, my daughters. Trust your heart, for there is the truth. Stop loving with your minds, love with your heart, your true heart: Acknowledge your need to cuddle; your need to cook and mend; your need to be still while looking into the eyes of your loved one as if he were a babe on your breast and silently transmit "I love you." The feelings in your heart must be aligned with the thoughts in your mind. When the two are joined, you will know there is a sacred union.

When you are in solitude and silence, come to me. Come in prayer and earnest will. Desire to know me, whatever you call me. Welcome me into your life. I will not lead you astray. I will not overpower your ability and right to choose yourself that which you think you want. What I will do for the daughters who come to me and honor me is teach you how to love powerfully, live peacefully, and grow wholesomely. It is my desire to recreate the love of the Mother in the world. It is my will that you be my instruments of divine light and healing. Will you not surrender your need to be right and in control to my will that you be righteously controlled by the divine light of my love?

The Valley of Light

2

*I*F WE REALLY UNDERSTOOD HOW SIMPLE IT IS TO LIVE IN PEACE AND JOY, BE ASSURED SOME INDUSTRIOUS sister would bottle and sell the formula. Then again, it is quite possible no one would believe life is simple enough to sell in a bottle. Many Black women do not trust the simple, obvious solutions. Instead, we take the hard way. We send away for the cellulite-reduction cream advertised on television at 2:00 A.M., wait four to six weeks for it to arrive. When it does, we rub, pat, brush it into those nooks and crannies on our thighs for two days before we forget about it, only to complain that we cannot get rid of the cellulite. This is so much more difficult than just eliminating fatty fried foods from our diet and drinking more water, but if it ain't hard, it ain't Black! Many of us believe it must be hard to be good. In some cases, the harder the better. In the case of life, this is just not the case. Life does not have to be hard! The simplest way to turn our lives into an easier, more peaceful process is to affirm, "Let there be light."

The Valley of Light is the womb of life. It is the sacred place to which a woman must retreat in order to reconnect her life energy with that of the Divine Mother, the spirit of peace, love, and strength with which we women have been blessed. A Valley of Light experience is one which many of us Black women resist because it is a time where we will find ourselves alone. When we understand the purpose of the experience, we find it can be a rewarding and enlightening time. It is a space of time in our lives for healing, learning, and empowerment.

Unfortunately, the standards of modern lifestyles have taught us that to be alone, to be quiet, is bad, frightening, and most of all, not normal. We believe that to be "by yourself" is to not be good enough, to not be right in the world. As such, we fear and resist being alone by accepting into our lives things and people which occupy our minds and give the illusion that all is well. To reap the benefits of the Valley of Light experiences, a woman must be willing to translate being "by yourself" to being "with yourself." When you are with yourself you receive the blessing of enlightenment. You can view an experience or the period of life in which you find yourself from a posture of introspection. Being with yourself is a time of *sacred aloneness* in which you can understand your lessons.

A Valley of Light experience is a calling from the Divine Mother. Whether you consider her an ancestral energy, a guardian angel, or a part of your God self, your spirit, she needs to spend time with you. In her love for and desire to heal our feminine energy, the Divine Mother surges forward in our lives, creating situations which lead us into solitude and silence. In this state, we can be nurtured and rejuvenated. She extracts us from the burdens of the world to give us an opportunity to reflect. "In quietness are all things answered and is every problem quietly resolved."* It is when we resist and fear being with ourselves that the experiences which take us into the Valley of Light are painful.

In my teaching, training, and travels, I have discovered that many Black women do not want to be alone. We need our friends, children, and mates to keep us company. We have been trained to welcome companionship as a statement of well-being. As young girls, we were not allowed to venture out alone. We were instructed to take a younger sibling, close friend, or adult

---

*Foundation for Inner Peace; A Course In Miracles, Tiburon, CA 94920 (1976) Pg. 363.

guardian. It was necessary that we be accompanied to ward off the dangers of the world which prey on young women who travel alone. We grew up afraid to travel alone, were uncomfortable eating alone, and eventually became averse to sleeping alone.

When children are in their rooms alone, if there is no noise, parents immediately expect there is a problem. "Hey! What are you doing? Why are you so quiet in there?" Could it be they are resting? You are out to dinner with a friend who is chatting away. He/she may be telling stories, revealing secrets or new insights. You are silent. The normal response to this is, "You sure are quiet. What's the matter with you? Something wrong?" Of course your friend never considers that you are listening. Silently, peacefully, you sit staring out of the window, looking at everything and nothing in particular. "A penny for your thoughts." People want to bribe you, pay you off, to buy into the hidden wealth of your silence.

In silence, we have an opportunity to reflect, listen, and gain new insights about ourselves. In silence, we can think, feel, and most important of all, breathe. You dare not open your mouth and take a deep breath in a room full of people because they might think "Something is wrong." Consequently, when you truly seek to be silent, you must also seek to be in solitude. When you seek guidance, understanding, clarity, or peace of mind, the first step is to master the art of silence and to rethink the value of solitude. Perhaps these two principles are so difficult for us to master because they are so simple.

The Purpose of Light

According to *Webster's Dictionary,* "to light" means "to lift up, reveal, enhance." In silence and solitude, we can rest our minds as we lift up the energy of our soul. It is an opportunity to cleanse and free ourselves from the pressures and expectations of living. There are times when you must step back from life in order to "lighten" your load and alleviate your responsibilities to others in your life. Silence and solitude will reveal what is going on in your mind by exposing what is weighing you down. If you talk or listen to ten different people in a day, it is absolutely necessary that you weed through your mind in order to separate those thoughts of yours that are original from those that have been implanted. "Be still and know . . ." what part of your world is your creation and which parts you have adopted. In the Valley of Light, the contradictions and conflicts you live will be revealed.

The Divine Essence of Woman

How much do you understand about yourself, your true self? Do you understand that there are unseen energies, aspects of your nature which come into play in every situation you experience? Do you recognize, can you discern the various aspects of yourself and how they are reflected in what you do? What you experience? Many of us Black women are out of touch and therefore do not understand the core of our true nature as women.

These energies within us know all we have been and what we must become. The simplest description of the instincts and identities is "spirit," your true identity. You are spirit expressing itself in the feminine form. For women, the purpose of the spiritual essence is "to mother." Not solely to have children, but to mother: to create, nurture, teach, heal, and love. The purpose of the mother is to receive and create harmony, balance, beauty, peace, and unconditional love as the tools she will use to nurture, teach, and heal the world.

THE LITTLE GIRL

The Divine Mother essence takes on many forms in our being as women. She is the little girl, the virgin, the mother, and the wisewoman, known as the crone. As the little girl, she is playful, curious, and loving. She is the energy within us that wants and needs to be protected, cuddled, and loved. She needs security, guidance, and freedom. The little girl wants to dance, sing, and show off for Daddy. She needs to be carefree, knowing that Daddy and Mommy will take care of her and her needs. The little girl wants her way. She does not care about rules and has no boundaries. As far as she is concerned, the entire world exists for her and is at her disposal.

Harsh, impoverished, often cruel upbringings kill the spirit of the little girl in many Black women. As children, we are taught to fear rather than investigate; to follow rather than explore or create. Our natural curiosity and instincts are interpreted as signs of trouble; our desire to be grown too fast as a demonstration of disrespect. Our instinctual urge to feel welcomed, to be cuddled, often goes unfulfilled as we are trained, watched, and disciplined to be nice, keep still, and be quiet.

As little girls, many of us are not told we are beautiful. Rather, we are dressed up to "look beautiful" for the pleasure of our parents and the world. In large urban cities, beautiful little Black girls are prey rather than treasures. We are taught to fear who we are and what we are for the dangers and hardships it will ultimately bring to us. In response to the danger our identity presents, we must hide who we are and what we feel because of the trouble, inconvenience, and competition sure to result.

Most damaging of all is that little Black girls around the world are force-fed religious doctrine which teaches them they are evil, lowly, disobedient, and born of sin. As females we are all held to the example of a disobedient "apple eater," destined to suffer in pain and disgrace until we find salvation. By the way, our salvation just happens to be a man. A dead man. A dead white man, but a man nonetheless. On cues from our parents, society, and church, we grow up frightened of doing the wrong thing. The fear numbs our natural instincts. Frightened, numb little girls grow up to be fearful, numb women, with no idea that they are divine expressions of life, divinely guided and perfectly protected by the Divine spirit in their being. In solitude and silence, that spirit embraces us.

THE VIRGIN

Also alive in our essence is "the virgin," whose purity and innocence wait to be filled with light and life. Like the young, delicate, desirable virgins of the ancient African villages, there are forces in the community scrabbling and competing to win the virgin's heart, mind, and body. Her innocence and purity are a prize. The virgin within us must therefore be instructed, prepared, and primed in order to be able to recognize who is and who is not a "suitable suitor." Under the watchful eyes of the mother in our physical lives and the essence of the Divine Mother in our own minds, the virgin is guided as to whom and what she should submit herself to.

When the energy of the mother is strong, wise, protective, and cautious, great energy is given to instructing the virgin well. A wise mother gives her blessing only to those people and things which have the most to offer her daughter and the innocence and purity in her being. These offerings may well be economic. They must be spiritual. Then there are those more common cases when the mother, numbed from her experiences as a little girl, sells her daughter to the highest bidder, without regard for what is offered in return. When the mother is numb and fearful, not wise or watchful, the virgin girl can find herself with a destructive, even abusive suitor. Whether the suitor is an actual person, a way of life, or an unhealthy desire, the early experiences of many young Black girls conspire to rob them of their innocence and purity.

The essence of the virgin is still alive in every Black woman. There is a purity and innocence in our hearts which wants to believe in and trust people. When we are betrayed, it is the virgin who requires nurturing, tutelage. When we lose contact with her or fail to recognize and honor her, we continue to submit ourselves to people and conditions which spoil her sacred energy. If the virgin is not handled gently, carefully, lovingly, she is hurt, damaged. She becomes bitter, reluctant, resentful, and frightened.

The virgin must remember the lessons the mother has taught her: Move slowly. Watch everything. Listen carefully. Tell the truth. When we honor our innocence in this way, reminding our heart to follow Mother's instructions, we tap into the joy that the time in the Valley of Light offers. We can be with ourselves, to nurture our wounds and to receive the guidance we need in order to be enlightened.

THE MOTHER

The Divine Mother knows the day will come when our innocence and purity will be replaced by the lessons of motherhood.

I did not say "lost" to motherhood. Our innocence is never lost. It is overcast by our changing roles. The mother in every woman rises to the surface when the virgin shifts her attention from fulfilling her dreams to giving others the opportunity of realizing their dreams. The mother is not concerned with "being taken." She is focused on preparing and instructing others on how to be taken and by what to be taken.

In ancient African societies, the mother is honored and cherished. She is left alone to nurse and fondle her child because the community understands the sacredness of a mother's love is the strongest foundation in a child's life. Today, the role and duties of a mother have been diminished to a chore, one which is squeezed into our responsibilities to the world and the pressures of the economy. Women are not taught to regard motherhood or the duties of a mother as sacred. Rather, we are made to feel ashamed or guilty if our "world" and our economics are not "just so" when we embark upon the role of motherhood.

The instinct of the ancient mother is alive in every woman, particularly Black women who watched their mothers care for many babies. The mother wants to hold onto the child. The mother wants to nurture, protect, and love not only the children born from her, but all children of God. What men call possessiveness, nagging, and dependency is the energy of the mother. Women who have not been given an understanding of this nature respond to it intellectually or defensively. It looks like jealousy, aggressiveness, being demanding of our mates and others in our lives. Men who have not been nurtured by or taught to respect the mother respond to the mothering instinct in women with egotistical fear: "Don't tell me what to do!" "Why don't you stop trying to control me!" In response, the woman shrinks away in fear, feeling she has done something wrong, she has overstepped her boundaries. Women are taught to know their boundaries and to stay in their place. In the American society today, void of cultural understanding, "her place" is subservient to the man.

In the Valley of Light, we get an opportunity to be a mother to ourselves. If we hold ourselves, nurture ourselves, talk to ourselves about our fears and dreams, the essence of the Divine

Mother comes alive and knows what to do. She may guide you to wash your hair, soak your feet, make or buy a new dress, purely for your own pleasure. As you move around, following her instructions, she is talking to your heart, helping you to reflect, learn, and heal. Mother has a way of making everything better. Perhaps it is the mercy with which she accepts us. Or the grace with which she guides us. One thing is for certain: If we make a sincere effort to make the most of our time in this valley, Mother will enlighten us.

THE WISE OLD WOMAN

Perhaps the most empowering energy of the Divine Mother essence is that of the wisewoman, the elder, the "Crone." You have seen images of her sitting on the porches in the South. You have seen her selling her wares in the open-air markets of the Caribbean and Africa. Everyone has seen her sitting in the pews of the Baptist, Pentecostal, or A.M.E. churches. Whether she is buxom and stern, or frail and gentle, her skin ashen or cold jet black, you know the Crone when you see her. It only takes one look, one experience, for you to know she knows exactly what to do.

Some women are born to be the wisewoman. Others grow into their wisdom. But all women have the essence of the Crone in their spirit. This formidable presence in your spirit knows exactly what to do at all times, under all circumstances. She is the first to yell out, "Hey! Watch it!" in your mind when you are headed for danger. When you do not heed her warnings, she does not give up. She points out to you certain details and inconsistencies about people and situations which the rational mind quickly silences. The wisewoman is the gnawing in your stomach urging you to ask certain questions. When you do not ask, she becomes the restlessness in your spirit. This elder wisewoman is the one who wakes you up in the middle of the night to tell you what is going to happen, before it happens. Do we listen to her, pay attention to her? Of course not! Why? Because we are afraid of her. We are afraid of her power.

In an African proverb the question is asked, "Who is more important, the king or the king's mother?" In their manhood training rites, the young men are taught that without the mother, there would be no king. The Crone, the wisewoman, is the king's mother. She gives birth to royalty. She has followed the right path, made the right decisions, and is now credited with the salvation of the village by the king's proper rulership. The king's mother does absolutely nothing. She may look, wave, smile, or nod—that is it. Her claim to fame is being wise, wise enough to give birth to a king.

We all remember being in church or at a public function acting out in some way. All Mother or Grandmother had to do was look. With one glance you knew she was willing and able to rock your world. You knew it then and you know it now. You know the look someone gives when something is not quite right. You know the sound they will make, the way they will tilt their head or shuffle their feet. That is the essence of the wisewoman, the same essence that was in Momma's look and Granny's wave of the hand. Unfortunately, we keep that essence, the wisewoman, the powerful Crone, in darkness.

Our journey to the Valley of Light is life's way of providing us with an opportunity to reconnect with the Crone, the wisdom in our spirit. We come into the realization that we know, and knew all along, what was going on and what to do. The Crone silences the wayward child who is stomping her feet to get her way. She soothes the frightened virgin who has been manhandled and hurt in some way. She silences the fretting mother who is trying to protect you. The Crone lays all your cards on the table, forcing you to say, "Damn! why didn't I see that before!" More often than not, she slaps you right in your face with the thing you saw but ignored, what you felt but rationalized, wanted to say but didn't, knew but couldn't figure out how to move. When the Crone finishes enlightening you, your natural response is, "Now what am I going to do?" Don't worry! The Crone will instruct you wisely and specifically. The question is, can you hear it? Will you accept it? Are you ready to do what you know you must?

If Black women began to do what we know we are capable of doing, what we know we must do for our own sense of well-being, many people would be very upset. This is what we fear the most: having people angry or upset with us. We sacrifice our feelings to placate others. We put ourselves down because others have told us it is not "right" to rise up. The essence of the Divine Mother and all of her identities has been misinterpreted. Her playfulness has been called irresponsibility. Her need to be nurtured and supported has been called dependency. The innocence and purity of her nature has been called weakness and stupidity. Her power has been called evil. The very people we love and trust tell us to ignore her and listen to them. As a result, we believe it is our duty to "please" other people.

Our desire to please others forces us to say yes when we want to say no. When we find the courage to say no, we are riddled with guilt. We sell ourselves short by accepting less than we want and convincing ourselves that what we have is good enough. We do not allow the little girl to question, the virgin to explore, the mother to nurture, or the Crone, the wisewoman, to direct. In numbness and self-inflicted darkness, we accept what others want to give us, tolerate their manhandling of us, and ignore the wisdom that speaks through our hearts. When our failure to respond to the urgings of our spirit takes us into dangerous situations, the wisewoman orders the palace guards to usher us into the Valley of Light.

A Valley Experience

Pam was a workaholic, a typical affliction of many Black women. We feel guilty, sometimes unworthy, when we have nothing to do. We tell ourselves we work because we have to work. Most of us work because we do not know how to stop. We are afraid to stop. Pam was a high-profile account executive with a major advertising firm. She worked ten to twelve hours a day, every day. She managed two of the agency's biggest accounts and several minor but important ones. Pam was also a detail-oriented perfectionist who feared criticism and could not delegate responsibility. She told herself, "Nobody can do it as good as I can." This was an outgrowth of her mother's old saying, "If you want something done right, do it yourself!" Pam, like many Black women, tried to do everything herself. She was pretty good at getting things done, but her demanding work habits had cost the agency six secretaries and two assistants over the three years she had been an account executive. Pam said she couldn't help it. It was just her personality.

Whatever tasks Pam did not finish at the office, she took home. She never got much of that work done, but it made her feel and look busy. It also gave her something to beat herself up about. Pam's evenings were reserved for choir practice, usher board meetings, aerobics, and a Spanish class. All of this went on much to the dismay of her boyfriends. Oh yes, Pam had boyfriends. She picked up a new one about every six weeks, at the disco. The disco was absolutely necessary to Pam's well-being. It was the way she chose to unwind. Pam spent a very good portion of her money on disco clothes. The rest went to pay the charge account bills for her work and church wardrobe.

Many Black women are on-the-loose "busy freaks." We have to be doing something every minute. If we are not busy, we are not satisfied. Pam was able to convince herself that she had a very satisfying life. She satisfied herself by working hard and having a good career. She satisfied her parents by remaining active in the church. She satisfied the world by being an "up and coming" executive, a Black female executive at that. She satisfied the men in her life by staying vibrant, in shape, and independent. Pam would never once have considered herself a "people pleaser." She was simply doing what she had been taught every young woman "should" do: making her own way in the world. In order to make it, you had to be busy. In those very rare moments when Pam had absolutely nothing to do, she would feel herself being overtaken by a wave of unhappiness, discontentment, and fear. It never lasted long. Just as the feeling came up, Pam would find something "meaningful" to do.

When we need to stop, slow down, and listen to ourselves, life finds a way to make it possible. Pam's agency lost three of the small accounts Pam was handling. It seems the clients wanted more personal attention and time. Of course Pam got blamed for not living up to her responsibilities. Her annual bonus was cut and one of her large accounts was given to another account executive. Right in the middle of the account shift, Pam's father had a heart attack. He recovered, but her parents decided to move back South. They knew Pam could take care of herself and they wanted to enjoy the rest of their retirement years at a slower pace. Pam was sad but relieved. Her parents were her lifeline, but their demands and expectations of her had taken over her life.

Most of the women Pam considered to be her friends were members of the church. She had begun to notice that a few of them were questioning her about her lifestyle. These women were either married to or dating men from the church. They spent most of their spare time on church committees and other church functions. They were suspicious because they never got to meet Pam's date and they did not know what she did with her spare time. Pam became defensive, which is what we do when we are in fear of being found out. She decided they were just jealous and ignored their questions unless answering them was absolutely unavoidable. Unfortunately, we do not realize that when we're living a contradiction, we are out of order. We are working against universal law and nature. You cannot want to do one thing and live another forever. We know it, yet for some reason we continue to ignore and resist the signs. For Pam, the women's questions were a sign. Her fears of being found out were a sign. She ignored the signs until they blew up in her face. The final blow came when Pam was confronted by the senior mother of the usher board who asked her to resign.

DARKNESS MUST COME TO LIGHT!

As the mother informed Pam, her latest boyfriend of three weeks was the husband of the sister of another usher board member. Pam had met him at the disco. They had been "keeping company." Unfortunately, his wife had found Pam's card in his pocket. Like any good wife would do, she staked out Pam's house on a Saturday night, the night her husband had begun to disappear. She wanted to catch a glimpse of him and the "floozie" who was taking him out of church and away from his family. She caught that glimpse at 3:30 in the morning when he brought Pam home. She caught another glimpse of him at 9:30 in the morning when he left Pam's house. In her state of distress, she told her sister, who, being on the same usher board, recognized Pam's name immediately. The sister had told the mother and the mother was now telling Pam that although she might not have known he was married, a "good" Christian woman has no business being in a dance hall in the first place. In the second place, no truly good single Christian woman has any business being alone in an apartment with a man at 3:30 in the morning.

The mother suggested to Pam that she study her Bible and take some additional classes to familiarize herself with the moral standards and values required for Christian living. Of course, it was the mother's duty to relate the whole story to the choir director. Who in turn had a responsibility to tell the head deaconess. Who had no choice but to tell her husband, who just happened to be Pam's father's best friend in the church. By the time Pam's parents got the news, Pam was trying to kill her mother and shame her father to death with her loose and lurid behavior. After three weeks' back-and-forth on the telephone, with her mother screaming and crying, while her father prayed for the salvation of her soul, Pam had a rip-roaring case of acne.

Pam fired her seventh secretary, which did not help her face one single bit. The acne had become so unsightly her supervisor suggested that maybe Pam should take an early vacation to give her skin a rest from the makeup. To Pam that sounded as if she had messed up again and "they" were trying to find an excuse to get rid of her. Pam responded hysterically, reminding her supervisor of all the money she had made the firm on their accounts. She went on to call the supervisor a racist thief who Pam would not hesitate to sue for discrimination.

The supervisor, a student of light, a very spiritual woman, did not take Pam's ranting seriously. Being more concerned about Pam's visibly distressed state, she ordered Pam to take two weeks' vacation, with pay, and issued a memo to the personnel office stating that Pam should not be allowed in the office before the two-week period had expired. She also rehired the secretary Pam had fired. The supervisor ordered a car to take Pam home, telling her to rest and pray. Reluctantly, Pam went home for a two-week vacation in the Valley of Light.

The Law of Self-Knowledge

Know thyself. Accept thyself. Love thyself. No matter what you have done, where you have been. Know, accept, love who you are. The Law of Self-Knowledge says:

To thine own self be true.

In other words, listen to your heart. Follow its prompting. Honor what you feel and act accordingly. When we break this law, the cardinal law of survival, we become pawns in the game of life. People can convince us that we are what we are not, and lead us to believe that we are not what we are. "Know thyself" means, know what makes you tick and why. Be able to identify your original thoughts from those you have adopted. It also means, trust that you can have an original thought and act upon it even when others are not "pleased" by what you are doing.

FACE YOURSELF, HEAL YOURSELF!

Self-knowledge presupposes that what you are doing is productive and satisfying for you. Self-acceptance means embracing all of you, the good and the not so good. You can always make a commitment to change those things about you with which you are not pleased. However, as James Baldwin reminded us, "You cannot heal what you will not face." "Love thyself" means, stop denying who you are and what you feel. Stop criticizing yourself. Take a moment to look yourself in the face, at least three times a day, and say, "I love you." It also means, do what makes you feel good without asking for anyone's approval or authorization. These three acts—knowing, accepting, and loving—are very difficult for Black women who are people pleasers. We become so derailed by what we have done or not done to make others happy, and understandably forget about ourselves.

One of the most difficult challenges Black women confront in knowing, accepting, and loving ourselves is accepting that we have made a mistake, been wrong about something or someone, or that we have made a poor choice or bad decision. Somewhere, deep inside, we believe that to say we are wrong is to admit, "Something is wrong with me." Even if we believe there is something not quite good or right about who we are, we do not want to admit it to other people. So we do not admit it. We make excuses for the way we think and behave. We create stories; tell outright lies; hold our parents, personality, or the zodiac accountable for our humanness. It's these very stories, lies, and excuses which take us straight into the valley.

Black women do not understand there is no wrong in being human. There are only lessons. No matter how outlandish, ridiculous, or irresponsible our behavior may be at any given time, we do what we do based on who we are and the information we have at the time. Know. Accept. Love. There is nothing wrong with you. There is, however, always room for improvement and change. Valleys are designed to help us improve who we are and what we do. But first we must know who we are.

We create our lives by our thoughts, particularly the thoughts we have about ourselves. Who and what we think we are today has been influenced by what we have been told throughout our lives. Repetition is the mother of skill. If we hear something often enough, we will become very skillful at believing and ultimately doing it. If we do not examine what we hear, we adopt it as a belief and incorporate it into our thoughts, emotions, and behavior. Eventually, we lose sight of and touch with our true identity, seeking instead what we have been told and have been trained to be. More important, we become what we have been told *not to be* because that is our most dominant thought pattern.

One thought will not make you or destroy you. It is the habitual thought patterns, reinforced by emotions, which eventually grow into a self-concept. If you grow up in a family where everyone wore a size five dress when you wore a size ten, you may believe you are fat. Your constant thoughts about weight, feeling and looking big, are sure to draw comments from the people in your life, such as "Are you gaining weight?" When you go shopping, you can bet you will find a rackful of size sixes or eights, but no tens. In your mind, this reinforces the idea that you are fat, when in fact, the idea has drawn you into the situation.

Don't Pick Your Scabs

Without self-knowledge you cannot have self-acceptance. Without self-acceptance, you cannot have self-love. When you do not know, accept, or love yourself unconditionally, one of the things you do is what I call "picking your scabs."

Remember how when you were young, if you fell or sustained any kind of wound, after the bleeding and soreness was over, a scab would grow to cover the wound? As children, we had a tendency to pick at our scabs. Out of our two legs, one leg would be beautiful, completely unscarred. That leg we paid no attention to at all. Instead we took advantage of every available opportunity to show the scabbed leg to any and everyone who would look. We had no shame about it. We would pull our pants leg up or our pants down, depending on the location of the wound, to show family, friends, or strangers the unsightly scab in the most private locations on the body.

Showing the scab was not enough; we had to pick it. We would pick the corners, the top layer, all of the loose, weak parts became subject to our filthy fingers and public view. As adults, we do the same thing with ourselves and our lives. We find the weak spots in our character, the loose parts of our lives and we pick, pick, pick. Pointing them out, showing them off, making sure everyone knows we have a scab, a wound, a weakness. What this looks like in our lives is the inability to accept compliments. If someone compliments us, we are quick to point out what is wrong, not good about the very thing they are complimenting. It is also our eagerness to put ourselves down: "Oh no, I can't do that! I'm too . . ."

We love to pick on ourselves. However, when someone else points to the very same thing, if they comment on a weakness or a sore spot, we are incensed: "Oh no! You can't pick my scab! When you do it, it hurts." I remember when my mother tried to put the Mercurochrome on my cuts and wounds, I screamed bloody murder. When she did it, the pain was unbearable. When I did it, I knew exactly how much pressure to apply, where to touch and how to touch. I also remember what my mother would tell me about picking my scabs: "Why don't you leave that thing alone! If you keep picking at it, it will never heal."

Self-knowledge is not about picking your scabs, beating up on yourself; feeling bad about your wound or weak spots. It means that you recognize you have them, make a commitment to nurture and strengthen them, and leave them alone to heal. Stop pointing out to people what you cannot do, how bad and weak you are. By all means, apply the right amount of pressure to facilitate your healing, but do not pick your scabs! At the other extreme are those of us who know we have scabs and wounds. We do not pick them or show them off. We cover them up. If you have an open, gaping wound which you keep covered, it will fester and become infected. The infection can travel throughout your entire body, creating a seriously life-threatening condition. Emotional and spiritual wounds can be just as infectious as physical ones.

A wound needs air in order to heal. We must talk about and expose those things which have hurt or harmed us in some way. Our wounds need nurturing care in order to heal. If we are to nurture and heal, we must admit that the wounds exist. We must carefully do what is necessary to help ourselves feel better. The minute we go into fear, shame, or guilt about having a wound, about how we got it or what we have done in response to the pain of the wound, we want to hide. When we hide our emotional and spiritual pain, it infects and affects who we are and what we do.

The Lesson

Pam knew or had reason to know that she was on a collision course. She had difficulty reconciling her commitment to the church with the fact that she picked up men in the disco, but she was wounded. She knew what her parents wanted her to be. She knew what the world expected of her. She knew what men demanded of her, but she would not allow herself to think about what she really wanted for herself. Her lifelong dream had been to be a dancer, but she had been taught dancing was an evil act. Pam had decided that what she wanted for herself was "wrong" and that what she *should* do was to make sure she followed the warnings her parents had given.

Pam is an example of many Black women who allow other people to "should" on them. We can become so preoccupied doing what we "should" do that we lose sight of and touch with the very thing which will make us happy. There were many instances in which Pam could do what she wanted to do in an honorable way. She could have been a dance teacher or a dance therapist, but she never took the time to think about it. She would not allow herself to consider it. For Pam, dancing meant using the body she feared, and losing her parents' love. Rather than risk that, she hid her dancing the way she had been taught to hide her body.

To compensate for the void we experience in our hearts and minds when we are doing what we *should* do, rather than what we want to do, we fill every moment with activity. Pam used work. Others of us use food, sex, drugs, children, television, caring for ailing parents, or any number of excuses to convince ourselves that what we need or want to do is impossible. We do not think. We do not allow ourselves to feel. On those rare occasions when we do think or feel, we berate ourselves. We push ourselves deeper into self-denial by becoming occupied with details of what we are doing. It takes time and energy to make sure whatever you are doing is done "right." The time it takes eliminates the chances for the brain to slip back to your "self" and what you want. It is a vicious cycle which keeps us in darkness and pain. It is this darkness and pain which comes rushing to the surface when we are finally alone.

Pam had many faces she worked hard to maintain. The Pam who sang in the choir or marched down the aisle in an usher's uniform was not the same Pam who twirled around the dance floor. The disco Pam was not the same Pam who showed up for work at seven forty-five in the morning. One of the first lessons we must learn in the Valley of Light is, "Be yourself." Pam, like many Black women, wore masks to suit the roles she played. The roles we live are not always a true reflection of who we are or who we want to be. They are the roles we have been given. They are the instruments which keep us from being true to ourselves. We always know when we are not being true to ourselves because we live in fear—fear of being found out. We fear being discovered. We try to run away from our true self and desires. But like the commercial told us, "You can't fool Mother Nature!"

Being clear about who we are, what we need and want to feel good about ourselves, is one of the basic lessons we learn in the Valley of Light. It is called self-awareness. The key to awareness is reflection. We must think about, reflect on, what we are doing and feeling in order to determine if it is good for us. As we reflect, we become aware. It becomes very clear which of the things we are thinking, saying, or doing create conflict in our lives. We become aware of the contradictions we are living. If we are honest with ourselves, if we resist the urge to blame others, if we can resist the urge to be ashamed or guilty, we will be guided into appropriate action. If we make any excuses for ourselves, however, we will be pushed deeper into darkness.

If you are willing to grow, pain and darkness often bring you to the light. If you can master the art of being still, you will get an opportunity to see yourself, where you have been and where you want to go. When you are alone, you come face to face and to grips with what you are doing and why. This is the process of awareness, figuring out what is necessary and unnecessary, wanted and unwanted, in your life. With awareness, you can differentiate yourself from the other people in your life. You can hear your thoughts and examine your emotions. However, if you continue to resist the light of silence and solitude, negative emotions will surface and put you back on a path which leads to an even deeper valley.

The Value of Awareness

Awareness is the value in the Valley of Light. By reflecting on ourselves and our experiences, accepting what we see, making choices and changes without fear or resentment, we become aware. Awareness enables us not only to know a thing exists in us, but also to recognize how it operates. When we know who we are, we become aware of how we function. When we are aware of how we function, we are not as ready and willing to accept what people say about us. The true value of awareness is that it provides us with the courage and strength to resist those people and conditions that do not reflect the true image of who we are.

Pam had no idea she was in a valley. She was just afraid. She was afraid of losing because losing meant she was wrong. She was afraid to reject the teachings of her parents, although she did not believe in them, because she was afraid of losing their love. She really believed she was doing the right thing by not honoring her feelings and pleasing other people. Because she put all of her time and energy into doing the "right" thing, she was afraid of being questioned or challenged. Questions made her angry and resentful. If you go into a valley experience angry, afraid, or resistant, you will not see the light. Anger and resentment often lead to overt and covert rebellion. If you are to benefit from the value of silence and solitude, you must first make peace with yourself and allow yourself to feel.

If there were a motto for the Valley of Light it would be, "Know thyself. Accept thyself. Love thyself." That is where the lesson begins. Who am I? How do I feel about me? What do I want? What am I doing? What do I need to know? These are basic questions to ask yourself when you are seeking the light. Take a bath. Listen to some music. Stare out the window. Ask the questions and wait for the answers. There is something, a force, an energy in you, that needs to be nurtured and healed. That is the value of the Valley of Light. It is the opportunity to nurture yourself. Born and raised to be people pleasers, many of us Black women are not aware of our own essence or energies. We believe as long as we are busy we are fine. Being in the Valley of Light is usually the opportunity to discover what we need to really be fine.

The Way Out

If I had a nickel for each time I really thought I knew what I was doing, I would be rich! I had no idea how confused and out of touch I was until I took a moment to seriously look at myself. I was not only blind, I was deaf and dumb about the things which really should have mattered to me. I thought I did not matter, so I did not, could not, trust myself. I believed no one really cared about me and concluded I must have done something to make them feel that way. Most of all, I did not like me. I was all wrong. The events in my life led me to these conclusions. However, I must admit I willingly accepted them. What is the lesson in feeling ugly, being wrong, believing you are worthless? The only way to understand is to have some light shed on your issues.

When you have a negative experience and find yourself alone, it is quite possible you have entered the Valley of Light. Remember to detach. Do not allow yourself to be dragged through an emotional frenzy. Get still in order to reflect on what has happened. Without judgment or criticism, discern—figure out what is going on in order to find the lesson. Admit to yourself how you have contributed to the experience by your own behavior. Integrate that information into your consciousness and make a choice to continue or discontinue that behavior. Make a commitment to employ whatever virtue is required to help you feel better. Make an honest assessment of what you need to do to avoid the situation again. Then and only then will you move up and out of the valley. Let us apply this concept to Pam.

Pam needed time to get in touch with herself. Her parents' absence and her forced leave from work provided just the opportunity she needed, although Pam misinterpreted this opportunity. Time off from work with pay, regardless of the circumstances which led up to it, is a blessing. This was time for Pam to take a look at life and decide whether she wanted what she had or something else. Pam needed to assess what part of her behavior and life was self-satisfying and what part was in response to her need to please. Reflection was a critical issue for her. No one had forced Pam to do anything. She had made choices to do or not do what she believed she "should" do. Her choice was really simple: Did she want to be happy or did she want to please her parents? As difficult and frightening as it seemed, Pam would be forced to go against everything her parents had taught her in order to pursue her dream of being a dancer. If she chose not to dance, she would then need to choose something else which would make her feel just as good and worthy.

There is absolutely no way to get clear about your life until you are clear about and comfortable with yourself. If there is anything you do not like about you, it will become an issue for you as you move through life. Most of the things we believe and do not like about ourselves are things other people have told us. The things we have been told, the things we witness and experience, create wounds in our emotional and spiritual psyche. Pam needed to work through some very serious issues about her body and sexuality. Very often, the religious doctrines to which we are exposed as children create distortions in our minds. As we mature and are exposed to different views, conflict sets in and we are forced to live contrary to what we have been taught and told. Life experiences and the lessons we must learn shed light on the conflicts and contradictions in which we live.

Parents have a way of getting over their disappointment, particularly if you are successful at what you choose to do. The little girl in Pam needed to know it was fine for her to play and dance. With all of the working, hiding, and living up to expectations, the fun had gone out of her life. Pam's virgin, her innocence and purity, had been damaged by the demands placed upon her and those she placed upon herself. You must give yourself the opportunity to make poor choices. If you do not make mistakes, you do not learn. In our innocence, we often choose things for ourselves which later prove to be unwise. This is how we grow. You can never do the wrong thing. If what you do does not work for you, you know what not to do the next time around. Pam had never explored the possibility of being a dancer. She chose her parents' work ethic to define the parameters for her own life.

There comes a time in your life when you have to choose what you want over what has been given to you. When the light hits an object, all of its imperfections become visible. That is what a Valley of Light experience does for us. Once we are able to pull back and look at our lives, we can see what is really going on. Once you can see, you can choose. Even if Pam chooses to stay in her current career and the church, she will still need to make some choices and changes. Her fear of her body and her fear of criticism and questions are related to feelings of being and doing wrong. Her need to please others is related to feelings of unworthiness. The fact that she never takes time for herself is a critical issue relating to self-love and self-acceptance. Before she can be or do anything, Pam will need to become aware of who she is and what she wants for herself. She is a human being, bound to make mistakes, incapable of controlling everyone or everything. Once she truly understands this, she will have less of a need to please others and the courage to please herself.

How do we know Pam is in the Valley of Light? The first clue is that she has been isolated. She is alone and has nothing to do. The second clue is that all of Pam's issues revolve around her, what she has done or not done. There is no one else playing a critical role in the situation. Her parents, the mother usher, and the boyfriend are all objects which were used by life to bring the situation to a head. The most revealing clue of all was the acne. The question which comes to mind is, What face are you showing the world? Not everyone who goes into this valley will get acne, but the body will let you know there is something going on which you must clear up. The fact that the supervisor was supporting Pam in her enlightenment is another clue. The universe always has a way of giving us exactly what we need even when we fail to recognize it. Two weeks with pay is a good way to get in touch with yourself. Unfortunately, it took Pam a week to be able to calm down enough to enjoy it. In the end, Pam left her job and went back to school to study dance therapy. Today she owns her own consulting firm.

MEDITATION
WITH THE
MOTHER

Forsake the foolish and live;
and go in the way of understanding.

—PROVERBS 9:6

Do you argue with your breath? Do you give directions, opinions, or doubt and question the ability of your breath to do its work, your work? I am as close to you as your breath. Yet you know me not. You embrace the symbols. Use the words. Wear the garment. And still you question the reality and relevance of your spiritual nature. You hate, you fear, you feel anger—emotions which are restrictive to your nature. Then you question whether spirit can provide for your needs, satisfy your desires, protect and guide you. You concern yourselves more with what you eat than how you pray, if you pray, believing the answers will come. This, my daughters, is the effect of your lack of understanding, your disconnection from the truth.

I am at your core. Beneath the lies, misconceptions, prejudices, and fears, I lie dormant at the gate of your soul, silenced by the hurt, anger, and burdens you accept from your experiences. I am sprawled, wounded, in your minds, covered by miseducation, social distortions, and the limitations of your human perceptions. Yet you know me. I am there at your darkest, weakest, and most troubling times. You doubt, yet I know: Not until you take the time to dig me up, dust me off, and listen to my murmurings will you know truth, build knowledge, and develop understanding. This, dear daughters, is your challenge in life.

The Valley of Under- standing

☙

3

☙

YOU ARE IN TROUBLE, CRISIS, OR CONFLICT. YOU DO NOT KNOW WHAT TO DO, WHICH WAY TO TURN, HOW TO get yourself out of a situation that you really do not understand how you got into in the first place. Your back is up against the wall. Suddenly, miraculously, something or someone comes along offering the prospect of salvation. You are not sure what to do, but you know you have to do something. You reach out to, grab onto, embrace this thing or person. At first, things seem just fine. As time goes on, you begin to notice that this thing or person is not what you need, want, or hoped for. Do you stop? No! You stay in the situation, telling yourself it will get better soon. It doesn't, and before you know it, you are in a worse situation than before. Once again, you don't know what to do.

I have watched this scenario over and over again. With family members, friends, friends of friends—for that matter, with myself. When we find ourselves in a difficult situation, we shift into fear, panic, or desperation. Rather than asking for guidance, praying for clarity, or refusing to do anything until we are sure of what to do, we keep moving. We move in confusion, unaware we are doing the very same thing, in the very same way, that got us into trouble in the first place. We start judging, thinking, where we "should" be, how people "should" respond, and guesstimating what "should" happen. We just do not understand "should" may have absolutely nothing to do with what "is"! We do not understand there is a part of our nature crying out for evolution. There is something we need to learn.

I will speak for myself here. One of the reasons I do not stop moving and doing when I know I should is I have convinced myself that if I don't do something, nothing will get done. There is the martyr in me. She thinks, "Since I'm the one who created the mess, and the one who will get blamed for it, I'm the one who has to fix it." Then I get scared. I am afraid I will do the wrong thing, afraid someone will find out I did the wrong thing. My fear makes me judge. I start "shoulding" all over myself and others. It's a vicious cycle which I have difficulty understanding until I find the courage to say, "STOP! I don't know! I don't understand what I am doing to create the mess! I don't understand what is really going on!" Please notice I do not ask "What am I doing wrong?!"

When you do not know what to do, don't do anything! When you are not clear, not sure, don't move. The time to get clear is at the very moment when your back is against the wall. That is when you have to stop grabbing, pushing, pulling, trying. You must suspend all judgment, surrender all fear. At the very moment you are at your weakest, in your most confused state of mind, that is when you have to tell yourself, "STOP! I don't know what to do here! I am in trouble! I need help!" This is what the average Black woman does not understand, and it is this lack of understanding that takes her into the valley.

JoAnne was young and attractive. She had finished college and was working in her divine position, doing what she loved. She was spiritually attuned, politically conscious, and dedicated to the empowerment of women. Then she met him. Actually, she had met him years before. This time they had an opportunity to talk and get together. They really got together for about four months. Things were fine and then *she* showed up, his daughter's mother. Unfortunately, she showed up just around the time JoAnne had told him she was pregnant.

He told JoAnne all he wanted was to be a good father to his daughter. He told her he wanted to be there for her when she had the baby. He even went so far as to indicate that he was not averse to getting married to her, if that's what she wanted. JoAnne watched to see how he handled the situation with his daughter's mother. She was not too pleased; his words and his action were in conflict. *If you don't want her, why is she staying at your house? If there is nothing between the two of you, why is she calling my house?* Time always reveals the truth of a situation.

When JoAnne was a young girl, she had some problems with one of her ovaries. There was a surgery. She had been told it would be very difficult for her to conceive and carry a child. When she discovered she was pregnant, JoAnne decided she was going to have the baby no matter what he did. She had prayed about it and felt pretty comfortable that it was the right thing for her to do. He still called; they continued to see each other. He sounded supportive, but time always tells.

He called one Thursday and told JoAnne he wanted to take her out Friday. They went to dinner and the movies and had a pretty good time. There really was a strong attraction and a good energy between them. He called on Saturday for small talk and promised to call on Sunday. Before he called, JoAnne called him to invite him over for dinner. He said he couldn't come. He was too busy. He was getting ready for his wedding, which would take place before a justice of the peace on Monday morning.

Understanding ourselves, people, and life is not like understanding algebra. In algebra, understanding means being able to apply a formula and with a little work, some manipulation of the elements, you will be able to figure out what is going on. There is a right answer because numbers are stable. Numbers are definitive. People are not! We cannot apply a formula to people believing they will come out exactly the way we expect. People are in a constant state of flux. There are times when they are moving up or forward. At other times, they move in the opposite direction. Most of the time, the average person cannot figure out how he or she is moving. In the midst of confusion, you cannot apply a formula, expecting that what you want to happen, will happen. Sometimes it does. Most of the time, it does not.

In the Valley of Understanding we encounter those experiences which teach us to stop what we are doing long enough to accept what we see without judgment. Judgment is the process whereby we label and categorize situations and people based on what they appear to be, without full knowledge of what they are. Judgment prohibits true understanding. The minute we start thinking we know what should and should not be, or what we should or should not be experiencing, we are judging. We set off an energy of resistance that prohibits a true understanding of ourselves and what is really going on.

"To understand" means to go beneath the surface and identify the truth. Truth is the consistent part of the thing. It is the natural outgrowth of a series of events in the process of life. Truth has nothing to do with what we think or what we know. There is so much that we do not know, cannot see, and without divine guidance, our ability to understand is limited. In times of confusion, we do not really want to understand, we want to get out of the situation. We panic. Our thinking becomes distorted. You cannot reach true understanding from a position of mental and emotional distortion and panic. This is why you must stop. Get still. Appeal to the universe for help. Once you are still, the brain slows down and you are able to gain some insight and understanding through the process of discernment.

You Have to Recognize What You Are Looking At!

The ability to discern is the ability to use spiritual vision and insight. It is the first step toward understanding. When you can see through what is taking place on the physical level and recognize what it is on the spiritual level, you will know the truth. Let us say you are in a heated debate with someone. In the midst of your discussion that person starts to call you names or talk about your mother. If you cannot discern or figure out that this person is angry about something that has nothing to do with you, you will react, respond, and retaliate in response to what is being said. If in the past you have judged yourself or your mother, you will immediately become defensive and allow the person to engage you in further debate. You will be hostile, angry, confused as to why this person thinks she or he has the right to say these things to you. Stop! Understand that what has been said has nothing to do with you or your mother. Know the truth. The person is angry or upset. Understand that you have no need to respond or react. Shut up, or let the person know she or he has overstepped her or his boundaries. Walk away, understanding that you are not responsible for whatever is going on with her or him, nor do you choose to accept it in your space.

Discernment takes the guesswork out of living because it eliminates the need to judge, guess, wish, or hope. Discernment eliminates the need to panic because it de-charges the negative thought patterns we have developed as a result of our past experiences and future fears. As we de-charge our negative experiences, we become less resistant to the truth of what we are now experiencing. Discernment leads to acceptance, which is the foundation of understanding. When we understand ourselves and what is going on, we understand why we respond the way we do. This is the level of understanding that leads to mastery of our human nature—the very nature which leads us into situations we do not understand.

You don't understand why your mother always criticizes you. You don't understand why your brother, sister, or best friend never does what he or she promises. You don't understand why your boyfriend or husband lies to you. It is not your job to understand other people. It is your task to understand yourself and your nature as a human being. Understanding or accepting other people is difficult because we have not been taught to accept ourselves. As we see it, there is always something to fix, change, or do to make others the way we want them to be and ourselves better than we are. If you are a Black woman, you always have the need to make a few tucks here, a few nicks there, in order to get it just right. Fixing people, changing things, doing everything in our power to make sure things are the way we think they should be, often leads to misunderstandings. We think the fault lies with other people rather than ourselves because we do not understand ourselves.

When people are treating me badly, I examine what I have been thinking about myself. When I am experiencing lack, limitation, or restriction of any kind, I analyze what I have been thinking and feeling about money and prosperity and my ability to enjoy them. More often than not, I discover, my past experiences—many of which I did not understand—have led me to draw certain conclusions about myself, others, and the situation I am experiencing. All experiences are lessons which demonstrate to us how we will respond and what we will do under any given set of circumstances. If we can learn lessons from our experiences, we can begin to recognize that all experiences come in response to some part of our nature, something we were thinking, feeling, or doing.

When we learn not to judge and label our experiences and other people, we cleanse our thoughts and that part of our nature. Your nature, what you are missing, what you do not understand about yourself, attracts your experiences. Human beings naturally want to fix what they have or adjust themselves to it, no matter how happy or comfortable they are at the time. We fear looking bad in the sight of others, and losing what we have. Most of us are so afraid of losing "the little" we have that we avoid the discernment process and thereby limit our ability to understand. Furthermore, most of us resist accepting the truth. We label what we have as something else, something it is not. It is our very own judgments, beliefs, and nature that we do not understand, that continue to create repeat performances of painful experiences.

Understanding the Lessons of the Valleys

If you are an honorary member of the Trials and Tribulations of a Black Woman's Life Alliance, I am sure you want to find JoAnne's beau and cut him down. STOP! We may not understand what is really going on. There are certain basic life lessons which confront all human beings on the path to enlightenment and mastery. In the search for a spiritual center, mastery of these lessons is a must as they are the keys to overcoming the challenges and obstacles which plague us. These lessons have nothing to do with what goes on in the outside world. They teach us what we need to know about ourselves. They strengthen our ability to master our nature and confront the world.

We must realize that as long as we see our problems coming from outside sources, there can be no solution. How can we hope to understand these outside forces which encroach upon us? We cannot. Are we therefore doomed to live in a state of fear and powerlessness, unable to determine when these forces will strike? Of course not. In mastering life's basic lessons, we understand how the problems we encounter are grounded in our own nature and inner conflict. When we begin to harmonize our internal energy, to master ourselves, we will neutralize our conflict by understanding we are the solution to all of our problems.

KNOW THAT YOU KNOW

We know. We always know what is really going on with us and around us. There are times when we know but the situation is too painful to face. At other times we know, but we let fear blind us in order to tell ourselves that what we see and know is not really happening. Most important of all, we always know what we are doing or not doing to cause our pain, our valley experience. We call it different things at different times, but we do know. A major challenge Black women face is taking the time to listen to what we know, in order to understand and become consciously aware of how to utilize what we know. Any valley experience is an opportunity to stop, listen, and learn about ourselves. The lessons are not new. They are things we do not realize we know because we are moving so fast, in fear or panic. Unfortunately, even when we know what to do, we make excuses for not doing it.

The minute the woman showed up on his doorstep and he could not get rid of her, JoAnne knew something was not quite right. To her credit, she slowed down, asked some pertinent questions, and made certain demands. People may say one thing, but their actions always tell us what is going on. If we love them or want them, it is difficult for us to see. If we are in fear of repeating old patterns, making the same mistake again, we will tell ourselves that what we see is not real. We can tell ourselves anything we like, anything we need to hear to get ourselves through the moment, but in the end we will have to admit, we knew the truth the moment we saw it.

STILLNESS

In order to master the lessons of the university of life, we must first learn to *"be still."* An ancient African proverb reminds us, "You cannot see yourself in running water." In order to see your reflection in any body of water, the water must be still. Spirit is the water of life, the essence of our energy in life. In order for us to truly see our lives, we must stop our activity and be still. Only in the stillness of mind and body can we come to "know" what action to take and in which direction we should move. In order to master stillness, we must learn to be patient.

If it were ten years ago and I were JoAnne, I would have been on his doorstep Monday morning with a whip in one hand and a butcher's knife in the other. Of course I would have accomplished nothing other than to embarrass myself and cause a scene. But I must admit I would have been there. Today, however, I realize that when a challenge is staring you in the face, you shouldn't move. Don't think. Don't speak. The first thing you must do is breathe. Focus on your breath. Focus on your heart. Let the thoughts float through your mind. Don't hold on to a single one. Let the spirit of the divine nurture you, guide and heal you. If you can get still for just a few moments, you will be shown or told exactly what to do.

PATIENCE

The Gallo wine slogan, "We will sell no wine before its time," is the best example of patience in action. No matter how hard we try, we cannot make things happen before they can happen. This is a difficult principle for many Black women to accept. Our belief in the lack of good, our belief that we cannot have what we want, and our need to be in control urge many of us to insist on making things happen before it is time for them to happen. This often results in our disappointment, which we then blame on others. Patience allows us to understand and accept that there is a divine order which prevails in life. Once we have done all we can do to the best of our ability, with good intent, we must learn how to wait for the final outcome. The reason we become impatient is that we have not mastered the ability to trust.

JoAnne was four months pregnant when the crisis came to light. No matter what she did or how she did it, she would have to wait another five months until she had the baby. Everything takes place in its own time, in its own way, the divine way. She may have wanted the answer right then and there. She may have wanted to know how the situation would be resolved or handled. Nothing she could do would bring her the answers any faster than they were ordained to come. She could insist, demand, stand on her head, hold her breath, but nothing would speed up time. That is why patience is so important. It teaches us that no matter what, we are really not in charge or control. We must wait for the final outcome. Patience does not mean we back down, lie down, or give up. We must understand that patience is a virtue which keeps us in alignment with the divine.

TRUST

We, as Black women, are taught to doubt our abilities and capabilities. We have been taught to doubt the small, still voice which speaks to us, the voice of spirit. We question whether or not this voice is real and whether or not it is right. The indoctrination to doubt self is the major challenge to developing and mastering trust of our spiritual self and developing enough understanding to stay out of valley situations. The key to mastering trust is in "knowing" we are worthy of the best. We must then trust that our good will arrive in divine time. When we know and trust there is goodness with our name on it, we become patient and peaceful. Those of us who have not mastered the ability to trust may also have missed the lessons of stillness and patience. However, we must master each of these before we can understand or master the lesson of faith.

JoAnne will have to trust that no matter what the father does, she and the baby will be fine. It may not be easy. She may not understand why this has happened or how it happened. She may want answers, need them to make sense of the situation. All of that is to be expected. What JoAnne must now focus on is providing a safe environment for herself and the baby. She must love herself, take care of herself, trusting that at the right time, everything she needs and needs to know will be presented to her.

FAITH

Prayer is asking for rain. Faith is carrying an umbrella. Faith is the inner sense of knowing that with divine order working on your side, all things will come together for your good. We must master faith in order to take the right steps in the right direction. We must also master faith because outward appearances make us lean toward believing the worst. When we cannot see what is going on, we convince ourselves that what we cannot see is bad and we become fearful. Faith is the only way to conquer fear. Faith is like planting a seed. Even if you cannot see the roots taking hold or the stem sprouting up, you know the seed is growing. With patience, trust, and faith, you can be still and wait, knowing that what is now invisible will become visible. Once you have planted the seed, your job is to know the truth and practice faith.

In our deepest, darkest moments, when we need it the most, we lose faith. We lose faith in ourselves. We lose faith in our Creator. We want to blame ourselves and others for whatever situation we find ourselves in. JoAnne had lost faith in men, found it, and was about to lose it again. She did not understand that faith has nothing to do with the way people act. Faith is knowing that there is a divine plan and purpose for everything in life. There are no accidents! Everything happens according to the Creator's will. That will molds us, shapes us, and teaches us what we need to learn. Every woman has loved a man who did not turn out to be exactly what she thought he would be. We lose our faith because we forget that people come into our lives for a reason, a season, or a lifetime. We put our faith in the person rather than in having faith that we will understand the reason, survive the season, or make it through the lifetime according to the Creator's plan.

TRUTH

We cannot be patient or trust and exercise faith when we do not know the truth. Truth is not telling ourselves what we want to hear or limiting ourselves to what we know. Truth is not seeing things the way we think they should be or want them to be. Truth is the consistent and natural flow of events based on universal laws and principles. The basic truth is, "God is." The supporting truth is, "I am because God is." Whether you believe, accept, or practice the truth that you are a unique and wonderful expression of God does not change the truth. You will, however, be affected according to your ability to recognize and practice it.

The truth is, God is the spirit in us, dependent on us to glorify the attributes and qualities attributed to God. The truth is, spirit is not limited to what we know or what we can do. The truth is, we limit spirit when we are impatient, when we do not trust, and when we do not recognize the truth. Our willingness to know and live the truth will determine how we view life and how life responds to us. Once we know the truth, it is easy to be patient, have faith, and trust that the spirit in us knows what we need.

We often mistake facts for truth. Facts are subject to change. The truth never changes. The fact is, JoAnne really believed the man she was sleeping with loved and cared about her. The truth is, the man JoAnne thought she was having a relationship with obviously does not love or care about himself. The fact is, JoAnne is pregnant by a man who, in the midst of her relationship with him, married someone else. The truth is, JoAnne is part of a divine, universal plan and she has been chosen to bring forth the life of a child of God. The fact is, a man JoAnne loved, cared for, and surrendered her body to, lied and deceived her. The truth is, JoAnne could only love this man as much as she loved herself. She shared a part of her life with him because she chose to in return for the joy it gave her. His dishonesty and deception have nothing to do with her. That is his issue, his problem, and his challenge. The fact is, JoAnne is alone, pregnant, hurt, and disillusioned. The truth is, with the spirit of the Creator moving in and through you, you are never alone. The hurt and disillusionment is part of a lesson. When JoAnne gets the lesson, she will get over the pain.

DISCIPLINE AND OBEDIENCE

When you understand the truth, that spirit is an active and essential part of your life, you will become less resistant to the voice of spirit as it guides you. Obedience means doing as you are inspired to do without doubt or fear, trusting faithfully that if you are patient the seeds you plant in prayer and deed will grow into viable conditions in your life. You cannot be obedient without discipline. Discipline harnesses the mind and strengthens the spirit. Like runners, we must practice discipline at every opportunity. We must pray, meditate, and conduct our lives in a disciplined manner. When we are disciplined, we are not easily led off the path that leads toward our good or into a valley. Obedience and discipline, once mastered, are the natural stepping stones to the next lesson, responsibility.

JoAnne decided to begin and end each day with prayer and meditation. She set aside a corner of her room, a chair, and a small table on which she kept her Holy books, a candle, and a glass of water. Her sessions lasted ten to twenty minutes. Some days she just sat and listened. Other days she cried and asked for strength. Each day she sat she realized she was getting stronger and feeling better. When she received a message or inspiration, she followed it. One day, she was guided to call her old beau, a brother she had had a good relationship with, but whom she had left because she was not ready. He was glad to hear from her, happy to know she was expecting, and asked her if she would like to go out for dinner.

RESPONSIBILITY

Responsibility is a critical lesson for Black women who seek personal and spiritual growth. We are responsible for creating in our lives the conditions we desire. As such, we are required to think and speak responsibly, to act responsibly, and ultimately to take responsibility for what we think, say, and do. When you are responsible, you are not willing to assume false responsibility for what others think, say, or do. Responsibility gives you a sense of vision, clarity, and purpose which will assist you in learning and mastering all of life's lessons.

If you make anyone or anything else responsible for your happiness, you will never be happy. If you make anyone or anything else responsible for what you do or do not do, you will not accomplish a great deal in life. No one is responsible for you but you! It is up to you, at all times, to do what needs to be done to advance your physical, mental, emotional, and spiritual growth. JoAnne could have held her beau responsible for her condition and situation. She could have been stuck in anger, resentment, fear, and guilt. She chose not to. She continued with her plans to work, have a baby, and build a life for herself and her child. She maintained close contact with a circle of supportive friends. She continued her spiritual disciplines. On her good days she was fine. On the bad days, the sad days, she did whatever made her feel good. JoAnne understood that the situation would be whatever she made it. It was her responsibility and she accepted it like a trouper.

SERVICE

We have been taught a great deal about servitude and very little about service. Service is giving of yourself and what you have without expectation of reward or recognition. Servitude is doing what you "have to" or "should do" to such a degree that you feel bad about yourself and what you have done or given. Service is the choice to do or give. Servitude is having your energy taken by unappreciative or unworthy causes or people. We cannot serve until we are in alignment. Grandma called it "being in the right place at the right time." I would respectfully add that service is also "doing the right thing, in the right way, for the right reason."

It is hard to do for someone else when you have your own challenges staring you in the face. That's what people think, but in fact, the best time to do for others is when you cannot do for yourself. Giving your time, energy, knowledge, or information to others is the best way to take your mind off yourself. Service, giving of yourself, is the best way to build an account in the universal bank. What you give comes back to you tenfold. As you give, you open your mind and heart to the joy of unconditional love. You find worth in what may appear to be an unworthy situation. You find strength at a time you thought it was waning. JoAnne continued all of her volunteer work and maintained a standard of excellence in her career. There is no doubt that the universe will repay her tenfold when she needs it.

ALIGNMENT

Alignment is the lesson which teaches us "our place," the place we are guided to by spirit, to do the things which make us feel good, are good for us, and benefit those around us. Alignment is the process of using your God-given talents, gifts, and abilities in a manner and under circumstances which nourish and fortify you. Alignment reaps the reward of independence, another lesson life requires that we master. Independence is the ability to stand on your own, fearlessly; the ability to think, speak, and act responsibly; and the willingness to do whatever it takes to get where you need or want to be, because you have clarity of vision and purpose. Independence is peaceful, cooperative, and loving because it is based on a critical lesson we must all master, forgiveness.

FORGIVENESS

Because we judge, we get stuck in what should have been done or should happen. We hold on to old hurts, past pains, because we believe we know the way things should be. The truth is, we don't know and we don't always understand. We want as much pleasure as possible and as little pain. When events, situations, and people create pain in our lives, we get angry or frightened. Holding on to the memories of events is what keeps us stuck in the pain. When we want to move beyond the pain, when we want to feel better, when we are ready to move beyond where we are, emotionally and spiritually, we must forgive. We forgive for our own evolution, not for the benefit of the other person. When we forgive, we are telling the universe we want to understand, are ready to know, can handle the responsibility of what we have done and the lesson it offers. Forgiveness is the spiritual laxative which cleans the crevices of the brain and the lining of the heart.

Without a doubt, JoAnne must learn to forgive. She must forgive her beau and forgive herself for being angry with him. She cannot get stuck in the whys and wherefores, she must simply forgive the deception, irresponsibility, lack of consideration, and whatever else she has labeled his behavior. She must ask for enlightenment, in order to be able to embrace the meaning of it all. She must ask for the gift of revelation, to understand why her, why him, why now. The only way she can open her heart and mind to receive, process, and understand the information is to forgive.

UNCONDITIONAL LOVE

This phrase has become a sort of catchall for the spirituality movement. However, if you can decipher what it means and master the lesson it offers, it will definitely be the catchall of any negative energy in your life. Mastering unconditional love requires that we suspend all criticism and judgment of ourselves and others, overcome all human ego-based fears, and surrender the desire to fix and control. Most important of all, unconditional love requires Black women to love and accept ourselves and one another exactly as we are.

You cannot give what you do not have. Until you can accept yourself for all that you are—a human being, bound to make poor choices and bad decisions—and love yourself without guilt or shame, you will continue to meet the challenge of mastering unconditional love, which is the first step in and out of the valley. Once you master unconditional love, you will find you have the patience to be still, the faith to trust, and the obedience and discipline required to be responsible for your life as you steadfastly maintain your purpose of providing loving service to the world and those around you.

The ego's view of life is that others are always gaining on us, prepared to take what we have or trying to keep us from getting what we want. Ego is the acronym for "Easing God Out." As we strike out or strike back at those we fear are out to get us, we "ease" the Godlike virtues out of our minds, hearts, and lives. To conquer the ego-enforced fears, we must practice the virtues of the spiritual realm. We must honor universal law. As a result, we develop the wisdom and the ability to recognize the power the virtues give us. We also develop the courage to live in and through our spiritual power.

You can fight your way into or out of any situation or you can love yourself into and out of it. To love someone even though your encounter with them has caused you pain does nothing for them and everything for you. Remember, what you give comes back! If you give scorn, anger, resentment, that is a debit in your universal account. To love, knowing divine order will prevail, is the greatest gift you can give to yourself.

JoAnne must love herself, no matter what. She made a mistake, a poor choice, a bad decision in choosing this man. So what! She is alive with the opportunity to do it again. She must love her baby. The baby chose JoAnne and this particular man to be its father because they provided the time and opportunity for this spirit to come into this life. JoAnne must love the baby's father. He was a tool spirit used to further her growth and evolution. She cannot change what has happened; she can, however, create the conditions in which she and the baby will now live. When we love without expectation of anything in return, we remove the limitations and restrictions from our willingness to be loved in return.

We may not always understand what is going on at the time it is happening. That's okay! Only when we are ready to understand and know will we truly understand. What we must do in our day-to-day living is learn to accept things and people as they are rather than trying to make them the way we wish them to be. All the people in our lives reflect a part of who we really are; they are a part of our nature which is manifested. When we do not observe, accept, and know the truth about the people in our lives, we are unable to master the part of ourselves they represent. If we cannot accept a person for who he is, by what he shows you, it is then difficult to make peace with that part of our nature.

Often we see in others what we have been told is bad about

ourselves. When we do not understand our nature, we will ignore what we see or call it something else. As a result, we fail to recognize the unhealthy, unproductive, and often destructive behaviors of others in our lives in fear of acknowledging the same issue in our nature. Our eyes are tainted by past pains and future fears. Our point of reference is incorrect, because judgments of ourselves and those made of us by others only take us down a symbolic path, a path of what we *think* is good or bad. We stumble over or get knocked down by people and situations because we did not recognize their true meaning in our past experiences: we missed the lesson.

When there is something about ourselves which we do not like, we must learn to accept that it exists before we can make a decision to change it. Instead, it is human nature to cover our eyes and refuse to accept or admit to our human frailties and weaknesses. When we see the same trait in someone else, we do not, cannot, accept it, even from a distance. Instead, we make excuses for the other person, just as we make excuses for ourselves. This does not work. Our issues manifest in others as betrayal, dishonesty, or manipulation. In fact, what others "do to us" are the manifestations of thoughts, emotions, and experiences encrusted in our hearts and minds. They are drawn out of us by the same nature in other people.

The Valley of Understanding teaches us about our own nature. The experiences which bring us into this valley show us how willing we are to hear, see, and act on what we know. They crystallize the character traits and spiritual virtues we are missing and demonstrate our willingness to learn what we need to know. The Valley of Understanding brings all of life's lessons into view, because at any given time we choose what we do based on our willingness to really see and know ourselves. For this reason, this valley is a potential Special Ed valley. The more excuses you make for yourself, the greater the number of judgments you must release, the stronger your beliefs, the harder your head and the tougher your hide—the greater the magnitude of your lesson and the longer your stay in the valley. All these issues come into play when the issue is looking at yourself. Remember, it is your attitude that will determine the outcome.

A Valley Experience

When she met him, she was doing okay. She was working, had a decent place to live, three beautiful children, and a car of sorts. She wanted so badly to be in a relationship, but she was scared, a little shy. Her last relationship had ended very badly. She was still wounded and she knew it. But what's a girl supposed to do when a sweet, gentle, rather nice-looking guy shows up, promising to give you the world? She is supposed to listen, discern, integrate the information, and make a choice based on what her inner self says is right. Faye did very well on step one; she listened. She failed miserably at steps two, three, and four because she was horny and he talked a good talk.

James had been around the block quite a few times. He had an ex-wife, an ex-girlfriend, someone he was trying to move away from, and several children in the mix. He was not looking for a relationship when he met Faye, but he was always on the lookout for good companionship. Faye was sweet, very supportive, in the midst of a crisis, and very attracted to him. They started talking. They had very similar concerns and interests in life. Talking led to hand holding—James loved an affectionate woman. Kissing began at the end of their third face-to-face meeting. Within two weeks of the first kiss, he had put his toothbrush in the rack.

Faye was in the midst of transition, ending a relationship, changing jobs, and relocating to another city. James was also in the midst of transition, leaving one woman, trying to find a job, and trying to find a place to live. Faye worked at night. James looked for work during the day. At first glance it appeared as if they met each other's needs perfectly. He needed a place to receive his telephone calls; she needed someone to watch her children until she relocated. It was perfect. Faye did not mind that James's older son would have to live with them; he too could help with the children. Faye did not mind that James had no income; providing child care more than covered his room and board. Faye did mind that James's ex-wife called her house and that his ex-girlfriend lived within walking distance, but James knew just what to say to make her feel better.

They talked. They made plans. They found a house in the city near Faye's new job. They moved together. Faye went to work. James stayed home and watched the children. Faye paid the bills. James worked on their business plan. Faye tried to talk to James about his inability to control his ex-wife. James told Faye to mind her business. Faye began to complain about James's inattentiveness, his verbal insults, and his son's unemployment. James told Faye she was a pain in the butt. Faye told James she was pregnant. He told her that was great. Faye told James her medical insurance would not cover the pregnancy because she had not been on the job for six months. James told Faye he would deliver the baby at home. They began to read books about it. Ask friends about it. Study and plan for the birth of Faye's fourth child, James's sixth. Before you shift into indignation about how stupid she was, how lowdown he was, let us get the rest of the facts.

In her sixth month of pregnancy, Faye very gently approached James on the subject of his and his son's employment. She was tired, she was having difficulty concentrating at work, and because she was the only one working, she was somewhat concerned. Faye believed James was doing his best to find work and that he was not going to force his son to take any old kind of job just to make her happy. James reminded her that he was there, taking care of her children, doing his very best, and that things would work out. You know how it is when you are pregnant and things are not going too well. You need more than verbal assurances. You need some proof positive. James could not give Faye any and she hit the ceiling.

All of the frustration she had been feeling as a result of carrying the relationship came spilling forth from her lips. James had a few choice words for her also. She was a nag, a whiner, a selfish, irresponsible airhead—and besides that, he didn't love her anyway. The only reason he was still around was the baby. He was in love with his ex-girlfriend. She understood him. She supported him. She simply did not want to be in a relationship. It was okay. He would wait. In the meantime, if Faye wanted the pleasure of his company, she would shut her mouth and get out of his face.

She did. She shut her mouth. She did not speak to James for two weeks. She spoke to her friends, most of whom told her to put him out. She didn't. She spoke to her mother, who asked her why she always got herself into this type of situation. She talked to her sister, who did not want to hear her story, again. Eventually, she talked to James, who told her he was sorry. He hadn't meant the things he said. He wanted their relationship to work. He wanted them to build a life together. He also told her he would make sure his son got a job and he himself would do something, anything, to help her with the financial responsibilities. Faye was eight months pregnant, tired and scared to death of being alone. She had no choice. She believed him!

James actively began to look for work. This meant he would leave the house. During his job search, he met several women, most of whom would call him in the evenings. He was able to convince Faye that these were strictly business calls. When James began to disappear on the weekends, Faye put her foot down. It was too late. She was in labor. The baby was here. The relationship was in a shambles.

When the baby was six weeks old, Faye caught James in a lie. She had given him some money to do one thing, and he had done something else and lied about it. Faye found out and invited James to leave. He asked her, where should he go? She didn't care. He asked, why was she doing this? She told him to take a guess. He begged and pleaded. She listened and cried. James was not allowed to come home for three weeks. During that time, he saw the light. He mended his evil ways. He got his act together and he was ready. Faye now had four children, problems on her job, very little support from her family and friends, and a fear of being made to look like a fool. She had no choice: she believed him! Again!

They tried, they really did, but the damage was done. Faye didn't trust him. She felt used, betrayed, and abandoned. James no longer found Faye attractive or sweet. And after she was fired from her job, not long after his return, she was no longer useful. The arguments turned into screaming matches. The screaming matches turned into shoving contests. Faye admits she hit James first. Of course he had no choice but to hit her back. Even after that, they tried. They tried to talk, to plan, to recapture that old loving feeling. Because they were about to be evicted, they had to talk fast, plan fast, and do a lot of recapturing in a very short space of time. It did not work. James eventually took Faye's invitation to leave. He went his way, back to his ex's and his search for employment. Faye went her way, deep, deep into the valley of understanding.

The Law of Human Nature

In *The Supreme Philosophy of Man,* Alfred A. Montapert outlines the Law of Human Nature by stating:

> ***Each individual has within himself the seeds of fear and faith, anger and love, anxiety and peace of mind, despair and hope. We are a strange mixture of good and evil, and as a result, we are inside ourselves, a battle ground.***

What we see in, and experience at the hands of, other people is a reflection of something going on inside of ourselves. What you refuse to accept about other people is what you refuse to acknowledge about yourself. There is within each of us the capacity to do absolute good or the exact opposite. We find this very difficult to accept. We tell ourselves we are good, even when we do not believe it. We set out to do good, even when we have no idea what it means. And we expect good in return for no matter what we do, good and not so good. Universal law, the spiritual foundation of the universe, does not reward us based solely on what we do. The challenges we face, the conditions under which we live, the standard of our behavior—all are based on what we believe. Beliefs are what make us and keep us in bondage to human conditions.

WE ARE SO MUCH MORE THAN WE SEE!

It is a mistake that we accept our human self as our true self. Our human nature is the result of our past experiences, social indoctrination, and ego-centered demands. The human part of us is attached to the physical world. Its quest is to find physical satisfaction and emotional and ego gratification. This human part of our being has a nature which is only attuned to what it can see, hear, taste, smell, and touch. Its goal is to control those things to ensure safety and pleasure. When the human self sees things which threaten its pleasure or safety, its nature demands that it seek to destroy those things or deny that they exist. It is our human self which gives rise to negative emotions that color our actions and ability to discern the truth. It is our human nature which requires the lessons we learn from valley experiences.

The battleground that exists within the human being is the space of consciousness which seeks to harmonize the human and spiritual natures. The quiet, gentle spirit nature must emerge through the clamoring, fearful determination of the human nature. It is difficult for us to accept what we cannot see. When what we see appears painful or undesirable, we want to fix it, to change it to look like something else. All of this we do on a physical level. We attempt to manipulate and change what we can see, hear, smell, taste, and touch. When we get it to an acceptable state, we feel safe again. Until our spiritual nature is stirred.

YOU ARE AT WAR WITH THE OTHER SIDE OF YOU!

Many Black women die in the battle between their natures. They burn out, stress out, drug out, or simply give up. The body becomes worn down from the struggle and battle of physical living. We know it is happening. We know we are dying, but we lose faith in our ability to survive, much less win the battle. It is because we have been taught to fight what we see rather than to listen to what we know. We look out rather than turning within. However, spirit is divine. It consistently provides us with opportunities to end the battle, alleviate the struggle. Spirit guides us into experiences, the pain of which lets us know we can change. We must change. These experiences are the valleys.

105

The truth under our human nature is an inability to stand in the reality that we have faults and weaknesses. We see very clearly in others what we cannot see in ourselves. It is simply easier that way. I can see your defects and faults. I can see very clearly what you need to do. I can see your potential and I want to help you live up to it. I can see in you what I cannot see in myself because to see it places me on the battleground with myself. How can I be good if I acknowledge bad things about myself? How can I prove to you I am right, when I know I have done wrong? Good and bad, right and wrong, are judgments, based on our past experiences and habitual thought patterns. Unfortunately, when we judge, we miss a crucial step in the process: acceptance.

Until we are willing to acknowledge our total nature, good and bad, we are powerless to change it. In our state of powerlessness, the universe will send people and situations into our lives to show us who we are and what we think, thereby providing us with the opportunity to make a choice. When those people show up, we must accept what we see. If the thing has webbed feet and feathers, and quacks, we must accept it is a duck. Do not tell yourself it is a swan because swans are better-looking than ducks. Accept the fact that there is something about you to which ducks are attracted.

When a part of you is manifested through the actions of others, you must choose whether or not you want to keep this part of you alive. If you do, embrace it. Welcome it. However, if you determine that what you see is not something you want in your life, if it is not a part of your nature that you want to cultivate, run! Run as fast as you can in another direction. Do not make excuses! Do not entertain the people or the condition in any way! If you stay, if you involve yourself by trying to fix or change what is going on, you are dancing with a demon. Take just enough time to bet you understand what you are dealing with and to be able to recognize it if you see it again. See it. Accept it. Then reject it and haul ass!

Don't Be Too Quick to Judge What You See!

When people do not turn out to be who we want them to be, that does not make them bad people. Remember: right, wrong, good, and bad are judgments we make about one another based on our experiences. People are going to be who they are no matter what we do. If we allow ourselves to believe it is otherwise, we set ourselves up for hurt, disappointment, and rejection. In all relationships, it is our assigned task to discern who the person is, and then accept them as they are or move them out of our lives.

It is not our job in life to judge what is right or wrong for somebody else. When another person behaves in a manner which seems to be unhealthy or unproductive, we must not judge. We must learn to accept. Once we accept this is how the person chooses to behave, we have the right to decide whether or not we want to participate. When we see the behavior, we cannot call it something else or ignore it. We can question people about their reasons and methods. We can offer suggestions for a different approach. We cannot fix or change them.

We know when people are being dishonest; when they make promises they cannot or will not keep. We know when people are irresponsible, inconsistent, inconsiderate and/or manipulative. We know because we have seen their patterns and heard their stories, or because intuition is screaming in our minds, STOP! When we know the person intimately, have been involved with them at other times, in other situations, we have seen how their patterns create conflict, chaos, or drama. We want to believe it will be different this time. We insist on banking on their "potential," which really means they have nothing to offer *now*. When things consistently go awry, we ask them, "Why do you always do that?" The appropriate question would be, "Why do I allow myself to be involved with you when you do that?" Ignoring what we know to be true about people and situations is a sign of our unwillingness to accept things. This failure results in the disappointment we blame on others.

We feel betrayed when people do their thing in a way which conflicts with our thing. We feel victimized. Why? We knew the pattern. We hoped they had changed or at least that they would not do it to us, again. The truth is, people are not always out to get us. They are simply being who they are and doing what they do. We should not take it personally. Particularly when we know the pattern. The truth is, we were not paying attention. When we do not pay attention, we must spend some time in the Valley of Understanding to figure out why it is so difficult to see and accept things as they are.

Acceptance does not mean we like what we see or what is going on. It means we see it and make a choice about the degree of our participation. One of the challenges to acceptance is, we do not know what to say to people about their behaviors. If the person is a loved one, family member, or someone in a position of authority, we do not want to upset or offend them. We feel uncomfortable speaking the truth when we have been taught not to trust ourselves. We do not trust our first thought. We do not trust our feelings. We do not understand that the way to build self-trust is to figure out what to say and say it.

The Value of Acceptance

We should never expect of others what we do not or cannot give ourselves. Yet we do it. We expect people to be honest when we are dishonest. We expect people to be loyal when we are not. We expect people not to behave in destructive ways when we ourselves are doing the very same thing. We say we do not expect it, but we do. In dealing with people and life, there are no surprises! We always get exactly what we expect. We may think we expect something else, or say we expect something else, but we always experience exactly what we expect to experience. We see it, we expect it, but we cannot accept it will happen. You can only expect from others what you yourselves are doing. If you are not expecting it, you should be running in the other direction.

You know you are in the Valley of Understanding when you expect a person to behave or respond one way and they respond in the totally opposite manner. They will always act the same way you have seen them act, the way you expected them to. Accepting the truth can be very difficult. The experiences which take us into this valley let us know we have not been listening. We have been hearing what we want to hear, or hearing what is said and thinking to ourselves, "I hear what you are saying, but I know you mean *this* . . ." We have not been paying attention to details. Details are an important part of the discernment process. So often, we let the little things people say and do, which are unpleasant or distasteful, slip by. We don't want to start an argument. We don't want to hurt people's feelings or embarrass them. We tell ourselves the little things don't matter, when in fact we know they do.

One little sperm meeting one little egg matters, does it not? One little cell with one little defective gene matters, right? The truth is, little things do matter. When we refuse to accept the truth we see in other people, we are rejecting that part of our nature. Human nature will not be denied! Our nature will rear its ugly little head at the most inopportune moments to inform us that there is something we need to know about ourselves. We have been operating with blinders on, seeing our nature and calling it something else. We have not been able to face the truth. We see it, but we cannot accept it. We stand on our own illusions rather than on the truth. Our judgments, perceptions, and fears get in the way. We allow ourselves to believe the truth is more painful than the fiction, the illusion, we have created.

The Lesson

Faye had never accepted her share of responsibility for her previously failed relationships, or any other aspect of her life. She had an excuse for everything. She allowed herself to believe that in each situation the failure had been the man's fault. He had done or not done something which damaged the relationship and her faith in him. Those were the facts. The truth was, Faye ran from one relationship to another, very quickly, without a clear idea of who she was or what she wanted or needed from a relationship. She could not accept the truth. Faye believed she was attractive, which she was. Intelligent, which she was. A loving, supportive woman, capable of making a man happy. This too she was. She also believed she was ready for a relationship. This she was not. Under all of her beauty and intellect, Faye had several very deep-rooted, unresolved issues with men. Many of Faye's issues stemmed from her relationship, or her lack of an honest relationship, with her father. Some of them stemmed from the verbal and emotional abuse she had sustained in previous relationships. Most of Faye's issues stemmed from her true feelings and beliefs about herself.

The Way Out

One of the most difficult challenges we face as Black women is to merge what we know and what we feel. The merger is called understanding, and for some reason, it escapes the best of us. We know we are worthy and valuable; still we feel unworthy, unvalued. We know we are human beings capable of making mistakes and correcting ourselves; yet we feel to make a mistake makes us unworthy. We know we are capable of doing, being, and having the best; still we feel to have something is better than having nothing or that what we have is all we deserve. We simply do not understand we are the designers of our lives! We design, create, our lives and the conditions therein by our willingness to know and understand the truth about ourselves. Equipped with the truth, we can build a stable mental and emotional foundation. We must believe in ourselves, have patience with ourselves, and trust ourselves to do the best we can at any given time. We must know that no matter what, there is a spirit of the divine in our being that gives us the power to change instantly.

We make or break ourselves through our thoughts and emotions. Our challenge is to bring what we know, think, and feel into divine harmony. When we do this, we have a deeper sense of well-being. When we are willing to see and know all there is, we open ourselves to a deeper level of insight and understanding. In order to do this, we must be willing to look at ourselves, examine what we see, suspend all judgments, accept who we are, and finally, make a decision to change those parts of us which keep us locked into negative thought and behavior patterns. We must be willing to know the truth, see the truth, and accept the truth. The truth always feels right. It never requires that we place ourselves in a compromising situation or accept less than what we know is good for us. When we cannot, for whatever reason, figure out what is true from what is false, we must be willing to dig—to dig deep inside of ourselves; to examine our thoughts, feelings, and beliefs; and to tell the truth about what we find.

Faye knew she had a great deal of anger and resentment toward her father. Faye knew she was out to please her daddy, to make him happy with and proud of her. She also knew no matter how hard she tried, she always failed miserably in this regard. She had long ago noticed how she always seemed to fail in making her partners happy with her also. Faye knew she was afraid of being alone. She knew she had a history of accepting less than what she wanted in a relationship. She knew she was insecure about herself, her talents, her ability to function on a personal and, for that matter, professional level. She knew all of this; still, she blamed other people for her fate. She blamed her father, her mother, her first husband, and the fact that she had stretch marks for her problems in her career and in her personal relationships. Faye knew from past experience that when she was at her lowest ebb, her loneliness moment, that was not the time to get involved in a relationship. But she allowed herself to believe that being in a relationship would make her feel better. The truth is, Faye used relationships to take her mind off the work she was not doing on herself. That is what made most of her relationships Special Ed experiences.

Just as Faye could not see herself, did not understand herself, she refused to see her partners. She refused to see James's unwillingness to sever or at least put boundaries on his relationship with his ex-wife. She refused to accept that a man who has no home and no job is capable of saying anything you want to hear in order to have a place to lay his head. Faye failed to examine the possible reasons why James, his twenty-three-year-old son, his brother, and his father were all unemployed. To her, their reasons, rationales, excuses, all seemed plausible in today's world, with them being Black men and all. Faye allowed James to verbally insult and abuse her because she was afraid that if she spoke out against it, he would leave. Faye knew a great deal. She just did not understand much. She was not willing to see anything at all. In the end, she was forced to face everything she had failed to explore when she had the opportunity to do so.

You Must Understand in Order to Understand!

There are two primary ways to gain understanding. The first is to follow the guidance of your spirit. Spirit will let you know what is honorable, honest, and right for you. In any given situation, simply ask yourself: "If this were not me, how would I handle this situation? What would I see if I were standing outside of myself looking at these facts, this situation?" Since it is always so much easier for us to see for others, we can remove ourselves from any situation and become a witness to it. Once we are able to assess what is going on, we must ask ourselves: "Have I seen this before? Have I done this before? Why am I willing to do this again?" No one said the path to enlightenment would be easy. There is a great deal of work involved in truly understanding ourselves, our nature, and what we do in response to who we think we are. The easy part is, we already know we can do it; we are now working to gain an understanding of how to do it.

The second, more difficult way to gain understanding is to move ahead blindly, following your human nature, and learn what not to do through painful experiences. That is called Spiritual Special Ed. In the first instance, the understanding given by spirit is felt as a "quickening." The mind is able to grasp the reality of truth in what you are experiencing by the quickening of the spirit. It is like a rush. It is a good feeling that lets you know you are on the right track. There is a level of comprehension which results in certainty. Quickening helps us to realize the only meaning an experience has is the one we give it. Every experience is merely a reflection of who we are, where we have been, and how we are thinking.

Truth leads to knowledge. Knowledge is the root of understanding. We must know at all times what we are doing and why. "I thought I knew you!" No. You thought you recognized the image. The image I projected. The image you perceived. Spiritual knowledge or knowing is not open to interpretation. The quickening of the spirit gives knowing a certainty which makes what you know concrete. Knowing is not based on physical interpretation of our experiences. All of our physical capabilities are subject to question and doubt. It is only when we are willing to accept the truth of who we are, to honor what we feel, and to accept what we know without judgment or fear, that we experience the quickening of spirit which implies understanding.

PAY ATTENTION TO WHAT YOU ARE DOING

The Valley of Understanding forces us to look at what we are doing. The human creature is a creature of habit. We are trained at a very young age to do things in a certain way. Very rarely do we deviate. As we mature, we develop a way of thinking and acting. It is rare that we actually stop to participate in the experience of what we do. This is most unfortunate. Habit reinforces our tendency not to pay attention to what we do—a tendency which hinders the mastery of our human nature. It is the automatic response mode which enables us to do the same thing over and over and over ad nauseam. It is the same response which allows us to see what people do and to call it something else. When we find ourselves in uncomfortable or unhappy situations, we say: "I don't want to see or know this, so let me call it something else!" We cannot accept it. We do not want to see it. If we cannot see, we do not pay attention.

John Roger, founder of the Insight Seminars, says: "Participate in your experience and experience your participation." This means that at every moment we must pay attention to what we are thinking and feeling. Furthermore, we must allow ourselves to think and feel at every given moment. Habitual behavior short-circuits thinking and feeling. We do our thing until we get done!

Once we learn to listen to our thoughts and experience what we feel, we can make a choice about what to do. It is called acceptance. This leads to participation. You are following the intuitive sensations of your inner being. You have an opportunity to explore and possibly to expand to new horizons of the "self."

When we experience what is going on within and around us, we can make a conscious decision. Decisions are wonderful. They keep the adrenaline flowing and cobwebs off the brain. With a little luck, we just might become interested in what we are thinking, feeling, and doing. We might try something new. It just might work. Think how wonderful that would be! We can trust ourselves enough to make a decision and it works out. The prospect of new thoughts, honest emotions, and conscious decision making is quite stimulating. This stimulation will probably alter the entire nature of your being.

MEDITATION WITH THE MOTHER

Fear is attracted to what does not see love.
What fear feeds upon, love overlooks.
What fear demands, love cannot see.
—A Course In Miracles

Fear is no thing! You fear no one! Your fears, my daughters, are but the ramblings of your minds which spew forth evidence of things which you have already convinced yourself may or may not happen to your liking or to your dismay. Fear is what happens to the daughters who are disconnected from their source. Even those who are connected must confront and sometimes battle the onslaught of fear which comes into their minds, filters into their thoughts, and hinders their actions.

Fear is what overtakes the daughters who are still in doubt, in question, about the ability of the Mother and the power of the Father. Fear is what the sons use against the daughters to keep them in "their" place. Fear is what the daughters use against one another when they convince themselves they are losing "their" place.

Fear has nothing to do with the etchings in the Pyramids or the evidence of life long before the etchings were made. Fear has nothing to do with ships bringing people to a land which they no longer desire to leave. Fear has nothing to do with chains, whips, trees, hounds, what someone has done, can do, will do to you in this day and time. Fear has nothing to do with man against man, man against woman, or woman's inability to stand against man. Fear is merely the evidence of the effect which plagues you when you remain disconnected from, disrespectful to, and disbelieving of the essence of your being. Fear is what happens to the daughters when they do not know where the Mother is.

115

The Valley of Courage

4

*T*HERE ARE SOME THINGS ONE CAN SAY VERY ELOQUENTLY. OTHERS ONE CANNOT. THIS IS A SUBJECT THAT CRIES out for eloquence but demands plain speaking. Simply put, you've got to have courage! If you do not have it, you must find it. Courage, the ability to stand on your own, for yourself, is the only way to free yourself from the obstacles that are sure to challenge you in this life. Courage, like most of the things which matter in life, is an intangible, somewhat indescribable element. You cannot buy it. It cannot be given to you. It must well up from the pit of your soul, fill your brain, surround your heart, spill forth from your mouth, and guide everything you do. Courage is a tool and a weapon. With just a little, you can build your life and use it to fend for yourself in the world. It is a breastplate and a helmet. Courage is the thing a peaceful, worthwhile life is made of.

Do you remember the lion in the Wizard of Oz? He is a classic example of someone taking a trip through the Valley of Courage. He hid behind others because he was afraid. He held himself back, refused to try to do anything because of fear. He allowed the Tin Man to criticize him, demean him, because he believed he lacked courage. In the end, he was forced to face the things he thought he could not do. Hopefully you noticed he was able to do for Dorothy what he was not able to do for himself. So many

Black women are like the lion. We hide behind excuses, shy away from situations because we tell ourselves we do not have courage. Is courage the issue or is it self-value?

It is quite possible that we are not as afraid of doing as we are of being criticized about what we do. Like the lion, we really do have the courage. We are endowed with the strength and stamina to confront anything. We know it and we do it under most circumstances. Most Black women can roar when we need to. We will take on an army of witches, goblins, and other folks who are just totally out of line. We find the strength and courage to do for others what we dare not do for ourselves. We come to the defense of friends and family members. We speak out against injustice in the world. But when we are forced to confront a situation which advances our own well-being, we freeze. Some of us freeze because we really believe we do not have courage. Others freeze because we do not believe we are worth the fight.

From a perspective of spiritual truth, criticism is one of the many ways the universe reveals to us those things we need to see but hate to admit about ourselves. It is also the way people project their fears, anger, and judgments onto us. Unless we know what to do and how to distinguish constructive criticism from someone's personal judgment, we will continue to be wounded by criticism. We will sustain mental, emotional, and spiritual wounds which could eventually prove to be fatal. We will die from fear of criticism by refusing to do anything that could possibly be criticized.

Those who believe they lack courage will be forced to confront the very thing they fear. That is the purpose of the Valley of Courage. They will have to face their fear of criticism, of being wrong, of being alone, of not knowing, and most of all, of not being in control. This is a very deep, very dark valley. Many of us shiver at the thought of confronting something we fear. Yet we are constantly asking and praying for a better life. We ask God, the ancestors, angels, and divine messengers to eliminate this problem or resolve that situation.

The only way to overcome a thing is to go through that thing. In order to resolve many of the situations we face, we may be required to confront and move through them. More often than not, we are simply not willing to face what we fear. It has nothing to do with courage or the lack of it. We just do not want to be bothered. Yet in order to move to a state of strength, freedom, and peace, we must learn to live fearlessly. When our prayers are heard and answered, indicating our willingness to be free of a situation, we must take a trip to the Valley of Courage to challenge the very thing which holds us back—the very thing we fear.

A Valley Experience

Shirley had worked overtime every night. She was tired. She was also both excited and apprehensive about her in-laws arriving that weekend. She wished her husband had asked her first, but since he was convinced she did not like his mother, she decided to let it go. They were just passing through on their way to their vacation home. How bad could it be? This week, however, had been so long and hectic that Shirley secretly wished they were not coming—but they were. She would have to get the groceries, clean the house, and make certain everything was "just so" for the arrival of her critical mother-in-law and her teddy bear father-in-law. Besides that, her period was due. Her feet hurt and her belly was swollen and she had planned to spend all weekend in bed, but Friday arrived quickly, about two minutes after 6:30 Thursday morning.

On Friday evening, Shirley fed the children and got them to bed. She changed the linen, cleaned the bathrooms, washed and waxed the kitchen floor, put the laundry away, and made love to Frank. It was his payment for vacuuming the living room before he went to bed. At 2:00 A.M., everything was done. Everyone was asleep. Shirley took two Midols and went to bed, to wait for the bat from hell to come and bite her neck.

Her in-laws arrived bright and early. Saturday was basically pleasant. The guys went off to do guy things. The children stayed in their room playing with the loot their grandparents had brought. Frank's mother spent most of the day educating Shirley about the benefits of wool shag over deep-pile carpet, the type

Frank and Shirley had. She also made sure to tell Shirley not to let Frank "touch" her until he had bathed. She reminded Shirley that the metal shavings he undoubtedly brought home from work could penetrate her skin, causing all sorts of "female problems," like cramps and swelling. Furthermore, she hoped Shirley was rationing Frank's sexual favors since that was the only way to keep a man in line (she hoped Shirley understood what she meant). "Too much sex affects a man's brain," she informed Shirley. "He can't write checks if you allow him to have too much sex." Even though Frank's mother and Shirley had very different ideas about sex, Saturday was bearable. Sunday, the Lord's day, was a trip to hell and back.

It started with the bacon. It kept burning. A pound and a half was tossed before Shirley could get a half pound cooked. Frank's father said he didn't mind burnt bacon if the eggs were loose. Frank teased Shirley about needing a degree in home economics, not medical administration. Frank's mother was sure it had something to do with the no-stick pan Shirley *insisted* on using. You cannot cook bacon in a no-stick pan. Why did these new mothers insist on filling their cupboards with the easiest thing to wash out instead of the best thing to cook in? Didn't your mother teach you how to cook in a cast-iron skillet? Oh, that's right, your father raised you. No wonder. Shirley's eyes were squinted. Her head was cocked to one side. She was just about to put her hand on her hip and ask, "No wonder what?," when Frank volunteered to finish the bacon, inviting his mother to go relax on the porch. Frank told Shirley to get the grits.

The grits! Oh, shit!

The grits were stuck to the bottom of the pot. Shirley had forgotten to turn the fire down. She and Frank peered into the pot in horror. Frank said, "I keep telling you to leave them quick grits alone! Real grits don't stick." Shirley was wounded but still angry enough to fight.

"No, they don't stick, Frank. They lump. I should have gotten some just to choke your momma on a grit lump!"

Frank wanted to, but he couldn't let that one go. "Maybe if you had a momma you would know how to treat and respect one!"

That was a low, nearly fatal blow to Shirley's PMS-wrought psyche. They were all against her and she was sick of it. In her most dangerously hushed voice, she told her husband of seven years, "Fuck you, Frank!," as she turned and left the kitchen.

Walking casually to avoid arousing attention, Shirley went to her bedroom and quietly slammed the door. Fighting back the tears, she cursed and pouted. By the time her five-year-old son knocked on the door, her head was pounding. She didn't answer until he had called her several times.

"Grandma wants to know what I should put on to go to Sunday school."

Lord have mercy! Sunday school meant she would have to comb Randi's hair. "Tell her you're not going . . . today."

"Mommy, what's Sunday school?"

"Shut up and go tell her what I said!"

Shirley tried to will Frank into the room. He had to defend her. To save her from his bloodthirsty bat of a mother. Unfortunately, Frank was in the kitchen trying to mash the lumps out of the grits.

Knocking, calling, and opening the bedroom door in one fell swoop, Frank's mother, in her spicy tone of voice, wanted to know why her grandchildren were not going to Sunday school. Shirley said she had thought it would be better if they stayed home, with their grandparents. That made absolutely no sense! They would be home by the time the breakfast dishes were washed. It was bad enough their parents did not go to church, but the children needed to know and fear God. That was the precise reason so many children beat and killed their parents. They did not know God.

This showdown had been ten years in the making. This was just the opportunity Shirley needed to get this woman told. "My children will not fear God! They will know and honor God and they do not have to go to church to do that. You live in the church and your heart is wicked and cruel! So what the hell is the point!"

Frank's mother had a few bones to pick with Shirley too. Ever since that day ten years ago when she found Shirley, half naked, pawing Frank in her den, she had known this "heifer" was a lowlife. But to challenge her faith in God—this was an abomination. "Let me tell you something! My Lord and Savior has prepared a place for me in the Kingdom. I have done my work. I honored my parents. Obeyed my husband. Raised my children. Earned my place. You were raised in the gutter. Married 'cause you were knocked up. Sent your children to day care so you could go to school, make money, and buy trinkets, the trappings of hell! So where are you destined for?"

Frank's father was at the door advising his wife that she had said enough. While he guided her out of the room, she informed him of what the "heifer" had said.

Shirley was stunned. She was wounded. She was ashamed of herself and of what had been said to her. She had no choice but to cry. The tears welled up from the hole in her heart and spilled out with a roar. She was screaming and thrashing around the room when Frank grabbed her.

"Shhh. Shhh. Come on. You know how she is. Why do you always get her started? You know how she is."

It felt good for Frank to hold her, but he was making her wrong again.

"Why! Why is it my fault? She is always criticizing me. I try to do everything perfectly so she won't have anything to say. Why can't she leave me alone? I am doing the best I can, Frank. You know I am."

"I know, baby, but you know how she is!"

"How am I, Frank!"

The bat was hovering at the door.

"I came up here to apologize, but before I do, please tell me, how am I? Good enough to raise you! Good enough to put you through school! Good enough to take care of your father! How good am I, Frank? Why don't you tell me!"

Frank, to his credit, did not respond. He asked his mother to excuse them for a few minutes. Disengaging his arms from Shirley's trembling body, Frank moved to close the door.

"If you touch that door, I will walk out of this house and never come back!"

Frank was in big trouble. He had to choose between his

mother and his wife. Shirley was whimpering. His mother was fuming. Frank's father saved the day—sort of, anyway.

"Shirley, you are much too sensitive. My wife talks too much, but she doesn't mean any harm. Frank, go wash your wife's face while I tape my wife's mouth." He shut the door and urged his wife to "be still."

The Lesson

If you want to get yourself into real hot water, criticize another Black woman who is hoping, wishing, trying, or struggling. Chances are, the minute you open your mouth, her heart will start racing, her mouth will drop open, her eyes will bulge, and you will be verbally attacked. On the other hand, if you are lucky, she will have so internalized her fear of criticism that your most well-meant comments will hurt her feelings. She will render herself helpless and cry. This will in turn render you defenseless with guilt.

Our indoctrination and socialization have fostered in us the belief that criticism amplifies and broadcasts those things which are "wrong" about being Black, being a woman, being who we are. It does not help matters any that our parents used criticism to shame us when we were disobedient. That siblings used it to ridicule us just for fun. Or that our playmates and classmates used criticism of our God-given characteristics, things over which we had absolutely no control, to show us affection, shun us, or keep us in our place. Adding to the impact of criticism is the fact that most people do not offer it in a constructive manner. They lash out in anger, with incomplete information, offending our sensibilities and sensitivities at the most inopportune moments.

When we believe certain people are out to get us, we open the way for them to do it. These people get on our nerves. They upset us. They get us to do and say things we would not do under normal circumstances. We all have somebody in our lives who has the uncanny ability to push our buttons. We think it is the other person. It's their attitude. It's their tone of voice. It's the fact that they are alive on the planet at the same time we are. Surprise, surprise! The problem doesn't lie in the other person, it lies in us! No one can push our buttons unless the buttons are connected. They are connected to something in our mind and our heart. The other person has no idea what it is, but we do. The only way to keep people from pushing our buttons is to disconnect our buttons. Detach whatever fear, guilt, shame, or anger we have attached to the issue and people will be unable to push us.

Shirley was afraid of criticism. She was even more afraid that someone would find out how her mother had died. Her mother was a delicate woman. Very fragile, but sweet. She was a manic-depressive who died from a barbiturate overdose. Shirley's father was a tall police officer, six foot two, who came home to eat, sleep, pay bills, and scream at Shirley's mother. When Shirley was ten years old, her parents had an awful fight. She remembered it was the first time her mother ever spoke back to her father. He threatened to "blow your brains out" when he came home if she had not found his . . . Shirley had forgotten what it was. After he left, Shirley's mother was trembling, so she kept taking her pills. For the first few hours, her hands were shaking so bad she couldn't hold the bottle, so Shirley gave her the pills. Shirley remembered her mother lying across the bed to take a nap. Shirley was to look for the thing her father had lost. By the time he came home, Shirley was asleep on the living room floor, her mother was dead, and her father was insane.

SECRET THOUGHTS CREATE REAL EXPERIENCES!

Although she never said a word, Shirley really believed she had caused her mother's death. Anytime anyone mentioned the fact that she did not have a mother, fear gripped her. She was convinced they knew what she had done. As she grew older, she figured out it was not totally her fault. Her mother had taken the pills to help her stop trembling. Still, Shirley believed that had she, her brother, and sister not lost their father's whatever-it-was, the whole thing would not have happened. Furthermore, she came to understand there was an awful stigma attached to her mother's illness. Only the family and close friends knew and they decided it was best to keep the whole thing quiet. After all, it was hereditary. People would think there was something wrong with the children.

Shirley feared that someone would find out she had helped her mother take too many pills. She had done the wrong thing and she was afraid of doing it again. Criticism created a paralyzing panic in her heart. She felt as if she were being attacked, so her response would be to attack defensively. If she survived the attack with only a deflated ego or a wounded spirit, she considered them cuts and bruises from which she would survive. She was always grateful that the secret had not been "found out."

Shirley, like many of us, did not realize her secrets kept her in fear. *You are as sick as your secrets.* Until you reveal, examine, and unpack the negative emotions attached to the secrets, thoughts, feelings, and experiences, you are held captive by them. Like Shirley, many of us have shame, guilt, pain, and anger attached to the things we have done or experienced. We internalize the wrath or scorn we feel will result if the secret is revealed. We go to great lengths to hide what we have done or what has been done to us. Most of us imagine a punishment far worse than the secret could possibly warrant. We punish ourselves not in response to what we have done or not done, but with the emotions we attach to the experience. Shame, guilt, and anger are toxic emotions which reinforce the belief that "something is wrong with me." The fear of someone discovering what that something is influences our behavior and limits our ability to see past the fear.

Fear helps to create drama. It is like living in a murder mystery. There is someone lurking behind every door. You are constantly trying to figure out what the person behind the door will do to you and how much they know. Who knows? Who does not know? Criticism is a telltale sign that the person may have a clue. You must defend yourself from that person. You must be angry with them. Run away from them. You are constantly living on the edge, planning your getaway or your attack. Since creating and maintaining drama plays such a big part in so many of our lives, we keep it going with our response to rather than examination of criticism. The most unfortunate thing is, we do not realize that by holding on to the secret, we keep it fresh in our minds. What you dwell on, grows. The very thing we do not want people to know, is the very thing we show them with our behavior and response to criticism.

The Law of Belief

Your mind is a dynamic and powerful instrument. Every second of every day, the mind sends thought waves into the universe. A thought is the brain's interpretation of the stimulus it receives through the five senses: hearing, vision, smell, taste, and touch. How you interpret and respond to the stimuli you receive is called consciousness, which determines the frequency or energy of the thoughts you transmit. The frequency of the mind is attuned to the brain's deepest thoughts, on both the conscious (physical) and unconscious (subliminal) levels. Many thoughts remain steadfast in your mind, regardless of the changes in the world or in your life. These hardened thoughts to which your mind clings are called *beliefs*. They are the sum total of everything you have ever heard, seen, or experienced throughout your life.

The Law of Belief, which is nicely summed up in Matthew 8:13, states:

> *As thou hast believed, so be it done unto thee.*

In essence, what you experience and perceive you will make manifest by your belief in its existence. If the thing you believe in does not exist, you will create it through your mind's perception of what actually is (*A Course In Miracles*). This is further supported by the Law of Thought, which in *The Supreme Philosophy of Man* is stated thus:

> *You move toward that upon which you dwell. You tend to become like that which you think about, most vividly, repeatedly, and most imaginatively.*

According to *The Revealing Word,* by Charles Filmore, "A belief is an inner acceptance of an idea as the truth." Although belief is closely associated with faith, a belief is accepted on both the conscious and unconscious levels of the mind. As such, beliefs are very difficult to erase. Whereas faith, a conscious mental activity, is reasonably questionable. Beliefs then are the conclusions of a string of thoughts laced with the emotions buried in the subconscious mind. Fear is a string of thoughts, the conclusion of which need not be true. However, since there is a belief in the conclusion, the consciousness accepts the beliefs as if they are true.

Just because a belief system is based on foregone conclusions which are not true, does not mean it is a weak belief system. The Law of Belief gives equal power to what is true as well as to what is not true. A great deal of the information Black women believe about themselves is based on conclusions created in someone's mind which have nothing to do with the truth. They are lies, very powerful lies. As Black women, our life experiences and interactions very often confirm the lies, thereby supporting even our belief in their veracity. If we choose to believe the lies, we stay in fear. If we choose to think differently, we will be forced to challenge the lies, withdraw from the belief, and act accordingly. More than likely, challenging what we have been told means we will be acting alone, which is something most of us fear.

FEAR IS THE STAGE ON WHICH WE ACT OUT DRAMA!

When I was a single mother, with three children, receiving public assistance, living in a roach-infested apartment, I did not believe I could do any better. The family members and friends with whom I surrounded myself supported my belief. Many of them believed that to be on welfare was bad but that to try to make it in the world alone, with three children, was virtually impossible. I accepted what they believed based on what I had seen of women who had attempted to get off welfare and ended up back on it. One day, when I was alone, I had a flash of inspiration. Without saying a word to anyone, I moved on that inspiration. I enrolled in college. Nobody believed I could do it. It would be too hard. It would cost too much money. It would take too much time away from my children. I did not know what to believe, but when I thought of spending the rest of my life fighting roaches, I knew I had to believe in something other than a can of Raid.

In order to change a belief, we must be willing to accept total responsibility for the behavior we have chosen in response to the belief. We cannot blame anyone. We cannot make excuses: "I did this or did not do this because I believed this." At the point we stop making excuses, we can make a choice. We can choose to continue in what we believe and allow it to govern our actions, or we can deny the old belief, choosing to behave in another manner. The choice to change challenges and ultimately denies the belief when we take action in support of the choice.

Fear is the belief in an undesirable outcome to an action or event. The mind produces fear. It is not produced or manufactured anywhere or by anyone in the world. Our belief that the undesirable outcome is real supports the fear and sends that frequency out into the world. In turn, we act in belief of the thing the mind has created, the thing we fear. We blame fear for our actions because we believe we are responsible for what we do, but not for what we think: "I couldn't help it. I was afraid. I can't help the way I think." The truth is, we are most responsible for what we think because it is in thought that we choose how to act.

Most of our fears are a sign of the conflict we experience between what we want and what we do. If we say we want something but believe we cannot have it, we are in conflict. If we then attempt to act on what we want, still believing it is impossible to achieve, we create a fear to prevent us from moving toward the goal. How many times do we say we want to lose weight because we fear getting fat? We are in fear because we know we just ate three pieces of fried chicken and two pieces of cake. The fear is not of getting fat, it is in our belief that we must have fried chicken and cake. We fear not having money, yet we resist the need to budget. When we get money, we have no budget, so we fear the money is insufficient. To live fearlessly, we must do whatever it takes to eliminate the conflict: "Fear not, for I am with you." Before you act or refuse to act in response to what you believe, examine yourself. Ask what it is that you really want. Ask for guidance to ensure that what you do is unified with what you want. Move consciously at a comfortable pace, being obedient to the guidance you have received. Deny the thing you fear by telling it, No! You cannot exist! Surrender the thoughts and feelings which support the fear to your higher self, your spirit, your God self, with trust and faith.

What Fear Looks Like

Fear dictates how you behave at any given time. We are not talking here about crossing the street when you see a stray dog, or avoiding a glance out the window because you are afraid of heights. We are talking about the gripping, toxic fear which is attached to what you do or what you imagine will happen to you because of something you have done. *A Course In Miracles* teaches, "There are only two emotions in life, love and fear." Either we are acting out of love, or we are acting out of fear. Hate is fear. Jealousy is fear. Shame is fear. So are guilt, anger, greed, the need to be in control, racism, sexism, homophobia, and any other negative response to people or conditions. When we act in response to any of these emotions, we are responding to the underlying cause of fear. Fear is the principle behind every emotion and every act that is not an expression of unconditional love. In our day-to-day interactions, our behavior is often motivated by what we fear may happen, what we fear is going on, or what we fear another person is thinking or doing.

We Attack What We Fear!

Attack, either verbal or physical, is the most common fear-motivated behavior. When another person does or says something which arouses a fear in our mind, we will attack them. Men are more apt to strike out physically while women resort to verbal attack. Attack in the face of criticism is a very common response for Black women: "Isn't that dress a little short for you?" "Well, look who's talking! At least I've got nice legs!" Women attack one another by pointing out what they believe is *wrong* with another person or by telling what they "know" about another person.

The purpose of the attack is to get the focus off yourself. In your mind, if people focus on you, they might "find you out." Gossip is the most common form of verbal attack among Black women. Passing stories around, betraying confidences, embellishing situations to make one person look bad in order to make yourself look good—all these are motivated by fear. When you live in fear, it is always necessary to have someone who is "worse off" than you are to keep the attention away from your secret.

YOU CANNOT DEFEND AGAINST WHAT YOU FEAR!

Some Black women are very defensive. No matter what you say to them, they have an excuse, a rationale, a reason to justify or explain the way they behave. Living on the defense is the way we cover our fear of being wrong. Defensive women always have somebody else to blame for their mistakes. Somebody "made" them this way or that. Somebody told them to do such a thing. Many defensive women blame men for "the way they are" because they have been so hurt by men in the past. Whenever you have need to defend yourself, you are in fear of something. Yes, there are those situations where an explanation will shed some light. However, an explanation is not an excuse. Unless you are willing to take responsibility for what you have done without blaming anyone else, you are living in fear.

FEAR CLOGS THE BRAIN!

Another common fear-motivated behavior is vagueness. All of a sudden, you do not understand. You did not hear it correctly. There was a miscommunication. You thought they meant this or that. "Huh? What do you mean?" is the most common response when we want to be vague. You know perfectly well that you heard the question, understood the instructions, or heard the statement. However, if it touches on a sore spot or weak area in your life or mind, you get vague. Vagueness is our most common response when we do something and our actions are questioned. Rather than being wrong, we get dumb.

IT'S YOUR THING!

"Doing your own thing" is the fear-motivated response of those who need to be in control. Some call it changing the rules. Lateness is the most common example. You know you must be somewhere at 9:00 P.M. You arrive promptly at 9:10 P.M. to announce you can never get anywhere on time: "That's just the way I am. I am always late." Your motivation for being late is to have people waiting for you rather than waiting for them. This is how you maintain control of the situation. Actually, your lateness indicates a lack of respect for other people and their time. Could it possibly be that you are in fear of not being respected? Could it be that you are in fear of not being noticed? Control freaks must be noticed and they must be respected because they fear they are not good enough.

YOU CAN'T PLAY WHEN YOU ARE AFRAID!

When you are in fear of losing something, or not getting your way, you take your ball and go home. You refuse to play. You have nothing to say. You do not want to be bothered. You politely inform all involved they can do whatever they want to do. You are done. This is the fearful response to feeling powerless: you just won't play. Black women do this at work. When we are criticized or feel blamed for some action we have taken with good intentions, we stop playing. We do not answer the telephone. We let the mail pile up and in some cases hide it. We eat lunch alone. We stop talking to other people, because we are in fear of not getting our way. We also do it in our relationships. When a mate does or says something we do not feel good about, rather than speak about it, we withdraw. We are allowing the fear of making our partner angry and the fear of losing to force us into silence. When we cannot speak what we feel, we are powerless. When we are powerless, we are in fear.

Everyday, commonly accepted behavior in the world, in our families, and among circles of Black women is motivated by fear and the toxic spillover of our secrets. Our fears create illusions of what we believe will happen to us if someone knows the truth about us. "Every illusion carries pain and suffering in the dark folds of the heavy garments which hide its nothingness."* The fear we have of what could happen, what might happen, is the illusion which creates the misery we experience, not the experience itself. Truth is the opposite of an illusion. Until we face the truth, we cannot overcome the illusions attached to our fears. To live fearlessly, we must have the ability to trust the universal order of life and the power of spirit at work in that order. In order to trust, we must learn to surrender.

The Value of Surrender

Let go and let God! Let go and let God. Well, what the heck does that mean? One of the first phrases we learn in the journey toward spiritually improving ourselves and our lives is, "Let go and let God." In her book *Mama*, Terry McMillan wrote a statement which crystallizes Black women's difficulty in letting go and letting God: "It's not that I don't believe in God. It's just that I don't trust His judgment." If we let go, God might do it the "wrong" way, at the "wrong" time, rendering the "wrong" results. That is our fear. Consequently, we must stay in control of the people and events in our lives to ensure they go the "right way"—our way.

Belief in lack of anything is a response to the fear of being out of control. When we surrender, we challenge those beliefs and fears which motivate us to be in control. Surrender is a conscious way of sending a message to the universe: "I have no needs or desires which are not met. I am not in control. The universe is and I am well provided for." Focusing your conscious attention on the joy and peace of total well-being cuts the channel of impulsive wanting and needing which you then fear will not be satisfied. When you surrender, you develop the "knowing" that you have no need to struggle or suffer. Surrender gives your mind the opportunity to relax and release. That is what is meant by "letting

---

*Foundation for Inner Peace, *A Course In Miracles*

go"—taking your mental and emotional energy off a thing. Surrender also gives the universe, your spirit, God the opportunity to support you to its highest capacity.

Another benefit of learning to surrender is that it provides us with the opportunity to respond to pure desire based on highest intent. For the most part, our wants are compulsive and impulsive rather than intuitive or necessary. We receive constant messages from the world about what we should have and should do, and what is necessary for a rich and rewarding life. Our physical senses are stimulated by the sights and sounds of the external world. In response to what we see and hear, we develop constructs of what we believe we need. We need a car. We need a television in every room. We need a microwave. We need a Milky Way bar! Years of sensory invasion give us the impression that unless we have certain things in our lives, something is "wrong" with us. Our lives are not meaningful or fulfilled unless we have the things we fear not having. As a result, our intent is not to satisfy our true needs, it is to satisfy the lusts of the senses based on social programming.

Surrender helps to heal fear-filled wanting and not having. As we empty our minds, we tap into the realm of "desire"; in spiritual terms, from *de,* the Latin word meaning "of," and *sire,* meaning "Father." Desire is born in spirit. "The things you desire in your heart are the things God wants for you." When we learn to surrender, to override the impulsive constructs of our senses, we begin to develop desire based on the purest intent of our spirit. When we surrender, our intentions shift from fear and control to joy and peace. We begin to desire those things which will promote joy, peace, and well-being in our lives. The focus shifts from *getting* and *controlling* what you want to *receiving* and *having* what you desire. The result is a more deliberate state of well-being as an outgrowth of our ability to let go of the ideas, habits, people, and conditions which create stress, imbalance, disharmony, and fear. When you can surrender, let go, you let God supply you with what you need.

When you are nursing a secret, surrender helps to disarm the illusions you have attached to it. Surrender the experience. Surrender what you think about it. Surrender what you think others will think if they know. Surrender all emotions attached to whatever the secret is. Surrender the pain, shame, blame, guilt, anger, and of course, fear. As you surrender, ask your spirit, God, the Divine Mother, to reveal to you the meaning of the experience. Ask for a word, a phrase, something you can use to help you find peace in the experience. No matter how bad you think the situation is, there is a lesson. When you surrender the fear attached to the experience, the lesson is revealed. When you understand the lesson, there is peace.

I once experienced a severe financial setback which caused me to question and doubt myself, as well as every good work I had done. I was in fear of being wrong. I could not believe that with the sales of two books skyrocketing, I could not pay my rent, my telephone was disconnected, and I had no aluminum foil to cover the burner trays on the stove. Still, I made my public appearances, usually praying that lunch would be served because I had no food at home. It was a truly humbling experience which I survived by learning to surrender.

The first thing you must surrender when you are a penniless public figure is your ego. You are being forced to make a decision between living the truth and living what you want others to believe about you. As Black women, we are indoctrinated to believe that our self-worth is attached to our net worth. When we have money, we feel valuable and worthy. We use money to buy things to support that concept. Our clothes, cars, doodads, and ditties often have nothing to do with what we want or need. They merely support what we want others to think about us and who we are. As our collection of "things" increases, we get comments and congrats about how well we are doing. Even when we are not doing so well, having things makes us feel better. We feel worthy.

When a Black woman has a cash shortage, in her mind it somehow translates to, "I am not doing the right thing. I should *be* more than this." We are not willing to let others know of our plight because of the aversion we have to criticism. We let our stomachs rumble rather than ask for a meal. We feign illness and stay home rather than admit we do not have carfare. We do not want others to think or know we are faulty in any way, so we suffer, silently, trying to figure out, "Where the hell am I going to get some money?" What we do not realize is that the criticism we want and try so desperately to avoid is born and lives in our own minds. The very things we think others will think about or say to us are the very things we think and say to ourselves.

Stuck in the blocked cash flow, I criticized myself for the things I did and bought when the cash was available. "I spent too much! I should not have gone there! I really didn't need that now!" In the midst of being cashless, I was bashing myself and, as always, promising to be more careful next time. And isn't it strange how hungry you can get when the cash is blocked? It seems that you get a taste for things you have not eaten in years simply because you cannot get them. This intensifies your fear of being wrong. The fear intensifies the bashing. You feel worthless, unable to fulfill even your smallest desire. Throughout the entire experience, you do not want anyone else to know.

There are some things which send out an alarm to the world that you are not doing so well. A disconnected telephone is one. During the first few days, I panicked. I thought of all the people who could possibly call me and what they would think if my telephone was disconnected. My solution was sheer genius. I went to the public telephone and called everyone I could think of so they would not call me. I told them I was out and that I would get back to them. It did not work. The very person I did not want to know had already called me. "I just called you and there is something wrong with your telephone." People try to help you out. They never know how to come right out and say it, so they hedge around the topic to see what you will say. I had a story. "I am writing and the telephone disturbs me." That worked for a while, but after a few weeks, you know everyone else will know. I cringed under the pressure of public scrutiny. Then it hit me. Forget what *they* think! What do *you* think!

I realized I had forgotten who I was. I had become so caught up in what the world thought I should be, I had lost touch with my "self." With or without a telephone, I am a child of God. I am beautiful! I am intelligent! I am worthy! I am valuable! Yeah, but I am also broke! No! I am not broke! I am temporarily out of cash! I still have all of the talents, gifts, and abilities I was born with. I still have meaning in life. I had to surrender my ego. I had to surrender the fear of being criticized. I had to surrender the need to be valued by others and find some value in myself. It was not easy. I had to detach from all the meanings I had attached to everything in my life. I had to surrender my life in order to get the lesson. In my case, there were several.

My first lesson was peace. What did I need to do to make peace with the situation? Surrender. I had to surrender this preoccupation with others, and what others thought about me, in order to find peace. Next lesson: trust. Did I really trust God to provide for me, protect me, take care of me? If I did, I would have to surrender my fear and worry. I had to trust that in divine time, my rent would be paid. That each day I would have a meal. I had to trust that the stove would survive a few days without aluminum foil on the burner trays. Next lesson: faith. I knew that my books were selling. I knew that both of my publishers would pay me royalties. I knew that I had done my work and that it would pay off. I also knew I could not have faith unless I had patience. I wanted cash now. I wanted it when I needed it. I knew, however, that life does not work that way. Everything comes on time and in time.

Surrender. In order for me to accept my lessons in the Valley of Courage, I had to surrender every thought, every emotion, attached to my fear of not having money. I had to surrender what I thought financial security meant. I had to surrender what I thought it looked like. I had to surrender what it felt like. When a thought or feeling came up for me, I said as loud as I could, "I surrender you!" Once I did that consistently for twenty-four hours, everything opened up. I got an American Express card in the mail. With that card I was able to rent a car and drive to any restaurant I chose. I used the card to secure an answering service to take all my calls. I bought some aluminum foil for the stove. I had found a state of peace. In peace, I stood back and looked at my life and realized the final, most important lesson of all: Never, never, be fooled by the way things appear on the surface.

Surrender requires trust. Surrender requires patience. Surrender requires obedience. The reward is learning to move fearlessly through any situation knowing that you will be provided for and protected. Each day, for sixty days, obediently practice surrender. You must obediently focus your mind on not wanting or asking for anything and not being in fear of losing anything. Focus your mind on joy. See joy in everything and everyone. Focus your mind on peace, remembering that what you focus your mind on will grow. With an obedient mind, focused on surrender, you weaken your attachment to things and people while developing patient, fearless reliance on the divine order of the universe.

Finding the Courage to Look At What You Do

One of the most profound statements of spiritual insight I have heard is, "Don't be afraid to look at your faults." If you know what it is you do, the good and the not so good, no one can ever use it against you. When I was in law school, I was told that the most effective way to diffuse the opponent's case against your client was to tell every bad thing the client had ever done. Yes, my client has been arrested fifty times. Yes, my client has been convicted of burglary, car theft, and assault. Yes, my client has spent many years in jail. That, however, has absolutely nothing to do with the charges presented against my client now!

When you are aware of and reveal the secret or hidden information, it takes the wind out of those who want to use it against you. This is how you disconnect your buttons. Put your stuff up front. Tell on yourself. It takes courage to admit that you are not an angel, that you do not have wings. Along with courage, it takes awareness. You must be aware of what it is that you do in order to be able to recognize it when it is done to you. Remember: Know, accept, love thyself. Know what you do. Accept that it is a part of you even if it needs to be worked on. Love yourself anyway. Think of it this way: if you do something you're not proud of, you are probably not the only one who's been there.

Lying To Yourself

When you know something or someone in your life is un-healthy or unproductive, that you have grown beyond where they are and where they want to keep you, you must let go. If you tell yourself you do not see it when you do, or you do not know it when you do, or if you tell yourself it will get better, you are not being honest with yourself. This is a common response to fear of change, fear of the unknown, and fear of being alone. The remedy: surrender. Stop trying to fix things or change things. Simply let go.

Lying To Others

Most of us tell little fibs to impress others or to hide what we perceive to be a weakness. To keep from being "found out" we are compelled to lie. There are those of us who become so accustomed to lying we no longer recognize the truth in ourselves or others. But remember, what you draw to you is what you are! If you are being dishonest with someone, someone will be dishonest with you. Dishonesty in general, and lying in particular, is the fear-motivated behavior of the need to be in control and a lack of self-knowledge.

Holding On To Limitations

"I would but . . . ," "I want to but . . . ," and "I thought about it but . . . " are the common reasons we find our butts in the Valley of Courage. If you believe you are helpless, powerless, or worth-less, the universe will eventually force you to put your butt on the line for something. Excuses are the common response to fear of failure and fear of success. Success more often than not means change and that is something many of us fear as well.

Procrastination

A sister-friend, Jewel Diamond Taylor, says: "Procrastination is a thief!" It steals the best years of our lives and the most blessed opportunities the universe sends our way. Procrastination is the fear of doing which keeps us stuck in hoping, wishing, and trying to do what we say we want to do. When you believe that you are not good enough, smart enough, or worthy enough, you will procrastinate until, like Job, you are forced to face your greatest fear. If you live in this category, your fear is having what you want. Courage is the key.

People Pleasing

We all want to be liked, loved, or needed. That is fine. What is not fine is what we are willing to do to make sure we are liked or loved or needed. When we make the needs and wants of others a priority in our lives, we devalue ourselves. When we devalue ourselves, we eventually believe we are not good enough. When we hold this belief, we must go to the head of the Special Ed class.

Not Asking For What You Want

I know your mother told you, "If you don't ask, you won't get it!" Did you listen to her? Of course not. Instead, you believe it is more important to keep people out of your business, or to do it all by yourself. Or perhaps you are the type who walks around wanting, being resentful of others who get and have. A spiritual teacher once told me, "When you do not ask for what you need, the need gets bigger."

Not Saying What You Need to Say

For some strange reason, we believe we must say "please" to the person who has his foot on our neck. We do not want to hurt his feelings, and we do not want him to be angry or upset with us. We sit and stew rather than say, "Get your #$$%@* foot off my neck!" This misplaced restraint comes from the fear of being wrong, which can only be corrected by courage, knowledge, and wisdom.

The Need to Be Right

Everyone has something she believes in. Everyone has something to say. When we insist that only what we believe is valid, becoming angry with those who don't agree with us, we are in fear. The fear is of not being in control.

Doing What Is Convenient

There is no easy way up, out, or over. You cannot fool Mother Nature, Father Time, and most of the everyday people. You will always get exactly what you give. If you think you can cut corners, get by, or get over, you are wrong. But that's your fear, isn't it?

Doing Too Many Things at One Time

It seems as if there is so much to do and so little time to do it. Life seems to be rushing by, leaving us behind. Many of us panic. We attempt to do it all, right now, today. Go ahead. Try it if you like. Your fear of lack and the need to be in control have undoubtedly taken you off purpose.

Not Following Your First Thought

You know that you know, don't you? Why, then, do you listen to other people and allow them to convince you that you do not know? Know what? You know exactly what I mean. When you know, but act like you do not know, you are in fear of being wrong again.

The Way Out

Dennis Waitley, a Life Transformation teacher, says, "Doing the same thing, expecting different results, is insanity!" We all have moments, days, and sometimes years of temporary insanity. This is to be expected in the experience of humans who believe they are disconnected from the power source. However, it goes beyond insanity to madness when we refuse to see, hear, or know what things we are doing that are harmful simply because we do not want anyone else to know about us or because we are afraid to do something else. The above list is by no means exhaustive. We all have our little idiosyncrasies. We all have fears. We all have our lessons to learn. There is a valley for you and your specific situation.

Grass growing through concrete is a courageous act. The grass never stops to consider the difficulty of its task. It does not seek advice or make plans. It has an inborn mission to grow. The grass does not consider all the possible ramifications of its actions, that it may be stepped on, ripped from its roots, or urinated on. The grass simply knows what it must do and does it, without question, hesitation, or complaint. When we are aware of our inborn mission and undertake that mission without doubt or fear, we become like the grass; courageous enough to do what is required of us in spite of the difficulty.

Like grass, we must develop the courage to grow despite hardships. When we consider the alternative of lying dormant as a seed beneath the surface of life, growing seems to be the wise, as well as courageous, thing to do. When we need assistance in determining what to do, how to grow, the Valley of Courage is available to provide us with all the incentives we need.

Shirley was not only miserable because Frank's mother criticized her. She was hiding what she thought was the truth about her mother's death. She was nursing a secret. She was in fear of being discovered. If the truth really be told, Shirley's life was built on a bed of fear and convenience. She did not love Frank. She had married him because he had stuck by her in the hard times. He helped her escape her father's house. Because she believed she was guilty and unworthy, she settled for marrying Frank, the first and only man who'd ever said a kind word to her. She told herself she loved him. She convinced herself that life with him was bearable. As the years went on, he and his mother had become a festering wound in the pit of her heart.

When the time comes for you to make a change, to grow, to do your life in a different way, the universe will make you so uncomfortable, so unhappy, you will eventually have no choice. If you insist on staying in a place you no longer belong in, if you do not grow the courage to do what is necessary to propel yourself forward, you will suffer the consequences, whatever they may be. For Shirley, the consequence was a mother-in-law who demeaned her and undermined her self-confidence. The only way for Shirley to escape her mother-in-law's criticism was to reveal the secret and confront the fear. Shirley had never spoken to

Frank about how her mother died. He was unaware that Shirley had never loved him. She rarely allowed herself to think about these things, much less felt the courage to speak about them.

If your mind stays in misery, your body will begin to suffer. Many Black women lose their health and their minds due to a lack of courage, an inability to say and do what they fear. Shirley will need to find a way and the words to talk to Frank. This does not mean she has to stand in the middle of the living room and scream, "I think I killed my mother and I never loved you anyway!" It means she will need to get clear about what she wants, and slowly, gradually, choosing her words very carefully, express those feelings to her husband. Being mindful that when we do things in fear or fail to do them because of fear, we drag other people into our issues, Shirley has to give herself and Frank time to deal with the changes that will need to be made. Frank's mother is really not the issue. The issue is Shirley's fear and what she has allowed herself to do because of that fear.

One of the primary reasons we do not take the necessary steps to move out of the misery of our issues is because we fear or become overly concerned with what the other person or people involved will do. We try to figure out what they will say. We create a scenario in our minds about what they will do. We do not want to hurt anyone and there is absolutely no easy way to break somebody's heart. The key is not to worry about what the other person might do, by staying focused on what you will do. This does not mean you become callous or uncaring. It means you listen, you offer as much support as possible, but you maintain your goal in your heart and mind by resisting the urge to give in to the needs and desires of the other person. If you really want to change your condition, you must have the courage to stand firm.

If you are unhappy, it may be because you have not been courageous enough to trust yourself to make new choices. If your life is not moving the way you want it to go, if you feel stagnated, closed in, it is quite possible a little courage will help to free you. If you are afraid of anyone or anything, what might happen or what they might do to you, courage is your ticket. You can eat your Wheaties. You can buy a Superwoman cape. You can talk to yourself in the mirror until you convince yourself that you can do what you need to do. Do whatever works. By any means, find the courage to make the decisions that will enable you to move forward. Shirley did. Two weeks after her mother-in-law's visit, she told Frank she was leaving him. Six months after she told him, he left and went back home to his parents.

As you move through this valley, the Valley of Courage, keep in mind: surrender, trust, faith, and peace. Fearlessness is not a state of namby-pamby spacing out. It is a state of "knowing." You must know at all times that your God self is in control. You must know, no matter what it looks like, divine order must and will prevail. If you get in the way by controlling, fearing, judging, you will cast yourself into darkness. The value in the lesson of courage is, not being fooled by how things appear. When you get that lesson, you will be able to stare down the thing you fear. When you can do that, you grow, you rise up, you evolve. No matter how bad the situation may be, you must realize that you will always be able to get out of a valley because you must be provided another opportunity to demonstrate what you have learned.

MEDITATION
WITH THE
MOTHER

*Obey my voice and I will be your God and ye
shall be My people.*

—JEREMIAH 7:23

*Let the Mother come to nourish you. You must have strength to
leave behind the trappings of the world. Let her nurture your heart
and your mind, so that they may guide your thoughts and words.
There is nothing you need which the Mother does not have, nothing
she has not already given you. She gave you love in your heart,
peace in your mind, strength in your will, power in your words.
You daughters have given it back. You have replaced the Mother's
gifts with things of darkness, things of the world—things which do
not honor your sacred energy.*

*Let the Mother nourish you, daughters, bring you back into the
fold of her pure and divine light, love, and energy. For there she
awaits to restore you to your station of grace. She wants to guide
you, daughters, for she knows your purpose and the plans by
which it shall be accomplished. She is the Ways and Means Com-
mittee, eternally elected to govern your completion of any assigned
task. She represents the President of the Holy Corporation and the
Chairperson of the Board of Your Life. She is with Him in mind,
heart, and spirit. She wants to share her post with you.*

*Let the Mother hold you up, daughters. She is a pillar of strength, a
guidepost of light and an able shipmate who has been on many
journeys. She has mended your sail many times. She has cleansed
your brow and hoisted your sail when you thought you were too
weary to continue. She knows the seas of life are not always calm.
No matter. The Mother is equipped to weather the storm with you.*

*Let the Mother bring you back to yourselves. To the shores of
peace. The post of plenty. The dock of everlasting life. All you need do
is enlist her help. She will hear you and come to serve you.*

143

The Valley of Knowledge and Wisdom

5

*I*F SOMEONE ASKED ME TO EXPLAIN IT, I COULD NOT. I SIMPLY KNOW WHEN I KNOW. I KNEW WHEN I MET HIM it was not going to work out. Did I listen? No! Who listens to me? I knew when I took the job it was not where I wanted to be. Did I leave? Of course not! If you have to pay the rent you keep the job. I knew it when I lent her the money. I knew I would not get it back on time. The minute she started making excuses for why she did not have the money on the day she said she would, the day I needed it so badly, I wanted to pinch myself. As she told me the long story, I knew she wasn't telling the truth. Like an idiot, I stood there, listened to her, and walked away smiling, when I was totally pissed off! Each time my gut, my spirit, tells me something and I do not listen, I find myself in trouble. Why is it so hard to listen to myself, while I willingly allow other people to tell me anything, particularly things I know are not true? It must be the orange juice. That's it! Too much orange juice has turned my brain to pulp!

Intuition, "teaching from within," is a fail-safe guidance mechanism with which we are endowed at birth. Through it, we always know what we need to know. We know what is going on with ourselves and with everyone else. Intuition never fails to operate. It warns us. It guides us. It provides us with helpful little hints and tidbits of information about everyone and everything. The issue is, do we know what to do about what we know? Usually not. We get the message or the information intuitively, but we do not know how to handle it. We may not know how, why, when, or what, but intuition sends us signals we generally ignore. We simply do not believe that what we are thinking or feeling is actually true. Not knowing what to do about what we know, not trusting what we know, and not believing what we know—these are the things that take us into the Valley of Knowledge and Wisdom.

In the Valley of Knowledge and Wisdom, we face those experiences that are the result of disobedience, failure to follow the voice of spirit—the quiet, still voice which speaks within our heart and mind. The information we receive lives in the marrow of our bones. It is the genetic memory of our DNA and the essence of who we are. We are at all times connected to the One and the ones who paved the way for our lives. They speak to us. They give us guidance. They tell us exactly what to do—but we don't listen. We are disobedient.

We are disobedient because we allow fear, doubt, habits of human nature, and the lack of discipline to silence our inner wisdom. We know, but we are not certain. In our uncertainty, therefore, we disobey the voice of our soul. The experiences which bring us to this valley are the forces of life urging us to develop obedience through disciplined spiritual practices. In this way, when we tune in to the voice of spirit, we will be assured we can move forward in certainty of the outcome.

Who Listens To You?

The American society is one which prides itself on information. The more information you have, the more valuable you are to the world and those around you. The trick is, you are expected to get the information from sources other than yourself, outside sources. You must have credentials, indicating how much information you have, before anyone will listen to you. You are taught to hash and rehash information which has already been discovered and discussed. If you come up with anything new, well, you can forget it. We learn this early in our lives. We are taught as children that we know nothing. If we think we do or insist we might, we are told we are arrogant and out of place. Some of us are lucky enough to be born to parents who believe children do know. Unfortunately, they send us to schools with teachers who keep their job as long as we do not know.

Those of us who are lucky enough to know, to prove we know, and to make others believe we know are considered geniuses. We are held out as some sort of freaks of nature, something to be honored and valued. The rest of the people, who may not know how to articulate what they know, are made to feel worthless in comparison to the genius. That is how it starts. In our childhood, we are taught we do not know and we believe it. We carry this feeling of ignorance into our adult life, feeling less than adequate unless someone, somewhere, has already proven what we know and feel in our hearts. This is not too difficult, since nothing is really new. Life is an educational process, a process of pulling information out, not putting information in. We are all here to express the same old things in new ways. Unfortunately, as a result of our childhood trauma, even when we think we know, we have been taught not to trust ourselves.

Rehashing and accepting already hashed information works fine in business, economics, sometimes even politics. It does not work well in our interpersonal relationships. Acting as if we do not know what we know, who people are, what they want, and what they are willing to do to get what they want can be hazardous to our physical, mental, and spiritual well-being.

We are taught to believe what other people say. When we are told that a person is wonderful and marvelous, we believe it, even if our intuition tells us something different. We are taught to believe what we see. When our inner self shows us something which contradicts what the physical eyes see, we generally go with the physical. Job interviews are a clear example. Most of us behave totally differently on interviews than we do at any other time in life. We dress up, sit up, speak up, and do exactly what we think is required. Interviewers know we are on our best behavior, but they buy it anyway. They buy what we are showing them rather than what is. I for one have been on many interviews where I lied through my teeth and had the paper to substantiate every word. I needed a job. I knew how to play the game, so I did.

What's Your Real Deal?

At some time or another, we all play the game. Whether interviewing for a job, meeting the parents of a friend or beau, or eating in a fancy restaurant, we put on a show. The problem comes about when it is time to be real. If we get real, saying what we feel and what we think, people get upset. If we get real by talking about what we feel and no one else agrees with us, we believe that we are wrong. When we get real and do what our hearts and minds lead us to do, we are afraid to stand alone.

Being real is frightening to most people. It is so much easier to put on a show and act as if we do not know. Each time we do, we sell our "selves" out. We let our "selves" down. As a result, we learn not to trust the "self" who we let down and sold out in order to go along with the crowd and do what was expected. Selling ourselves out to play the game is an insult to the teacher within who provides us with all the knowledge we need at any given time, free of charge.

Knowledge is having information. Wisdom is knowing what to do with the information you have. Most of us are very knowledgeable. Few of us are wise. Spirit is very well aware of our dilemma. Consequently, when we will not listen to the spirit within, the information will be presented to us through the world around us. We will hear or see things which spark an interesting thought or an idea. Thoughts often provide us with some form of information about ourselves, others, or what to do at a given time. Thoughts give us clues about the possibilities and opportunities which lie ahead of us. People in our lives also give us information.

A Valley Experience

Sylvia and Alex had been married for twenty-three years. Twenty-three long, often hard years, which produced three beautiful children of whom they were both very proud. They "loved" each other, but they were no longer "in love." Sylvia knew it. Alex knew it. Neither of them knew how to say it. They had stopped arguing long ago. Now, they ate their meals together. They attended all the obligatory functions together. They were civil to one another and they slept at separate ends of the bed. Sex had stopped about three years ago. All touching had ceased about two years ago. One of them needed to do something. Neither of them did.

Sylvia was forty-six. Still very attractive, very active, secure in her career. Their youngest child was ten years old the first time she heard it: her husband was actively involved with another woman. She began suffering from panic attacks. "Leave this marriage." It was more of an idea than an instruction—an idea she considered absolutely absurd. She had no place to go. Everything was in his name. Besides that, the children loved, no, idolized him. Alex was not a bad person. He just liked other women.

When Sylvia decided to go back to college to get her degree, the panic attacks calmed down quite a bit. She was feeling a lot more confident and a lot less dependent on him. Their oldest child was preparing to go to college. She had been promoted on her job. Alex was talking about buying a new house. Things seemed bearable. Until the idea started plaguing her. "Leave him. Leave him now!" It now had a sense of urgency. Every time Sylvia heard it, she could feel the panic rising in her body, threatening to take her breath away. It was happening every day, several times a day. She was relieved the day it happened at her mother's house. It gave her just the opportunity she needed to talk to someone about it.

When she told her mother she was thinking about leaving Alex, her mother said: "Good! I never liked him anyway."

Sylvia was shocked. But she also felt the need to defend him. Alex was her husband. The father of her children. "Why? Why don't you like him? He has never done anything to you."

"First of all, he thinks he is the cat's meow. He acts like everybody owes him something for being great. Alex acts like he thinks he did you a favor by marrying you. I always told you to marry that nice guy from your grandmother's church. Oh no! You had to marry Mr. Wonderful!"

"That nice guy from Grandma's church had buck teeth and wore bifocals."

"Good! Nobody else would want him! Everybody wants Mr. Wonderful! There is something funny about him. I don't know what it is, but I know there is something which must come to light."

"How do you know?"

"Because I'm your mother. A mother knows when her daughter's husband has another woman. It changes the color of your skin. I can smell it. I know it is poisoning you and you should leave him."

"I can't."

"Why not?"

"I don't know, I just can't."

So she didn't.

Until she had that discussion with her mother, Sylvia would not allow herself to think about leaving him. That day, in spite of what she said, she knew she had to do it. It was not just that he had other women—he just did not make her happy. Alex was as nice as he was mean. Not moody—arrogant was a better word, just as her mother had pointed out. But he was a good provider. He paid all the bills, her money was her money. If there was something he could not pay, he always *asked* her to cover it until next time. Those instances were very rare.

Sylvia spent her money on the children, herself, and anything she wanted for the house. Basically, she did whatever she wanted to do. Alex never asked her about money. He never asked her where she was going. He never asked her anything. He told her everything. That was it! Alex never asked her opinion. He never elicited her help. He treated her as if she were ignorant, and she had been playing the part. If she left him, maybe he would realize how smart she was. Still, the thought of it made her weak.

They bought the new house, in his name. Their second daughter went off to school. He was coming home earlier. Must have ended another fling. Sylvia was in her last semester of school, six months away from her degree, when the unthinkable happened. She met a man. A wonderful man. He was gentle, polite, easygoing, very intelligent, and divorced. He sat next to her in class. If she was late, he saved a seat for her. When class was over, he always offered her a ride. One night, because her car was in the shop, Sylvia accepted his offer. They stopped for coffee. He asked her questions. He listened to her answers. They laughed together. He took her home, and she knew: something was about to happen.

She could not get to sleep. She walked the floor. She drank tea. She watched television. She woke Alex up twice getting in and out of the bed. She told him it was cramps. Right part of the body. Wrong affliction. It was lust. Pure and simple. There was a raging lust burning in her that was about to burst. She was frantic, so she did what most frantic people do: she prayed. "Please help me! Tell me what to do! Take him away! I'm confused! I'm weak! I'm sexually frustrated! I know it is wrong, but I can't help myself. Please help me." The prayer helped her calm down somewhat. Within seconds, the answer came to her loud and clear: "Leave him! You have no excuse to stay." "I can't! My children will hate me. He will hunt me down. I will be penniless. I love him, I just don't want to be with him. I can't leave." And so she didn't.

She told him about her marriage. He told her to do whatever she thought was best. He would be her friend no matter what she decided to do. Both of them decided an affair was too risky at this point. She needed to be sure. He did not want to be her excuse to leave. They discussed and decided to keep things as they were until she figured it all out. Her best girlfriend told her to keep both of them. One for the money, the other just for the hell of it. Her sister told her adultery was a sin and that she would burn in hell. She reminded her sister that her husband would be there burning with her. Her mother told her to be careful. "Every shut eye ain't asleep." Her theory was that the guy was a plant, either a plant by her husband or a plant by God to see what she would do. By the time she had spread her business all over town, she was more confused than ever.

The voice had become an obsession. Each time Sylvia saw Alex, it screamed at her, "Leave!" She began to think she was losing her mind. She could not figure out if she really wanted to leave or if she just wanted peace of mind. She thought they were mutually exclusive. After graduation, Sylvia would meet her friend on the weekends. They went to the theater, they shopped, they did all the things she and her husband had stopped doing. One Saturday afternoon, when they were in the middle of having lunch, she saw her oldest daughter Ivy, who on the spot demanded to know who the man was.

Sylvia decided not to lie. "He is a friend of mine from school, whom I like very much and spend most of my spare time with."

"Is he your lover?"

"That is none of your business."

"Well, it is my father's business."

"Yes. He is." Again, Sylvia decided not to lie.

In the middle of this lovely little cafe, twenty minutes away from her house, her oldest daughter screamed, fell into her chest, and cried hysterically.

It did not matter whether or not the daughter told the husband. Sylvia would never live through the guilt and shame. She was convicted. She had never considered how this would affect the children. She had only considered her own selfish needs. This was their first child. Alex's favorite child. He was her hero. They were best friends. Sylvia decided, no matter what else happened, it would stay that way. He helped Sylvia and Ivy to their car. Ivy cried all the way home but she never said a word.

Thank God Alex was not there when they got home. They both went to their rooms and closed the doors. Sylvia called her mother to tell her about the mess. Her mother replied that it was bound to happen. Thank God it had happened. Sylvia did not have to live like a thief in the night. She was a grown woman. Her children were practically grown. Leave him! Right now! Today! Sylvia decided to talk to her husband about the possibility of a separation. She would do it as soon as he came home.

When Ivy knocked on the door, Sylvia's heart began to race. Ivy came in, crawled into the bed, curled up next to her mother, and began to cry. Sylvia and Ivy both cried until the daughter spoke. Ivy was sorry Daddy had pushed her out of his life. She knew about the other women. She had met one of them. She was sorry her mother had been so unhappy for so long. She had tried to help her, though. She used to pray they would not argue. It worked. Now she was sorry her mother was leaving Daddy, but she understood. Why had she waited so long? Why had she let Daddy treat her this way? What was the man's name? Did he have any children?

You just never know. The very thing you believe is virtually impossible is the very thing that often happens. Of all their children, this is the one Sylvia had thought would crumble under the pressure of a divorce. If the children had to decide between their parents, Sylvia thought for sure she would lose this one. To find out that Ivy knew about her father and felt bad for her mother was completely unexpected. Sylvia was angry but elated. She was hurt, but for the first time in a long time, she was strong. Now she could leave. As her oldest child lay sleeping in her bed, she ran downstairs to call her friend. As she was explaining what had happened, he burst out laughing, telling her, "You just never know, do you?"

Sylvia skipped right past separation to divorce. There was no longer any reason to wait. If Alex would not agree, she would go to Mexico. She had the money. She wanted the car, the china, and of course, the youngest child, whom Alex would put through college. If he didn't agree, she would fight him tooth and nail. Sylvia practiced her speech over and over. She paced the floor. Peered through the window. Paced some more. Peered again. It was 5:30 in the morning when the voice said, "He isn't coming home."

The sun came up at about 6:10. She realized that for the first time in twenty-three years, her husband had stayed out all night. She was livid. This had to be a new one, one who did not know the rules. But he knew the rules. She remembered their first big argument about his infidelity. He had come home at 3:00 A.M. She told him if midnight ever caught him on the other side of the door, she would leave and take him to the cleaners. Since that night, he had never stayed out beyond 11:00, 11:30 at the latest. Considering he closed his office at 5:00 and was off on Wednesdays, that hadn't been so restrictive. Now she *knew* she was making the right decision. By 7:30, she was praying for the opportunity to tell him.

Don't you hate it when the telephone and the doorbell ring at the same time? At 7:43, it happened. Her mother was on the telephone. The police were at the door. Mother said she would wait. The police had found Alex's body slumped over the wheel of his car about an hour ago. Everything was intact. No signs of foul play. Must have been a heart attack. She would have to come to identify the body. Ivy became hysterical again. The police were very sympathetic and very supportive. How old was he? Fifty-one. What a shame. Very nice-looking man. Mother was screaming into the telephone, "What's wrong over there? Pick me up, I'll go with you. This is your father all over again."

The lawyer waited two weeks after the funeral to call. He wanted to stop by to talk to Sylvia about a few things. There was no will, but the property was joint. Sylvia had to refrain from telling him, "And I am free." When the lawyer showed up, he was embarrassed. He was as shocked as she was. He was so sorry. He would help her any way he could. Had Sylvia divorced him, no one would have ever known. Now there was sure to be a lengthy, costly legal battle. "The law is very clear. The wife takes everything. That marriage was recorded two years before Sylvia and Alex's marriage. The woman has the papers and all of the checks dated up to three weeks ago. The one child is grown." It didn't really matter, however. That wife and that child would have everything Sylvia's name was not on. That wife owned this house, her car, and every dime in the bank he left that was not for the support of minor children. She wanted it all and chances are, she would get it. The lawyer could not figure out why Alex had not taken care of this long ago. Whatever the reason, he had not. Now Sylvia was in the valley.

The Law of Obedience

Follow your first thought. Be obedient to what your spirit guides you to do. If you are not clear, ask for clarity. Do not be so willing to doubt yourself, to abandon yourself. You cannot know you are on the right track unless you move. The truth has a way of vibrating in your soul. It lets every part of you know when it is present. "Be still and know" the truth in you. Lies are what we accept from the world, not what you have been given in your spirit.

How do you know you know? Because we cannot *not* know. That would mean we were set up for failure from the start. Why would we be given the essence of all that is good in life and be doomed to fail? Our knowledge was born within us. It is intelligence that we must develop along the way. Unfortunately, it is our intelligence which leads us to doubt what we know.

We live in such a vicious cycle. We are told we do not know so we must be educated. As we are educated, there is a criterion for the measurement process. Where we get knowledge, and who provides us with the knowledge, determines the value the world places on the knowledge. And how do we get this knowledge? We read it in books. The books we read, we are expected to remember. The question then becomes, do we know or do we remember? How can knowledge be substantiated without experience? Yet our experiences are limited by what we know. How can it be that every vital thing we need to live is inside of us, but the knowledge we need to live is outside of us? These are just a few of the questions which keep us in doubt and conflict about what we know and how to use it.

In the Valley of Knowledge and Wisdom are the experiences which allow us to examine and test what we know. When our intuitive learning presents us with information, we must test its veracity by being obedient to what we hear. We must suspend all judgment and intellect long enough to examine whether or not what we are hearing is consistent with what we know, what we want, and what we are doing. We get caught off guard when what we hear inside is inconsistent with what everyone else is saying or doing. We question ourselves and ignore the messages we receive. We have been trained to do it. We have a fear of moving out from the pack, looking different, being different. If we have not developed courage, it is difficult to be confident about what we know.

THE WISE OFTEN STAND ALONE

Eagles do not flock. You find them one at a time. They fly higher than all the other birds. Chickens flock and get caught in the slaughter. Very often, chickens are eaten by eagles. In the Valley of Knowledge and Wisdom, revisit the fear of being alone. The conditioned response to being different is that it's wrong. If it's so wrong to be different, then why do we all have different faces? different bodies? Why don't we all have one uniform way of looking and living? That would be our death. Life is diversity. No two things are the same. No two paths cover the same ground. No two people can express the same uniqueness. God made Chihuahuas and He made Saint Bernards. If either loves you, it will look different. If either bites you, it will feel different. We must each learn to become comfortable in our uniqueness—what that looks like, what that feels like, and what we know as a result of it.

In *The Supreme Philosophy of Man,* the Law of Obedience states:

> *To obey means to submit to rule or to comply with orders and instructions. Obedience then is the governor of all movement, whether it be mechanical, literal, or spiritual. Once this law is understood, we hold the secret of eternal happiness, peace, and domination or mastery over all forces around us.*

Obedience to spirit is the only way to master our lives. We must learn to be obedient to develop courage. We must be obedient to see the fruits of our faith. We must be obedient if we practice trust. Obedience to the internal voice is the only way to master our human nature which lusts after external appearances. Many of the challenges Black women face in their lives arise not because we do not know what to do, but as a result of our failure to listen to what we know. We get confused. We are not sure whether to follow the laws of earth or those of the invisible realm—the laws of spirit.

The laws of earth, physical laws, promise us things we can see and have. They offer us immediate gratification. But the laws which govern the invisible realm take time to manifest our desires. Our lives, for the most part, are measured and quantified by outward appearances, the way things look. We accept these measures of our worth by paying first homage to the law of what is tangible. The error we make in following this logic is we forget that everything we can now see is an outgrowth of something which has taken place in the realm of the invisible—the realm of spirit.

We see a beautiful, shiny, brand-new BMW. This is more than just a car. It was first an idea in someone's mind. Obediently, that person nurtured that idea, held a clear picture of what it was, what it would look like. Drew a picture. Obediently, others followed instructions, crafting, designing, until they produced the prototype. Wrote it down. Following instructions, they listed everything about this car that would make it different from all other cars. They obeyed, not knowing if they would be embraced or disgraced. The rest is history. As a result of someone's obedience to the invisible, today we have not just a car, but a masterfully crafted machine for our driving pleasure and safety.

Disobedience is the refusal to do what you know. Spirit always provides guidance and instruction. We doubt. We fear. We worry. We question. We forget the powerful workings of the mind. Whatever we give the mind, it will produce. If we feed the mind seeds of worry, doubt, and fear, it produces situations to increase what we worry over and fear. That is the law. Worry in. Worry out. Obedience in. Rewards out. If we learn to obey the voice of spirit rather than the appearances and conditions around us, our rewards will become tangible experiences in our lives.

The Lessons

TRUST WHAT YOU KNOW

"Can't you do anything right!" "Why can't you do what you are told?" "This is wrong! You did it wrong!" "I don't know when you will learn to do things the right way!" That is where it all starts.

Between the ages of three, four, and five years old, our parents and other caregivers, in their frustration, anger, or impatience, let us know how wrong we are. It is the job of adults to convince children they are wrong. Remember when you got one of those big, fat red F's on a test or homework assignment, which you quickly hid in the desk so no one else would see how "wrong" or "bad" you were? What about when you received the red-circled 60's, 55's, or lower on your report card, for which you were punished? Punishment always lets you know how "wrong" you have been. It's a pure setup! We are measured against standards which have absolutely nothing to do with us. If we don't live up to the standards, we are considered wrong. If you are wrong, you cannot be trusted. If you are wrong, you do not know what is right or good for you.

The setup continues when, as children, we see people do things and they tell us we did not see what we know we saw. If we walk in somewhere we should not be, if we interrupt acts adults would rather we didn't see, if we find things adults thought were well hidden, we get blamed. "What are you doing in here?" "Where did you get that?" "Get out! Get out right now!" Somehow, being a curious child has made you wrong again. You don't know what you are doing that is wrong, but you are doing it. Let us not forget dishonesty, while we're at it. When we hear adults say things we know are not true, which adults insist are true, we doubt ourselves. After all, we are usually wrong anyway.

We fall into the real trap when we say true things and are scolded or punished for saying them. My classic was, "I don't like Grandma. She's mean." My parents would sit me in the corner each time I said it. As children, we have an uncanny way of telling the truth. The truth is not always nice. The truth is not always convenient. As children, we don't know that. We just speak. Unpleasant and inconvenient truths sometimes result in a pop across the chops. We remember these experiences when we are adults. We have a difficult time telling unpleasant or inconvenient truths. We may have valuable knowledge or information about people and situations, but if it's unpleasant or inconvenient, we remain silent. This is not a wise thing to do.

DO WHAT FEELS RIGHT FOR YOU

We must each learn to feel comfortable in our own uniqueness by rising above the fear of being wrong and the aversion to being different. We witness the experience all of the time. We see a wonderful singing group. We enjoy their music and believe they work well together. Then, we see one member strike out on his or her own. Diana Ross. Patti LaBelle. Sheila E. Be assured it was not an easy task for them. Alliances had been formed. Plans, goals, dreams had been shared. Yet there came a time when that one individual had to be obedient to the urge in her soul. And what happened when she left the group? Did the group flourish and survive? In some cases, yes. In others, no. When it comes to being obedient, what will happen to those you leave behind is not your issue! We get stuck in worrying about what the fate of others will be if we follow our heart. The danger is what Dr. Vanessa Weaver, author of *Smart Women, Smart Moves,* calls "analysis paralysis." We become so bogged down trying to figure out what could happen, what might happen, we do not move and nothing happens. The key to finding a little tummy comfort when you know you must be obedient to your spirit is to be honest, tell exactly what you know and feel, and act with love.

Never use what you call obedience as an excuse to harm another person. Always examine the quality of your intent. If you are out to get someone, to flex your ego, or to pursue your own personal hidden agenda, you must keep your mouth shut. When we know an unpleasant truth about a situation or a person, we must evaluate the quality of our intent before revealing the information to anyone. A few very simple questions will reveal the truth:

1) Why am I revealing this information?
2) Who will be helped/harmed if I reveal this information?
3) What is the source of the information? Is it reliable?
4) What do I expect to happen once the information is revealed?

We are not talking about hearsay or gossip. That stuff is never reliable. We are talking about a strong intuitive sense, a personal experience, or information which has come directly to you from a reliable source. If your intent is not honorable, the information will probably blow up in your face.

Ask for guidance every step of the way. There may be times when the messages or information we receive are not clear or complete. Ask in prayer or meditation what to do and what to say. Be obedient to what you hear. Do exactly as you are told or what feels right to you. Spirit is usually very specific. Do not add or omit anything, no matter how ridiculous or insignificant it may seem. Remember, the little things do matter.

This is where I always get into trouble. I get the instructions, clearly, specifically, but the control freak in me always finds something to add or subtract. Very often I add what I think is needed to keep other people from being upset or angry with me. Or I subtract the thing that is most uncomfortable for me, the thing that will challenge my fear. Whenever I am disobedient, I must deal with the unpleasant outcome. There are times I can regroup and still move forward. However, there are those times when not paying attention to the details sends me right back to the drawing board.

It ain't easy being a queen. Somebody is always ready and willing to dethrone you. In order to hold on to your royalty, you must plant yourself firmly on your throne and refuse to move. People are going to challenge your royalty, your right to sit where you are and do what you are doing. Just know that it is their job. If you give up the throne to the first person who comes along to challenge you, you are proving you are not worthy. Be obedient. Sit tight. No one is running around challenging the paupers. Trust that you have what it takes to rule your own life.

DEVELOP DISCIPLINE

If you do not have some degree of discipline, you cannot be obedient. There needs to be a prescribed manner in which you communicate with and contact your higher self, your spirit. You want to know there is some place you can go or something you can do to get guidance when you need it. This can take the form of a daily ritual or routine. It may also be a sense, a feeling you get.

One reason we do not trust what we know is that we are not sure what it sounds and feels like. We must learn to spend time with our innermost selves. We must learn to love, value, and honor who we are. Quiet time is the best place to start. Spend time alone with you, listening to your thoughts. Begin to filter out those things you know are not true about you. Ask yourself simple questions about yourself and listen to the thoughts which flow. The answers will be revealed.

Learning to trust yourself and what you know takes time and work. You cannot expect to eradicate a lifetime of misguided information overnight. You must make a continuous, conscious effort to get on good terms with you. Try spending the first twenty minutes of your day in conscious contact with yourself. Sit quietly and think good thoughts about yourself; speak loving, encouraging words into the mirror while looking into your eyes; write yourself a love letter and read it aloud to yourself. Just as in our relationships with others, trust must be built between you and your "self."

Trust is based on your ability to depend on yourself. When you say you will or will not do a thing, keep your word. If you cannot honor your original commitment, renegotiate. You cannot let yourself down and expect you to be there for you in a pinch. Tell yourself the truth about what you feel, what you want, what you will and will not do. There will be times when you falter. In those cases, do not beat up on yourself. Get still and ask yourself, "How can I do it better next time?"

Each and every day, make time for a self-inventory. This is best done at the end of the day. Mentally reflect on the day's activities. Did you honor your agreements with yourself and others? Did you act with integrity and an honorable intent? Did you honor what you were feeling throughout the day? Did you ask for guidance and follow it? Did you give thanks for the guidance you received? What were the things you did today which you want to do better? What were the things you did well today? Did you celebrate your successes today? What are you willing to work on about yourself tomorrow? These questions can be asked and answered mentally, or you can keep a journal. Self-evaluation is the key to self-understanding. Self-understanding is the key to trusting yourself and what you know.

ACT WITH CERTAINTY

Knowing is not the issue for many of us. Translating the information into words or action in a wise manner seems to be where we experience the greatest amount of difficulty. How do we speak the unpleasant truth in a manner which will not get us thrown out of the nearest window? Ask for your own inner guidance. If you can get still enough and calm enough to ask what you should do or say, you will be guided. The exact words will come to mind. You will be guided as to what to do. You must trust what you are feeling and go with it. If you allow fear, intimidation, or doubt to overtake you, the guidance will not be clear. If you are afraid of what someone will do to you, or what will happen as a result of what you know, you will be thrown off track. If pleasing other people is your ultimate goal, you're doomed from the start.

There are times when it is wise to be silent and observe. There are situations when you must speak directly to the person or people involved in what you know. There are times when you must say what you know, say it loud, and say it repeatedly until someone hears you. Ask for guidance. You will be directed and you will know exactly what to do. When the guidance comes forth, trust it! Do exactly as you are told! When you have done what you have been directed to do, with an honorable intent, sit back and observe. It may take a while for something to happen. What you expect, may never happen. That is not the issue. Taking what you know and using it in a wise way is the only way to keep yourself out of the Valley of Knowledge and Wisdom.

BE OBEDIENT

Some of us are bold, some are arrogant. Some of us are insensitive, others are intimidating. Some of us are powerful, some are intelligent. Few of us are obedient. It takes a great deal of wisdom to develop the discipline required to do what you know is necessary for your growth and well-being. Only with disciplined obedience can you develop the skill to know what to do, when to move, and how to accomplish the task. Discipline and obedience replace fear. If you are obedient to the laws of nature, moving consistently in a disciplined manner, you have no need to fear or doubt the natural outcome of your actions will follow, with the best intent for all involved. Certainty is not bold or forceful. It is a gentle energy which, because it is intangible, is often mistaken for something else. Certainty is not boastful or self-seeking. More often than not, it is silent and modest. Certainty, the outgrowth of discipline and obedience, is the ultimate testimony of faith, trust, and truth.

Knowing is the foundation of certainty. You must know that the universe and your spirit will protect you from all harm. You must know that no matter what happens, the truth of who you are cannot be touched. You must know that you are valuable and worthy of being heard, honored, and respected. Knowing is an active function of intuition. You develop it from the inside in order to see it operate on the outside. When you can trust yourself and what you know, and act with the most honorable intent, at the appropriate time, in the appropriate manner, without fear, doing what needs to be done without expectation of reward or recognition, you have developed obedience.

The Way Out

No one is saying it will be easy to do what you know is right or good for you. That is what the valleys are about. Valley experiences force you to do the hard stuff that makes you better for life. Life and the laws that govern it are consistent. Hard lessons make you better. If you have a bad habit, you *better* stop it! If you have an unhealthy body, you *better* heal it! If you are in a failing relationship, you *better* get out of it! Sylvia knew the marriage was over. She knew Alex was cheating. She knew it was only a matter of time, and still she stayed, trying to squeeze water from a rock. There are plenty of rocks in the Valley of Knowledge and Wisdom, which is where she ended up.

No matter what anyone says or does, you cannot move, will not move, out of a situation until you are ready. To the outside world, the situation may have seemed unbearable eons ago. But you, who live in the midst of the garbage, you find a way to cope, to hang on until you are ready, willing to let go. The wife was very clear that she was not ready to leave. She told her mother. She told herself. What she did not do was sit down and make an attempt to figure out why. Why was she willing to stay? Was it fear? Was she staying for convenience? Was she hoping for the best? We do not know, and she, it seemed, did not care to know.

Everybody has a fleeting thought, an idea which sticks out in her mind. It may pass through and keep going, or it may plague you, hound you, haunt you until you pay attention. The wife had more than a fleeting thought. She had an obsessive drive to make the first move. She did not obey. She did not examine. She found excuses and reasons to ignore the thought and stay in the marriage. Spirit really does want to support and guide us. We get in the way of the very support we need with our questions and fears. If the human self cannot figure it out, or see the way out, we pay little attention to the spiritual urge. We want to know how and why. We want written directions and concrete instructions. Spirit does not work that way! Spirit prompts, sends signs and signals. It is up to you to obey. Trust, faith, and obedience are what spirit requires of us. Without them, we drive ourselves face first into the very mess spirit will have to get us out of later on.

If there is something which continues to stay to the fore of your mind, pay attention to it. If you are being prompted, guided, to do a certain thing, be obedient. Your spirit has no reason to play tricks on you or send you up the river. If you go, it goes with you. If you are in bondage to people or conditions, your spirit is in bondage with you. You already know when it is time for you to move up or out. If spirit is prompting you, it means the universe is ready and willing to support you. Take advantage of a good thing when it passes through you. Spiritual guidance is the best guarantee that the time and conditions are right for you. Do not limit yourself to what you think you know. Be obedient. When spirit says jump, simply ask, "How high?"

MEDITATION
WITH THE
MOTHER

He told me I was his property; that I must be sub-
ject to his will in all things. My soul revolted
against the mean tyranny. But where could I go
for help?

—INCIDENTS IN THE LIFE OF A SLAVE GIRL

There is peace in the midst of your mind. That peace makes your
decisions. That peace governs your choices. In that place of peace,
there is no doubt, no fear, no illusion. There is only the certainty
that for all time, in all places, God's love for you is your peace.

In this place of peace, you cannot make a mistake, no error can
stand against you, no battle can be formed. There is but one thing
for you to do: to know that in your peace, the light of God shines
upon you and lights your way. Why will the daughters not seek the
peace? Have you become so attuned to the clamoring of the world
that you believe your peace is gone forever? Or is it that the daugh-
ters do not trust peace? For in peace there is no conflict, no ques-
tion, no fear.

Come, daughters, and seek my peace. As I hold you in my arms,
there can be no conflict in your heart or mind. There can be no
one to please, no roles to fill, no loss to fear. In peace, I gently urge
you to choose me over the world; to choose my peace in the place of
shame; to choose my peace in lieu of anger; to allow peace to erad-
icate the lusts of the mind and body.

There is no place I cannot be. Seek me and I will come to bring
you the assurances that will ease your mind and open your heart
to the abundance of my good. Rest assured that in the peace she of-
fers, the Mother knows her daughters. She will respond if they will

but call. She will enlighten them, lift them, heal them, hold them in a state of peace, mercy, and love forever. So, let it be that no daughter who seeks peace and freedom be left unprotected, unguided. Let them know that in the Mother's heart, there is a jewel of peace waiting to be plucked by the abiding daughters who make peace, above all else, their priority.

The Valley of O.P.P.

6

*L*ESTER WAS RAYNELL AND RON-
NEL'S BIG, STRONG, PLAYFULLY LOVING DADDY. HE WAS A CROSS BETWEEN A
giant teddy bear and a superhero. He would do anything, be anywhere, to save, protect, or entertain his daughters. In return, they
looked up to him, around for him, and always knew, no matter
what, Daddy would always be there. Then one day, something
happened. One day, something clicked in Lester's mind. On that
day, he changed from a teddy bear into a worm. From a superhero into an animal. On that day, liquor became more important
to Lester than his daughters' love. Power became more important
than peace. On that day, Lester began to fight in the street. More
important, he began to fight at home. Without warning or provo-
cation, Lester began to fight with—actually, it was more like beating the hell out of—his daughters' mother.

Raynell was the oldest of the two and therefore had the longer
memory. She remembered the good times, the good days, when
Lester had loved their mother as much as he did them. Ronnel
could not remember back that far and so she paid close attention
to the very present memories. Screaming in the hallway, the dining room, the living room. Blood on her mother's face, arms,
neck, and legs. Police at the door, running through the hallway,
crashing to the floor in the dining room, guns drawn in the living

room. Lester sitting in the police car crying, then screaming to his daughters to help him. Mother on her hands and knees scrubbing blood off the floor. It was all too much for Ronnel's short memory and tiny brain. She watched in horror, becoming more and more frightened. Even more, angry. Raynell was always there, holding her, rocking her, reminding her of the good old days. At first, Ronnel simply could not remember them. Then she chose not to remember them, choosing instead to hate her father and to hate her mother for bringing her father into her life.

Lester eventually died from too much liquor and fighting and too little peace. Raynell would stop by her father's tiny, stinking, dismal room on her way home from school every day. She would bring him the fruit from her school lunch and anything she could rummage from the refrigerator at home. Ronnel would never go up with her sister to see their daddy. She would sit on the stairs pouting and cursing, telling Raynell how stupid she was to waste her time on that drunken pig. But Raynell would remind her that he was still their father and he had not always been this way.

One day, Ronnel finally convinced Raynell to eat her own fruit and let the pig sit in his own crap for a day because she deserved to play. It was that very day that Lester got into an argument with one of his drunken neighbors. In his staggering stupor, he lunged at the man, who was just sober enough to push Lester backwards onto the rusty fire escape, which broke, dropping Lester, head-first, down three stories. Their mother cried when they called her and told her. Raynell blamed herself. Ronnel got even angrier.

Their mother's grief took her into the church and a vow of celibacy at the age of thirty-four. Ronnel's anger took her in and out of the principal's office, juvenile court, reform school, and eventually, the state prison for women. Raynell's guilt took her off the honor roll, out of college, into a dead-end job which kept her near her family; in and out of church with her mother, up and down the road to the state prison; alone most of the time, and sad the other part. Lester, although he had been dead many years, continued to run his ex-wife and his daughters' lives from the grave. They were either so devoted to, afraid of, angry with, or despondent over what he had, or they had, done or not done, there wasn't much room for anyone or anything else in their lives.

When we are children, we have no idea that our parents and their issues are temporary, transitory conditions in our lives. At every moment, parents make choices or fail to make decisions which turn the course of their lives and ultimately affect their children. When we are children, we have no choice other than to accept what is going on. However, as we mature, in learning how to make our own decisions, we must separate "their stuff" from "our stuff," their issues from our own issues.

When I was growing up, somebody told me that I didn't like okra. Whenever it was served, my brother or grandmother would quickly remind me, "Oh, that's right, you don't like okra." I was a thirty-year-old woman with children when my next-door neighbor invited my family and me to dinner. On the menu was okra, mixed with butter beans. It looked and smelled delicious. I decided to try some. It was absolutely wonderful. I got the recipe, went home, and prepared a huge pot. Whenever I prepared the dish after that, I wondered where I could have gotten the idea that I didn't like okra.

Their Issues Are Not Your Issues!

For Raynell and Ronnel, it was their father's alcoholism. For me, it was okra. For many Black women, our minds and lives have been drastically altered by O.P.P., things other people have told us or done to us in response to their issues. Things we have seen other people do and their experiences become our own. It begins in childhood and spills over into our adult life. We are weighed down by burdens which have little, if anything, to do with us. We suffer, sometimes giving up on ourselves because the weight is too much to carry. The woman's inborn instinct to serve, nurture, and protect leads to needless sacrifice as we attempt to help, save, and fix other people. We pick it up as children, carry it on as adults. A few lucky ones are able to recognize it in their lives, and still cannot figure out what to do about it. In all cases, O.P.P. is like a lasso. It holds us back. Pulls us down. Ties us up in situations which are not of our own making.

We are not indebted to anyone in this life. We are accountable to some, responsible for others. We are never, however, obligated to take the weight of another's life on our shoulders. When we do, we become toxically poisoned by the dreaded affliction of O.P.P.: other people's problems, priorities, principles, perspectives, purposes, presumptions, and in some cases, other people's people encroach upon and infest our lives. Some of us are so bogged down with O.P.P. we have no life. There are so many things others want from us, expect of us, or do to us that we get confused and begin to believe it is our duty to be whatever other people need us to be.

Are you so embroiled in the lives of others and their conflicts that you have lost track of your own life? Other than your children, is there someone you believe that you cannot leave? Someone you must help? Someone who needs you in order to survive? Are you angry? Are you so angry with people for what they have done to you, or said to you, that you have spent a major portion of your life trying to get back at them? prove them wrong? keep them out of your heart? mind? life? Are you where you want to be in your life? Or are you somewhere doing what someone told you to do, believing you cannot do anything else? O.P.P., Other People's Problems, Perspectives, and Purposes, is the number one killer of the spirit of Black women.

In the Valley of O.P.P. are the experiences we have when we fail to develop and honor our inner authority, the authority which gives us the strength to stand on our own. Each time we give our lives over to the issues, priorities, and problems of other people, we dishonor our inner authority. Without it, we are not free to pursue our dreams, goals, and personal fulfillment. When we do not believe we have the authority to choose for ourselves, or have been trained to believe that someone else knows better than we what is good for us, we lose sight of and touch with our mental and spiritual authority. When we acquiesce, give up our lives to the problems, perspectives, and purposes of other people, we lose our sense of personal power and freedom. We are bound by responsibility to others. We act from a place of anger toward or fear of others. Our inner strength wanes. Our mind is confused. We cannot identify what we want from what others have told us to want. Our perspective on life is not our own and the purposes of others motivate our behavior.

I am always amazed at the number of Black women who claim the limitations and restrictions of their families and environments. Reverend Johnnie Coleman, a Christian New Thought teacher and founder of Christ Universal Temple in Chicago, says: "You don't have to claim the konkus and the bonkus because it runs in your family!" Your grandmother's high blood pressure is not your issue! Your grandfather's big ears, flat feet, or crooked nose is not your issue. Just because all of your family, since the beginning of time, lived on X street, in Y city, in Z state, does not mean you have to live there with them. You are free! You have the power, authority, and most of all, the right to create your own reality. If you insist on hanging onto the family tree, you may very well find a noose around your neck.

ISSUES BY PROXY!

Jesse's mother had a bad heart. Even as a young woman, there were many things she could not do. She considered Jesse's birth to be a blessing from God since all the doctors had told her she would never be able to give birth. Jesse grew up hearing from her mother what a blessing she was, how lucky she was to be alive, and all the things she could not do because her mother had a bad heart. It didn't help matters much that Jesse's father had left the home. He helped to make a bad matter worse. Without him, Jesse's mother did not have enough money to take care of herself, never had a moment of rest, did not know how she was going to make it, and could not stand men.

Of course, Jesse got it all confused. To her, men gave you a bad heart, took your money to keep you from doing what you needed to do, and wanted you to work all your life for nothing. Jesse did not go out much as a teenager because her mother needed her rest. She could not wait up for her. She did not go away to college because her mother could not make the trip to see her. Jesse never wore makeup because she was so lucky to be alive it did not matter what she looked like. She never dated because she was afraid of men. What Jesse did to occupy her time, overcome her fears, and alleviate the impact of her mother's heart condition was eat. Jesse ate all of her pain, fear, and anger away. She ate until she could not do anything or go anywhere because she weighed 319 pounds. At that point, she was too ashamed to go anywhere

Some of us eat. Some of us drink. Others sleep around. Some of us hide behind religion, real and imaginary illnesses, and obligations to family members. A few of us run away, not sure of where to go or what to do. When we get where we think we are supposed to be, we cannot function. We are afraid. Many of us just sit. We sit and make excuses, wondering why we can't stop sitting. We sit because we have a pile of O.P.P. in our laps. We carry the burden of O.P.P. on our shoulders. It bends our backs, warps our minds, and sometimes, if we are not careful, it will break our spirit.

Lay Their Burdens Down!

In response to your gender, your ethnicity, your economic background, the neighborhood in which you live, the schools you attend, the shape of your body, and the length of your hair, the world holds a particular view of you and has a purpose for you. White people are expected to be wealthy. Black people are expected to be poor. Fat people are not expected to dance. Thin people are expected to be good runners. Italians run the Mafia. Irish run the bars. Jews run the banks. WASPs run the corporations. Chinese run the laundry. Koreans run the vegetable markets. Blacks just run. The world and the people in it have a perspective of you based on what is individually and collectively believed about you in response to your God-given, unalterable characteristics. You are, with or without knowledge of that perspective, expected to live up to what others think about you and want from you. If you rebel against your prescribed place, you are wrong, again.

O.P.P. is particularly insidious as it operates against Black women. As people of the darker hue, we are still perceived as lazy heathens, unworthy of trust, incapable of self-sufficiency. We are expected to believe these perspectives no longer exist. As women, we are still perceived as useless, powerless subjects; beasts of burden, tools of pain and pleasure. The purpose of this perception is to maintain masculine dominance as the all-powerful and controlling factor in our lives. The world despises as much as it fears us. While marveling at our ability to survive, the world still fears that Black women may eventually evolve in such a way as to disrupt the status quo.

We respond to the unspoken perspectives and purposes by despising and being fearful of our individual and collective energy. We know we can, but we are afraid to honor the inner authority which will tell us how. We discount that inner authority because we are taught it does not exist or cannot be trusted. Black women are reared to be dependent on and in some cases addicted to what others tell us, expect from us, or demand of us. The social indoctrination of Black women is the basis of O.P.P.

Someone asked me about the sometimes obvious "martyrdom syndrome," a special kind of O.P.P. that operates among Black women. This woman, a white woman, explained how several Black women she knew seemed to be burdened down by taking care of and doing for others the very things those people should be doing for themselves. I had never thought about it. As a Black woman, I accept that there are simply certain things you must do, are expected to do, as a function of your identity. If your mother gets sick, you take care of her. If your sister dies, you take her children. If your husband, boyfriend, mate is not working, you support him. It is a given, as a Black woman, that you step in and do whatever needs to be done. It is your responsibility.

The woman asked, what if you do not want to do it? What if it causes disruption in your life? Or takes you off your course? So what? I said. We do not put our parents in homes. We do not leave parentless children alone in our families. The woman understood about the parents; she had read a lot about the extended-family concept. She also understood about the children, although she thought the family member who was best situated financially and emotionally should be the first to volunteer. Her point was that many of the Black women she knew seemed to get "stuck" doing for others, often to their own detriment.

Her belief was that adults must learn how to take care of themselves. That they should make provisions for emergencies. Based on her personal observations, her assessment was that Black women more often than not allowed family and friends to emotionally blackmail them into doing what they should do for themselves but were too irresponsible to do. I was beginning to get upset with this woman, but I was also listening.

A woman she worked with had been offered a promotion and a substantial raise to take a managerial position in another city. This woman had worked very hard for the position and she was good at what she did. She was excited about the prospect of being the first Black woman to head a corporate division. In the end, she did not accept the position. She could not leave her mother and her boyfriend did not want to move. The woman's mother had assumed custody of three grandchildren, her youngest crack-addicted daughter's children. The mother depended on her other daughter to pay the child care expenses and to pick the children up from day care every day. Although this new offer was the chance and the job she had dreamed of, she could not leave her aging mother with the responsibility of three young children.

Her boyfriend was a sanitation worker, with ten years of service. He was waiting to be called to work at the Department of Corrections, after which they planned to be married. She had been with the man four years and did not want to leave him. How could she give up a six-figure salary and the chance to do what she dreamed of doing, to help people who were quite capable of taking care of themselves? The only explanation I could offer was O.P.P.

We all know people who have given up their lives or pieces of their lives to the benefit of others. Black women will not return to school for higher education or seek career advancement until the children are grown. They will not leave toxic or abusive relationships because the other person needs them. They give their time, energy, and money to family members or friends who do the same thing, in the same way, and get the same results: no change, no growth, no healing or evolution. Many Black women seem to be addicted to helping and saving others. We do whatever we believe is necessary to make others love us; we keep them dependent on us in order to give our lives meaning. There are times when we are so angry and resentful about what we are doing that we make ourselves sick. We develop diseased conditions which give us an excuse to stop doing the thing we do not want to do but believe is expected of us.

A Valley Experience

Maria married Joseph because her mother told her she would never make it in this life without a man. It was a well-known fact in the family and among anyone who would listen that the only thing Maria's father could do for Maria's mother was satisfy her needs and pay her bills. She was grateful that he had given her three beautiful children, of which Maria was one. But the fact still remained, he was a man. A man is useless unless he has money and an imagination in the bed.

Maria was not sure she believed her mother. None of her girlfriends felt that way. They were in love or wanted to be in love just for the pleasure of it. Some of them made out pretty well. On the other hand, Maria saw quite a few of them heartbroken and sick when a relationship failed to work. She was confused, but she was also twenty-four years old. According to her mother, no one would want her soon. She was getting old. If she started working and making it on her own, the only men she would attract would be freeloaders and gold diggers. As fate would have it, she met Joseph on the eve of her twenty-fifth birthday.

Now you must remember the lesson from the Valley of Understanding, "What you draw to you is what you are." Maria was in conflict. She was confused. She was looking for a husband not because she wanted to get married, but because her mother told her she should be married. When you are lonely, confused, desperately in conflict, and you go out on the prowl, just what do you think you are going to attract? That's right! Your mirror image! A man who is lonely, confused, and desperately in conflict. Also remember that human nature forces us to chase the symbolic representation. We go after what the thing we want looks like without understanding what it really is beneath the surface. So you know Maria was in trouble, right? So here we go.

Joseph was a tall, aggressive, very handsome man. Like his father, he was well-read but had little formal education. He had completed the tenth grade. Like his older brother, he had worked for many years as a servant/chauffeur in the home of a very wealthy family. He saw what it meant to live in wealth and he was determined to live that way. His father and brother told him he was crazy. He would never make it to the top in the "white man's world." He was almost convinced, but then he met Maria.

Maria was beautiful and well-educated. She seemed to have it all together. When his employer was out of town, he would take Maria to the house and entertain her. As a matter of fact, the first time they made love it was in his employer's house. In his employer's king-size bed. Joseph told Maria he was a stockbroker. He took her to all of the private clubs and establishments to which he chauffeured his employer. Of course everyone knew him. Maria was impressed. When Maria took Joseph home to meet her parents, he had all the right answers to all the right questions. The fact that he gave Maria's mother a crystal vase, which he had told his employer was broken, only helped him get his foot in the door. Maria liked Joseph, but she was not sure. She sensed that Joe was not being completely honest. He never did what he said he would do when he said he would, but at some point, he always did what he said he would. Maria's mother kept telling her, "This is too good to be true! This man is too good to be true! A man who wants you to stay home and look pretty. A man who has the means to provide you with the opportunity to live in luxury." Maria kept saying she was not sure or ready. Her mother told her to get ready because she was ordering the wedding cake.

Joseph's employer helped him secure the country club so he and Maria could get married. He also gave them the use of his villa in Hawaii as a wedding present. On the day before the wedding, Maria had a panic attack and needed to talk to Joe. She drove herself to his house, the house he worked in, and found him polishing the Benz. He tried to make up a good story. He almost succeeded, but when his employer came running out of the house to tell Joseph there was an emergency at the office, Maria came face-to-face with Joe's lie, her own confusion, and her mother's face.

A Ditch in the Middle of Nowhere

Your back is up against the wall. Your greatest fear is upon you. Everything you have been told you wanted, hoped for, wished for, has just crumbled around your feet. Your mind is racing. Your heart is pounding. When you close your eyes, you see little white spots floating around. You think you are going to faint but you are too damned mad! What do you do? Do you start swinging? Do you run? Hide? Break down and cry? Maria did not know what to do. She knew only one thing, she could not, would not, tell her mother! She would marry Joe and make the best of it.

For the first few years, they did pretty well. They told Maria's mother that Joe had decided to sell the house and invest the money. They bought a very nice house in a well-to-do neighborhood, on Maria's credit, with a good word here and there from Joe's employer. Then, they invented even more stories to save Joe's ego and ward off Maria's mother. Maria had to sneak off at night to work in order to keep the house going. Joe kept "breaking" things at work so he would have them to give to his mother-in-law. When either of their families came over, they played the game very well. When the "where are my grandchildren" questions started, they quickly had two children, and then all hell broke loose.

Almost overnight, Maria realized she could not stand the sight of Joseph. She tried to talk to her sister about it, but she was in a similar situation. She had married the man her mother thought was right for her too. She reminded Maria that her mother would "simply die" if she knew the truth. To her it would mean that her daughters had failed and that she had failed as a mother. When she tried to raise the topic of separation with her mother, she would rant and rave about how ungrateful and stupid Maria was acting. Joseph went to the other extreme. He begged and pleaded with Maria. He promised to do anything she wanted as long as she did not leave him. He told her he would die without her. Maria was caught in the middle of O.P.P. with what seemed no way out.

It had started out as a bad day. Her mother had called at 7:00 A.M. wanting Maria to convince Joseph to give her a trip to Hawaii as a Mother's Day gift. Joseph had come into her bed, trying to force himself on her. The baby was teething and running a fever and had not gone to sleep until 4:00 A.M. Then, at 4:30 in the afternoon, Joseph called. He was in jail. Joseph and his brother had been arrested for armed robbery and attempted murder. His bail was set at fifty thousand dollars. Maria was to go to his employer and ask for the cash.

She was in the car, backing out of the garage, when the voice screamed in her head, "STOP! This is not your issue!" Obediently, Maria jammed on the brakes. She put her head on the steering wheel and cried a four-year cry. She cried because she was married to a man she did not love. She cried because she was afraid of her mother. Then she cried because she was on her way to ask a stranger for fifty thousand dollars to bail her husband out of jail. Finally, she cried because she was miserable, confused, and about to break under the pressure of O.P.P. She cried because she didn't have the time or courage to really break down.

She got the money. Joe got out of jail. They hired a lawyer. Joe stayed out of jail. He was placed on probation for seven years. About a year later, Joe and his brother successfully pulled off a robbery. He quit his job because he and his brother had more than enough money to start their business. Maria knew what it was, although she and Joe never talked about it. She simply took the money he gave her, lavished it on her children, herself, and her mother, and kept her mouth shut. She was quiet until Joe brought his business and his business associates into their home. Maria told him she would not have it. He told her to take the children shopping and shut her mouth. She and her mother took the children to Spain to buy some shoes.

Three years can whiz by so fast that you wonder how you failed to notice your life is not at all what you hoped it would be. On the other hand, it can seem like an eternity when you are miserable. Maria teetered between those two states of consciousness. She felt that she could not leave, yet she knew she had to go. She thought about what would happen if she left, what her mother would say, what Joseph would do. She knew it would not be pretty, nor would it be easy. She was afraid to go. She was afraid of what would happen if she did not go. Back and forth in her mind. Up and down with the women she knew. Around and around with Joe. Maria was trapped. Joe needed her. The children needed him. Her mother browbeat her. She leaned on her mother. It was a vicious case of O.P.P.

The Law of Sacrifice

Where do other people end and we begin in our lives? It is a challenge we must all overcome, figuring out what we want from what we have been told we can have. I believe Black women expect less for themselves and from themselves than women of other persuasions. We are taught it is our responsibility to give of ourselves to benefit everyone else, without complaint. We are trapped in a vicious cycle of being everything to everyone except ourselves. We give and give until we have no more to give. When we run out of things to give, we go out and find something else. We are expected to do what other people cannot conceive of doing. If we do not measure up, we beat up on ourselves and allow others to beat up on us. We sacrifice to the point of suffering because we do not know the law.

When we are not sacrificing ourselves to the point of suffering, we sacrifice ourselves in order to avoid *perceived* suffering. The first principle of the Law of Sacrifice is:

> ***Something always has to be sacrificed in***
> ***order to gain something else.***

Everything in life has a price. In order to have what we want, we must give up something we have. In order to have good health, we must give up heavy, greasy foods. In order to have good friends, we must stop people pleasing and allowing people to have their way with us. To obtain and maintain peace, we must sacrifice the need to be in control and be right. The key to working this particular law in your favor is to understand what you will be required to give up and what you want to obtain.

It is not necessary that we lose our self-value or self-worth in order to have the "finer things" in life. We are not required to sacrifice our own thoughts, feelings, ideals, needs, and desires in order to support others in fulfilling their needs and desires. Never are we expected by the universe of life to sacrifice who we are or what we want to mimic others or to have what they say we "should" have. Success is not one-size-fits-all! No one can tell you how to secure your blessing or your success. When, however, we are unable to separate ourselves from the perceptions, priorities, and problems of other people, we unconsciously sacrifice who we are to what we see and what we are told.

Beverly spent her teenage and young adult life reading, listening to, and following the dictates of the cultural nationalist and revolutionary theory of several organizations and leaders. As a Black woman, she felt it was her duty to always put the needs of "her people" and "community" ahead of her own. She was never quite sure how to do it, but she had enough theory and dogma to live up to. Beverly truly believed poverty was the honest way of the revolutionary. According to the party line, she believed that it was her duty to spend her money in the community, obtain any service from a community-based business, and contribute all of her time and energy to those people and organizations which looked like her. Beverly went so far as to spend seven years in school, incurring a forty-seven-thousand-dollar debt to obtain a law degree in order to "serve her people." The fact that she did not want to practice law did not matter. But the fact that her clients were indigent, that her loan was in arrears, and that she felt like her life was being wasted eventually overshadowed the revolutionary indoctrination.

Beverly moved ahead, but not too far away. When she changed careers, she saw to it that everyone who represented her came from the community. All of her sales agents were Black. The suppliers she used were Black. Everything she did was focused on the needs and availability of someone in the community, until she became dissatisfied with the quality of their services. She grew tired of the work she ordered not being delivered on time. She was disappointed that her workers were often late or did not show up at all. She was suspicious that she was not being respected because she was Black and a woman. Overshadowing it all was Beverly's fear of being called a "sellout." To avoid that, she sacrificed her needs and the quality of her work for the party line.

The deeper you go into the realms of your spirit, the clearer the picture of your life becomes. How do you stay Black, live Black, and buy Black and still meet the standards you have set for yourself? It can be quite a dilemma. In my own very similar situation, I had to pray. Eventually, spirit brought me the answer: *"The issue is not Black, the issue is freedom. You have the right and the ability to choose what you want. What are your standards? What color are they? If you can secure the standards you want and still honor your commitment to the community, that is fine. If, however, you reach a point where one must be sacrificed for the other, you are always free to choose."* It made sense but it was not good enough. I would not believe I could not get the quality I desired in my own community, from "my own people." The next answer I received was this: *"You can. The two are not mutually exclusive. The squeaky wheel, however, gets the oil. Those who speak the loudest, make the most noise, are the ones who attract your attention. Rather than sacrificing your standards to what you see as being available, call forth what you need and want from a place of peace and assurance in your own being."*

Today, my literary agent is a Black woman. My attorney is a Black man. I have two publishers, one a larger predominantly white-owned corporation, the other a small African-American-run press. I have two editors: one is a Black female, the other is not. My personal agent is a white female. In each instance, I have chosen the person who can provide the quality of service and support I need which enables me to further my work on all levels. What I eventually figured out was that I, like Beverly, had been stuck in O.P.P., what other people expected of me and said I should do. When I called forth what I needed—people of a like mind—the quality of work I desired and the support I needed took precedence over their color. I am receiving those things which keep me peaceful and I am still "serving my people."

Very often when we want to avoid something, we sacrifice ourselves to the other extreme. To avoid poverty, we sacrifice our time to work. To avoid loneliness, we sacrifice ourselves with people who neither respect nor value us. To avoid criticism, we sacrifice ourselves by doing what our major critic says we should do. We give up our freedom to consciously choose for ourselves in order to avoid what we believe will be an unpleasurable experience. Self-abandonment, self-denial, and the failure to consult your own inner authority before making a decision or choice have nothing to do with the true meaning of sacrifice. It is O.P.P. which we have unwittingly embraced as our own stuff.

The second principle of the Law of Sacrifice states:

> ***Give of thyself only that which nourishes thyself and prepares thee to share nourishment with others.***

According to the law, sacrifice means that we be willing to give and do what we can, when we can, to improve our lot in life. For Black women, this means having the willingness to give up the mundane, unnecessary, and mediocre elements of our lives to pursue excellence for ourselves. Excellence means, giving one hundred percent of your time, attention, and energy to those activities which nourish and enlighten you.

When you are fully capable of taking care of yourself, you are prepared, and must be willing, to share what you have with others. Black women have been taught that sacrifice means totally giving up yourself for the benefit of someone else. The most obvious purpose behind the erroneous teaching is that if we expect nothing for or from ourselves, we will have more to give to everyone else. The results have been devastating on the minds and bodies of Black women. We give to the point of hypertension, stroke, breast cancer, uterine cancer, or until our heart attacks us.

I watched my grandmother sacrifice herself for her family. She worked from sunup to sundown, first in her "Madam's" house and then at home. I am not sure I ever said thank you to her. I would bet no one else did either. We expected her to do it, we depended on her to do it. I watched my mother sacrifice herself for my father, my brother, and myself. I never realized what it took from her until I became a mother and a wife. Each day, I become acquainted with sisters who cannot tell me what they want for themselves, while they are able to articulate, with exacting clarity, that which they want for their children, their community, and the world. It is O.P.P. at its finest hour.

If there were a slogan which could be used for the social indoctrination of Black women, it should be: "God first. I am next. Everyone else take a ticket and get in line." Only when we internalize and memorize this slogan can we forget everything we have ever been told about ourselves and follow our heart's desire. The things we want in our heart are the things God wants for us. It is our duty to pursue our dreams. Even if we fall down in the process, we owe it to the spirit within us to move ahead at our own pace without interference from anyone else.

We cannot ignore our political reality. We cannot float through life in a state of meditative bliss. There are certain realities and issues which are as real as we are. What Black women can do is take the time to honor ourselves, to give to ourselves, as we are learning to trust ourselves. We must dig deep into the essence of our being, pull up the wisdom and the courage which are buried there, and at appropriate times, in an appropriate manner, enable ourselves and be willing to say, "No! That is not my issue!"

Our great-great-grandmothers were wounded. They were slaves, property, chattel; denied the basic right to think for themselves. They were mentally, emotionally, and spiritually wounded by O.P.P. They passed their wounded images and ideas on to our great-grandmothers, who passed them on to our grandmothers, who passed them on to our mothers, who passed them on to us. We are today the walking wounds of our foremothers, sacrificing our lives to the ancient images other people held of our ancestors. Are we tired of sacrificing ourselves? Are we tired of dying unfulfilled?

I believe the universe is tired of receiving the worn-out, lifeless bodies of Black women. In response, life has created the Valley of O.P.P. to teach us how to differentiate our issues from those which have nothing to do with us. We cannot live up to, help, or save anyone until we can live up to the standards we set for ourselves, in order to elevate ourselves and save ourselves. In order to do this, we must understand and appreciate the value of freedom and honesty.

The Lesson

Terri Cole Whittaker wrote a book entitled *What You Think of Me Is None of My Business,* which should be required reading for the descendants of African women born in America. This book, in great, painstaking detail, describes how the average person becomes enslaved to the problems, principles, and often, whims of other people in their lives. It warns about people pleasing, as well as clarifying how the need to be needed, the need to be wanted, carries us into the zone of self-loss and self-denial. For Black women, in addition to the common pitfalls, there is also the unconscious, often unrecognized need to suffer. We suffer at the hands of others to whom we give free rein and the right to control our lives.

Black women straighten their hair because we are told, probably by someone who is not Black, that our hair should be straight. Although this defies everything we are or hope to be, we do it to the tune of six billion dollars every year. O.P.P.! The things other people tell us and impose on us are bad enough. Complicating matters even further are the things we tell ourselves about the things other people tell us: "If I don't do this, they will . . ." "If I'm not like this, they might . . ." In the end, we get confused and embroiled in inner turmoil. Few of us realize we have the divine right to choose what to believe and what to do. Most of us have not mastered the self-empowering virtue of honesty.

We are not born to live in turmoil, struggling to make a way out, only to have dirt thrown in our faces before we can realize a state of accomplishment. We are born to live in peace and free-

184

dom, giving and receiving, loving and being loved. You might ask, "So what goes wrong?" Lessons. In our peaceful, loving freedom, we must learn lessons which will eventually make us stronger, wiser, and better people. Lessons, not life, create turmoil. We struggle to get what we want, while resisting what we need to learn. We fall from grace in life when we resist and rebel against our lessons. Life is a consistent, orderly flow of events, which will carry us to a desired outcome when we learn how to work through our lessons and ultimately to avoid their pitfalls by accepting them. People create turmoil in their own lives when they accept the issues of others and when they rebel against the natural order and the flow of life.

The Value of Freedom

If you go into a restaurant and sit quietly at a table, you may never be served. You know there are people available to cook what you want and others who will serve you. You also know if you just sit there and do not open your mouth, you will not eat. Knowing we can do a thing is not enough. We must realize we are free to choose. This is the lesson we must learn through the experiences which take us into the valley of O.P.P. Allow your inner authority to guide you. That guidance gives you the freedom to do what you know you must do. Or else, you must suffer the consequences.

Once we give ourselves over to what we can or cannot do based on the expectations of others, we are no longer free. When our vision is restricted to outer appearances, we are enslaved to the way things appear to be. The physical evidence of life is the truth working its way out. We must be willing to get to the bottom, patiently waiting for the truth to reveal itself. When we seek authority from within ourselves, we act on what we know from the core of our being. We are not talking here about moving through life doing whatever you want, whenever you want to do it. We are talking about taking care of your needs, doing what feels right for you, exercising your divine right to choose for yourself the course and direction of your life. Other people may not like it. So what! They will get over it! If they choose not to, if they become angry or upset with you, it is not your issue! O.P.P. is a given in life. It is given to us, but we do not have to accept it.

The Way Out

Nina Simone sang a song which could be the theme song of the valley of O.P.P., "Ain't Nobody's Fault But My Own": "If I die today and go straight to hell, ain't nobody's fault but my own." If we live in the hell of poverty, ill-health, toxic relationships, professional or personal unhappiness, chaos or confusion, we have no one to blame but ourselves. The law says, "What you draw to you, is what you are!" Look at what is going on in your life. Like it? Who is responsible for it being there? The thing we think is our life preserver usually turns out to be a shark. That's the law working to show us where we are.

When we are under the spell of O.P.P., we may feel like victims. As victims, we do not pay attention to our behavior patterns. We sacrifice ourselves to conditioned responses which take us to the experiences we believe are safe or give us what we want. Very often, the experiences are not safe at all. They may provide temporary relief; however, as long as the core issue remains the same, the outcome will be the same. As long as we are not aware of our patterns, we cannot understand how or why the unwanted experiences continue. Any psychologist worth the name will tell you that if you are experiencing the same or similar events in life, you must get to the core. I am not a psychologist, so I will approach it from a different perspective—a spiritual perspective.

Maria was bullied by her mother. In an attempt to escape, she ran to Joseph. This was definitely a Spiritual Special Education experience which took Maria into a dungeon. You cannot support others in wrongdoings! No matter what your reason, rationale, or excuse, you owe it to the universe and your own personal integrity to remove yourself from the evil doings of others. Many human beings have a need to impress other human beings. To do so, they will tell little white lies. However, when we discover that what we thought was a harmless little story is actually a giant, man-eating shark, we owe it to ourselves to extricate ourselves from all parts of it.

Let us call a spade a spade. A man who tells you he works one place when he does not is one thing. A man who leads you to believe he is something he is not is another thing. A man who tells you a home is his home, a bed is his bed, a life is his life, when they are not, is not a man you want to marry! It does not matter what your mother or anyone else thinks or wants—do not under any circumstances involve yourself with a person you know is actively violating someone's trust. If your mother is that attracted to the things money can buy, let her marry him. That was Maria's first mistake: she married a man she knew was dishonest.

Maria had many opportunities to leave Joseph. She really didn't need a special opportunity. Maria failed to choose what she wanted and to make a decision about how to get it. She was caught up in appearances and people pleasing. She never even tried to fix Joseph. She accepted him just as he was, knowing he was not what she wanted. Fear of what her mother would do; too much concern for what would happen to Joseph; failure to acknowledge her own needs; dishonesty, deceit, and self denial; surrender of her personal freedom; failure to acknowledge her inner voice; fear, threats, and intimidation; talking to the wrong people—what it all boiled down to was Maria selling her soul to the devil of O.P.P. In her case, it was more like a demon.

Joseph did not love her. He loved what she represented— which by the way is also true when we turn the table, Maria to Joseph. The fact that he turned out to be a criminal is not the issue. The only issue which confronted Maria from the very beginning was her willing surrender of her will to her mother's will. She did eventually leave him. Then she went back. Then she left again. She went back and forth for six more years. When her mother found out what was really going on, she gave Maria hell for being so stupid. She told her to clean out the bank account and get the hell away from him. Maria did it. She moved to the outskirts of the city. One day when she was in town visiting her mother, Joseph saw her. He followed her home. When he knocked on the door, she let him in. When I last heard from Maria, Joe was still in jail. He is doing fifteen to twenty-five years. Maria visits him once or twice a month. She is still confused. Still miserable. Still trying to figure out how to escape the clutches of O.P.P.

Some of us do not make it. As a matter of fact, millions have not made it. I wish I could tell you that spiritual laws and principles work for everyone. That would be dishonest. The key is, you must be open to them and willing to accept them into your life. Some of us are open and willing. Many of us do not have a clue. The manner in which the social constructs and gender roles operate in the lives of women is a function of O.P.P. We are almost expected to do certain things in order to have other things. It is a given that we must sacrifice some part of ourselves to get what we want. The issue is, what part do we sacrifice and under what conditions? What is the honorable margin of return? We live in a society where property ownership determines economic status, which in turn determines social mobility and the degree of social acceptance you will enjoy. This is the operation of O.P.P. The requirements of property ownership restrict the independent mobility and economic viability of women, who were, until eighty-seven years ago, themselves considered the property of men. This, too, is a function of O.P.P.

SPIRIT GETS MY VOTE!

I am often asked how spirituality or spiritual empowerment provides one with the necessary tools to address the issues of the political reality. How can prayer, breathing, meditation, honoring the ancestors, all of the practices we consider spiritual, help anyone overcome the reality of racism, sexism, classism, ageism, homophobia, social injustice? How can you fight hate and political disenfranchisement with a crystal or a deck of tarot cards? My answer is that spiritual consciousness does not make your problems go away; it does, however, help you to view them from a different vantage point.

Politics and political issues are not living, breathing entities. They are based on mental constructs and the laws of man. Life is based on the laws of God. Life, as it is created by God, operates from the inside to the outside. In the hidden, secret realm of the internal order of God, life is created, formed, and shaped. When life appears in the outside world, it does so to continue its development, not to be created. Politics are based on the way human beings perceive themselves and the world, not the way the world was created by God to be. If we are to successfully redress the constructs of the political environment in which we live, we must each go back to the drawing board. We must begin within ourselves, developing a clear understanding of our ability to create what we want, rather than being locked in an endless battle with O.P.P.

Growing up as a poor Black female in the 1950s, the political reality of my family as well as the world was extremely limited as it applied to me. When I was three years old, I could not ride in the front of a bus or drink water from certain fountains, nor could my grandparents or parents vote in their hometown of Smithfield, Virginia. It was a very vague possibility that I would ever go to college or earn a law degree or own property or be able, if I so chose, to marry a white man or a Black woman, in full public view, without fear of being burned at the stake. In 1953, that was my political reality, the facts as they existed at that time. Facts are subject to change. Truth is not. O.P.P. are transitory facts. Spirituality examines and reveals the truth of your being.

When I was in an abusive marriage, my political reality was a very angry, six-foot-two-inch, 240-pound husband who could, and did, break various parts of my face with one blow of his fist. It was a fact that on numerous occasions, he broke several of my ribs, blackened one or both of my eyes, choked me into unconsciousness, and threatened to kill me if I left him. My experience was real. At that time, I saw nothing spiritual about it. Ultimately, my reality was not changed by the spiritual transformation of my husband's mind. It changed when I began to realize that the only way he could continue to beat me was if I stayed with him. And that whether I died trying to get away from him or died because he beat me to death if I stayed did not matter. The only thing that mattered was that I decided I was not going to get beat by him or anyone else ever again. I was willing to die rather than live with abuse. I made my desire to get away from him more powerful than his threats which had kept me in fear for nine years.

Racism and sexism in and of themselves are not what limit Black women in America. It is our perception of them and how they can or will operate against us that gives them so much power over us. Your political reality is determined by your personal reality. How you see things determines what you believe you can do. The political realities which operate to limit Black women are not nearly as powerful as our fear of them, belief in them, and reliance on their operation as an excuse to operate within the status quo. When Black women are taught to *be* the thing we desire, rather than to seek external authorization and approval to *have* what we desire, O.P.P. will lose ground in our minds.

If you want peace, be peace. If you want wealth, be wealth. Think it. Talk it. Prepare yourself to have it. When we become faithful enough to seek guidance and authority from within ourselves, being obedient to the voice of the Creator's spirit as it speaks to our hearts, we will rise above O.P.P. and the politically factual constructs it uses to keep us in bondage. Whether our political reality is passed on to us by our parents, reinforced by an economic reality, or thrust upon us by others as the circumstances and conditions of our lives, O.P.P. cannot survive in the presence of a made-up mind, a faith-filled heart, and a trusting reliance on the power of spirit.

Some of us are born to be active warriors and revolutionaries. Others are born to be teachers, healers, helpers, and servers. Not all of us will march in the picket lines, rally folks to go to the polls, or boldly go where we have been forbidden to tread. Some of us must stay home, in the background, to do the praying, crying, healing, and teaching it will take to move us all forward. A spiritual consciousness will not only move us beyond the limits of O.P.P. as a political reality, it will help us each identify what it is we have come to do, so that it will all get done and we will not be in each other's way. O.P.P. keeps us all stagnated. Spiritual empowerment deploys divine legions of spiritually empowered soldiers to their and to our divine destinations, with the clarity of vision, exactness of mission, and freedom to create whatever is needed at any point in time.

MEDITATION
WITH THE
MOTHER

*When you hate, you become that which you hate.
When you struggle, you become that which you
struggle against. When you protest, you take on
the very qualities of the thing against which you
protest. How else would you know so well the in-
tricacies of that which you despise?*

—YORUBA PROVERB

*Dear daughters, the Father has given everyone something they
must grapple with and resolve in order to become whole. There is
healthy conflict and unhealthy struggle. How you are impacted is
determined by whether you have healthy or unhealthy thoughts
and desires. Healthy conflict pushes you beyond your self-inflicted
limitations, causing you to reach, to stretch, and in moments of
need, to ask for divine intervention or guidance. Unhealthy conflict is that which causes you to push, shove, demand, struggle,
and ultimately, hate when you do not get what you want.*

*It is the Father's pleasure to give you the goodness, peace, and
joy you seek, when it is based on healthy desires. When you grapple with life's difficulties, seeking divine guidance in pursuit of
healthy pleasure, the Father and I delight in your victories. When,
however, you set your sights on things which push you further
away from that which is divine and deeper into a sense of hope-
lessness, helplessness, it is then that healthy grappling becomes unhealthy struggle. You look outside of yourself, away from the
divine, for solutions and resolutions which cannot redeem your
sense of self. There is nothing beyond you which will enable you to
reach a state of grace-filled peace. From an external perspective,
your healthy human dilemmas become soul-disruptive struggles*

which lead you to hate the very thing which has been divinely ordained to help you grow.

Dear daughters, do not believe you are being punished or that you have been forgotten by me when you are grappling with the mysteries of life. You are here, in this form, at this time, to bring forth blossoms of beauty which are buried in your heart. Do not become dismayed when you miss an opportunity, misunderstand a direction, or are delayed in receiving rewards. All that has been ordained for you awaits you. Rest assured that a day of sorrow is but a moment in the divine plan for your life.

The Valley of Come- uppance | 7 🍃

🍃

I WANT TO STATE VERY CLEARLY, RIGHT AT THE START, THAT THE LESSONS OF THIS VALLEY ARE UNDOUBTEDLY the most difficult to recognize and the hardest to accept. The experiences which take us into the Valley of Comeuppance are those that we bring upon ourselves when we are unaware of the powerful impact of our thoughts and words. The drama, hysteria, heartache, confusion, anger, and depression often associated with the lessons and experiences of this valley are the direct result of our resistance to admit to ourselves, "I had something to do with the situation I am in." It is in this valley that we are tested, pushed, and prodded in order to determine our willingness to remain victims, doormats, martyrs, flunkies, and fools. The issue with which we come face-to-face in this valley is looking in the mirror of self and realizing that whatever we see, really see in and for ourselves, is what we will experience and live through.

The primary issue for Black women, like everyone else in life, is that we do not understand the laws of the universe. It may seem as if we are downtrodden and beaten down. In some cases, this is true. In most cases, particularly those issues with which many of us struggle, we simply do not understand the rules of life. When I was broke and destitute, the issue was not that my welfare check did not provide me with adequate funds. I discovered the main issue which kept me in poverty and lack was a misunderstanding of the laws of prosperity and ignorance of the spirit of money. In addition to being totally unconscious about those two things, my very own mouth kept me in a state of poverty.

Wealthy people never talk about how much money they have. On the reverse side, you always hear how broke a broke person may be: "I'm so broke I can't buy a mosquito a hair net!" "I'm so broke, I can't remember what money looks like!" We are never broke! We are only temporarily out of cash. When we speak of being broke, tired, fed up, or any of the minor dilemmas we face daily, the laws of the universe immediately go into effect. They create for us those things we believe exist and ultimately speak into existence. In response to our "being broke," we may experience a broken heart, a broken home, a broken leg, or worse, a broken spirit. The universe does not care that we are ignorant of its laws. It creates what we demand. We create with our thoughts. We create with our words. In our ignorance, we create the very things we do not want.

I once worked with a support group for Black women. One woman had a habit of talking about how fed up she was with her husband, children, job, and life. "I'm fed up! I'm just fed up with all of it!" Sound familiar? A few weeks after the group started meeting, this same woman began to complain about being constipated. The constipation grew into a block in her intestines. Several months later, she ended up in the hospital. Her small intestine was impacted and it became necessary to have a portion of it removed. During her recovery we talked about it. As the woman spoke in detail about the events of her life, it became very clear that she was in fact fed up. She could no longer digest what was going on in her life. She did not know what to do and she did not know how to let go. In response to her affirmations and her emotional state, her elimination organs shut down. Her issues came up as a physical condition. Common declarations used by Black women, such as "I'm sick of this," "I can't take this anymore," and "You make me sick," frequently show up as physical conditions. "Your body believes every word you say." In addition, the law is always operating, creating and bringing into existence exactly what you think and speak.

In the Valley of Comeuppance, we come face-to-face with our thoughts, words, and secret feelings as conditions in our lives. If you think you cannot take it, make it, stand it any longer, it is a guarantee that your life will be plagued by situations and people who will reinforce those thoughts. Some of us think we can fool the universe by saying we can take it when we are thinking we can't. Forget it! Remember, spirit searches your heart first. Your thoughts and words must be consistent. When they are not, the universe acts upon the most dominant influence, which is your mind, not your mouth.

More often than not, we are responsible for the creation of the very things we hate, fear, and struggle to get away from. Because we are ignorant as to the operation of universal laws, our tendency is to hold people and conditions outside of ourselves responsible. How many times have you said, "Look what you made me do!" No one can make you do anything! Your body responds to your mind regardless of what is going on around you. After a few moments of reflection, you will find it is a sure bet that somewhere deep inside, you did not want to do what you are doing. In response to the mere thought, you messed up somehow. When you do, you want to blame someone else. We do not realize we are held responsible for everything we think, say, and do. It all comes back in the mirror of self somehow, someday, someway. When it does, we find ourselves in the Valley of Comeuppance.

You know you are in this valley when you find yourself surrounded by negative people, in negative situations, having negative experiences. You cannot figure out what is going on and why it is going on with you. If you are addicted to drama, struggle, and hysteria, you begin to fight, to struggle, to run away from the very things you have created with your dominant thoughts, words, and actions. This is an active valley; consequently, whatever you do serves to intensify the situation. If you are not aware, if you are not willing to surrender, to change your words, actions, or thoughts, the situation will persist. The Valley of Comeuppance is a potential Spiritual Special Ed valley because we so often fail to recognize how we contribute to our own drama and hysteria.

Waiting until the last minute to do something and then being dissatisfied with the results is a ticket into this valley. Affirming thoughts such as "I'm so stupid!," "I don't know," and "I'm too fat!," which then result in somebody saying the very same thing to you or treating you in the same manner, is a function of this valley. There are also some more difficult examples to recognize. In 1979, someone lent you money. You did not have the money to pay them back when you promised to pay it back. Rather than telling the truth, you ducked and dodged the person. You felt bad, but what could you do? You were broke. Eventually the person went away. You never repaid them. In 1993, you lent someone some money. She did not pay you back when she said she would. You called, but she was ducking, dodging, giving you excuses. Of course you are furious! You need your money! For the life of you, you cannot figure out why this person would do this to you. You forgot what you did in 1979. Furthermore, you fail to realize that when you withhold from the universe, the universe will withhold from you! It will catch up with you and come up, somehow, someway, someday.

I had a friend who staged car accidents. She did it to get the money. If another car were to slightly bump into her car, she would scream whiplash or lower back pain. Once, she was crossing the street and a car tapped her. She lay down and swore she could not move. Over the course of a number of years, she collected thousands of dollars from her "injuries." About two years ago, she fell on the ice, threw her back out, and has a great deal of trouble bending over and walking to this day. When she starts whining and complaining about her back bothering her, I gently remind her of all the accidents she has had. Perhaps she should use some of the money she got from them to get some help now. She gets angry, but I recognize the law in operation.

A belief will keep you stuck in a situation, afraid to move beyond your perceptions. Your thoughts and words actually come to life. When we see them, we cringe, blame somebody else, and fight against them. Unfortunately, the law is at work, showing us who we are and what we have been thinking. There is nothing in your life but you and that which you create in your inner self. It does not matter how ugly it is, how terrible it may seem—it is you! It looks like you, walks like you, talks like you, shakes its finger in your face just like you. If it is not you, it is a lesson. If it is a lesson, do not give it the drama or hysteria required to keep it alive and growing in your life.

Remember, detach! Do not get emotional. Deny it the right to exist by keeping your thoughts and words positive. Find what principle you must practice to eliminate it and move on. If a negative situation persists in your life, rest assured that it is you, some part of you, which needs healing. If you cannot or will not take the time, make the effort, to figure it out, you are probably in the Valley of Comeuppance. If you choose to fight rather than learn, you will find yourself in Spiritual Special Ed . . . again!

A Valley Experience

Karen hated her job. Actually, she hated her supervisor who served to make the job unbearable. Each day, she went to work expecting a negative exchange or confrontation. It was rare that she did not get exactly what she expected. All of Karen's friends hated the supervisor too. Their nighttime telephone marathons were spent discussing what she did, what she said, and how she looked—which frequently led to off-color presumptions about her sexual preferences. If she was not so bad one day, it was suggested that she had used fruits and berries. If she had gotten on Karen's nerves particularly badly, everyone assumed her attitude was caused by intimate dealings with baseball bats and pepperoni. Everyone knows that most supervisors on most jobs are hatched in hell to become sexual deviates and porn queens. They try to fool us by holding down nine-to-five jobs.

Karen was never threatened with termination. She did not resign. She spent six and a half years in mental and emotional warfare with a woman who gave her rave reviews and timely raises, but who obviously hated her guts. Karen never made an effort to ask the woman whether or not she had a problem with her. Instead, she talked about the situation with her friends. It never crossed her mind that her attitude was the major cause of strife between her and her supervisor. She chose to blame the other party. It was not until Karen developed severe hypertension that she was prepared to take the bull by the horns—which by the way, can be very bad on the nails in addition to being quite dangerous.

Karen blamed her hypertension, chronic eating, betrayal by her best friend, and failed relationships on the stress caused by her supervisor's treatment of her. When her best friend told her neighbor that Karen was a fat, lazy pig who did not deserve a nice guy like Mitchell, Karen was stunned but not surprised. She had always known that she should not trust women around her man. When Mitchell married her ex-best-friend's sister, Karen spent three weeks stuffing her face with chocolate cake and ice cream, on top of her regular visits to the fast food establishments. In discussing her problem with the friends she had left, she decided that her supervisor was really a white witch who stuck pins in a doll named Karen. She went to a reader who confirmed her suspicions and gave her some moth flakes to sprinkle around her desk. Everyone knows that supervisors are afraid of moth flakes! Karen swore for three days that the woman was acting better, but she hated her anyway.

Karen had graduated summa cum laude with a bachelor's degree in English. Since teaching was "hard work," she had taken a job as a clerk-receptionist in a fast-paced medical benefits and insurance claims firm. Her job was to receive and open the mail, answer the telephone, and pass the mail on to claim-adjusters who would process the paperwork. The supervisor, the senior claims adjuster, relied on Karen to get the claims date-stamped and on her desk. It was also Karen's job to get the checks in the envelopes and to the mail room, which was thirty feet away from her desk. Most of the incoming calls were from frantic benefit payees. If they were calm and polite, Karen responded in kind. If they were hurried, confused, or the slightest bit annoyed that they had not received their check, Karen would leave them on hold. She would not be treated like "that" by anyone.

Karen was extremely intelligent but quite insecure. Her constant battle with her weight made her even more uncomfortable. She thought that her employers thought she was too fat and too stupid to do anything besides open the mail and answer the telephone. Only those adjusters who were nice to her got anything other than their mail from her. In addition, most of the adjusters were white, non–college graduates. Like Karen, most of the receptionists had some form of college education but could not seem to get ahead in the firm. Karen told her girlfriends how deep the Black-white thing was at work. They all agreed, "they" always think they are better than you are just because of who they are. Unfortunately, Karen and the crew did not understand that when you think for them, you end up thinking like you think they think. It is real simple. What goes on in your mind comes out in your life.

Mitchell was Karen's third beau in four years. She did not seem to have a problem attracting men. Sustaining a relationship was a completely different issue. Karen liked hardworking men—men who did not mind spending money on her or giving her money to spend on herself. Karen was smart. She knew better than to ask a man for money outright. Instead she would complain about her low salary. It was in the low thirties. She told them of her need to look nice at her front-desk position and her desire to "outdress" the snotty little white girls who got designer clothes at a discount. While she was complaining, whining, or crying, Karen fixed her beaus candlelight dinners. She ran them nice, fragrant baths. On occasion she would reduce herself to a foot massage or back rub. As she told the crew, "Men are so stupid! They really think you rub their feet because you like to do it. I only rub feet when it will bring me an Andrew Jackson. I do not rub feet for George Washingtons."

Mitchell was different. He did not come bearing or offering gifts. He told Karen how annoying her complaining was. He also let her know he thought she was wasting her life and her talents by not putting her degree to use. Mitchell worked at the post office all day so that he could go to school at night. He had a dream. He wanted to own his own business. He talked about it constantly. In her weaker moments, Karen would become engaged in Mitchell's dream and help him plan the future. Mitchell liked to go out, so they frequently had their conversations on the way to the theater or a sports event.

Mitchell taught Karen how to drive and helped her celebrate when she got her learner's permit. When she was in her whining or complaining mood, he would go home and call her the next day. Karen knew he was good for her and good to her, but he was a man and all men are dogs. Karen knew it and the crew knew it. They couldn't seem to figure out what role the supervisor played in making him a dog, but they knew it would come to light eventually. Mitchell called off his relationship with Karen on the very day her supervisor accused her of being rude to the callers. Of course, Karen had no idea what she was talking about.

In addition to being insecure, Karen was frightened, bitter, and angry. The unabated work she did, the failed relationships, the constant battle with Big Macs and Lay's potato chips—all supported her feelings of unworthiness. Karen's motto was, "It ain't gonna work so it doesn't matter anyway." When confronted with an exciting opportunity, she recited her motto. When a challenge or obstacle arose, she affirmed what she thought to be the truth. By age thirty-two, Karen had given up on herself and her life. The most exciting events she faced were the daily mental sparring matches with her supervisor, which she hated and enjoyed immensely.

Here is the scenario: Your best friend is trashing your name in the street. Your beau is cruising around town with your ex-best-friend's sister. You are eighty pounds overweight with chronic hypertension. You are in a state of panic, depression, and confusion. A friend suggests you go to someone for counseling. When you get there, that person tells you, you are creating this mess for yourself. This person, who does not know you from a can of paint, looks you dead in your face and says all that is going on in your life is the result of what you have been thinking, feeling, and doing. This person wants you to believe this is "coming up" to give you an opportunity to change. The person is trying to convince you that change is a good thing. With all due respect, you tell that person she is out of her mind.

When Karen came for counseling, the hypertension had resulted in so many missed days from work that she had been placed on probation. The fear of being unemployed sent her blood pressure even higher. Compounding the situation was the fact that Karen was eating like a butcher's dog. The doctor was insisting that she lose at least fifty pounds. Karen was convinced she was starving to death when at 2:00 A.M. she could not sleep. For many people, food is the drug of choice. Food helps us stuff what we are feeling. It pushes down what is trying to come up and numbs the emotional pain. Karen had been in pain for quite a long time. Eating was the way she avoided dealing with what she was feeling. She was resistant. Karen was so resistant that her experience in the Valley of Comeuppance was a true Spiritual Special Education.

The Law of Cause and Effect

Everything happens twice, first on the inside and then on the outside. Life begins in darkness, the silent realm of spirit. A seed planted in the earth takes root. Buried in the darkness of the soil, life begins. Weak at first, the seed, determined to live, to grow, to flourish, pushes its way through the earth. It is not an easy journey. The seed cannot speak, cannot see; there is no one to assist it. Still it grows. At the end of the journey, the seed becomes a bush of tomatoes, a field of beans, a mighty tree producing apples, oranges, or bananas. Inside the tiny acorn sleeps the mighty oak. The tiny seed blooms into a life-sustaining force, a valuable source of nourishment, supported by its environment as it gives to those around it. The seed is the cause. What the seed produces is the effect.

The cause is planted on the inside. It produces what we see, the effect. No matter who or what you are, this is the universal law which governs the creation of life. As a human being, the cause of your life is the sperm fusing with the egg. You are the effect—that which grew in the darkness of the womb. In your life, your thoughts and feelings are the seeds, the cause. What you think, fused with what you feel, produces the effects, the conditions, those things which you see in your life.

The Law of Cause and Effect operates whether you plant positive seeds or negative seeds, good thoughts and feelings or negative ones. It does not matter. Seeds will produce in kind. The laws of human nature and the universe are eternal. They are the unseen forces which come to our attention as events, circumstances, and conditions. When we lack knowledge, when we are ignorant of the law and our ability within the law to create, enact, and enforce the unseen power of the universe, we perish because we are unable to bring ourselves into alignment with nature.

The Law of Cause and Effect states:

Whatsoever [you] soweth . . . that also shall
you reap. (Galatians 6:7)

Whatever you plant, you will see in your harvest. We are like farmers. We plant seeds of thought and emotions in our lives. That which we plant will produce effects in which we must live. There can be no effect without a cause! Trees do not spring up from the earth unless a seed has somehow been planted. The seed can fall from a tree, take root wherever it falls, and produce an unplanned tree. Or the perfect site can be selected. Seeds planted with care will produce a carefully planned, ideally located tree. Conditions do not come to life unless we plant seeds to encourage them. Unfortunately, many of us are unconscious as to the types of seeds we are planting with our thoughts, words, and actions.

In the Valley of Light, we come to understand that we are the most important ingredient in the workings of our lives. What we need and want guides and directs what we do. What we avoid or fear determines how we respond. Through the learning process of light, we can see how we are in fact the cause. The Law of Cause and Effect is the foundation of that understanding. This law is the foundation of every other universal law. The cause is what we believe, how we act and react to what we experience. The cause lies within us. It is the essence of our being, our spirit. The cause is brought to life as outward manifestation based on the seeds we plant, our responses and reactions to every experience we have or have had in life.

My experiences with my father, brother, uncle, and all the little boys with whom I interacted early in life helped to shape my opinions about men. Whether they were good to me or not is not the issue. The issue is how I responded to what they did or did not do. My responses, based on my perceptions, created my opinions. My opinions, embedded in my mind, supported my expectations and beliefs. Those expectations and beliefs were the cause of every experience I had with men. My father was emotionally unavailable to me. My husband was a carbon copy of him. My brother was distant and aloof, very secretive, and verbally abusive. He was my brother. I loved him. As a result, I accepted into my life men who responded to me exactly as my brother had. After a series of abusive and unsatisfactory relationships, I began to question why I continued to draw a certain type of mate. Once I developed an understanding of the Law of Cause and Effect, it became quite apparent that I was creating, with my own thoughts, the very relationship I did not want. I was thinking, "All men are emotionally unavailable," "Men are secretive," and "It is all right for men to be verbally abusive." These were the conditions created in response to my thoughts.

The same is true regarding our thoughts about women. As young girls, we are "schooled," educated about women and what to expect from them. My aunts, cousins, and friends all warned me about women not being trustworthy, about their talking too much, about them being sneaky. I carried these thoughts in my heart and mind. I expected women to behave a certain way and they did. Back to the Valley of Courage for a moment. "What you believe will be established unto you." The difference between belief and cause is action. What we believe causes us to act or behave in a particular way. Our own actions draw corresponding effects into our lives.

Very simply stated, if you are dishonest, people will be dishonest in their interactions with you. If you think or speak negatively about others, someone, somewhere, will return your deeds. If you cut corners, skim off the edges, behave irresponsibly, recklessly, or unwisely, the conditions you encounter will be the result of someone doing the very same thing you do. The situation will come up in your life in order to make you aware, to teach you a lesson. As children we are taught that what goes around, comes around.

From a spiritual perspective, what goes around in your mind, will come around in your life. The real kick is, it may not come from the very same people who were involved in what you did. It may come months or years later. When it comes back to you, it may be more devastating than anything you have intentionally done to anyone in your life. Rest assured, the Law of Cause and Effect always operates, creating the effects we have caused.

The Lesson

When I first started my own business, I experienced many delays in my cash flow. People who owed me money seemed to always be late in paying. There were delays in contract payments, delays in people paying for services I had rendered. It was very disheartening and very difficult to figure out how to continue on my path and purpose. In speaking to a dear sister-friend of mine during one particular dry spell, I was bemoaning my fate. I was owed in excess of seven thousand dollars for work I had done. My telephone was about to be disconnected and my rent was late. I asked her to pray with me in an effort to figure out the underlying issue causing the problem.

After we prayed, we spent a few moments in silence. My sister-friend asked me, Who do you owe? Who do you owe money to that you have not paid? I told her, Everybody! I owed bills I had not paid. I owed people I had borrowed from with the expectation that I would get paid for services I had rendered. Since I had not been paid, I could not pay the people I owed. Another period of silence. Finally she said to me, "Don't think about who you owe now, think about the past. Think about who you owe, who you have not paid, how you paid when you did have money, and how you feel about paying or not paying what you owe."

Prayer always sheds light on the subject. If you are really willing to see yourself and the light, prayer will open the way. I had to admit I had not been an "on-time payer." Each month, I paid bills late. There were many occasions when I would allow my bills to double up. When they did, I would make a partial payment. Since I was being honest, I admitted there were times when I had the money to pay my bills and chose to do something else. At other times, I would pay what I thought was important and leave the minor bills until more substance was received. I also told my friend there had been people in the past who had helped me financially, whom I had never repaid, about which I felt very guilty, somewhat ashamed. Another period of silence.

Finally my sister-friend revealed to me that I believed in lack. She explained that when you do not pay what you owe because you believe you will not have enough left over, you are giving lack the right to exist in your life. She went on to say that if we believe that our substance, our income, is what we must live by, we are limited to what we know. When we believe that spirit is our source and supply, we know the source which sustains us is unlimited. Even when we cannot see where it will come from, we must know that it will come. We must believe we will be provided for in all of our needs. What we believe will cause us to act. When we act, we create the means by which the effects must manifest. In other words, write the check even when you do not know how the money is coming.

At the core of the lack issue for me was my own guilt and shame about owing money. By holding onto the mental images of those I had not paid, I was creating an energy in which I could not get paid. By borrowing and not repaying, I had depleted my account in the universal bank. There was nothing for me to draw on. Complicating matters even further was the fact that I had spent what did not belong to me. I was in visible and invisible debt. When you owe and you receive, you must pay what you owe. The universe does not accept excuses. The spirit of money must not be violated. If you are provided a service or given support based on your promise to repay at a certain time, the spirit of money will hold you to your word. If you have money which has been allocated for one thing and you spend it for something else, you are in effect spending money that does not belong to you. It belongs to that to which you have promised or allocated the money.

It does not matter how much you know or how much information you have: when you find yourself in difficulty, you need help. I was not about to spend another semester of my life in Special Ed. I wanted out and I wanted out now. Realizing this could be my last telephone conversation for a while, I asked my friend how to break the cycle. Forgiveness. Very simply, she told me the only way to release yourself from the mistaken actions and beliefs of the past is to forgive yourself and others. When you forgive, you clear the way for a new energy to enter.

The Value of Forgiveness

The application of the principle with regard to the Law of Cause and Effect is very clear with respect to money. It becomes a bit more difficult to accept as we apply the same principle to those matters which are close to our heart. It is difficult for us to understand why people behave a certain way. More specifically, why they treat us in certain ways. The first thing that comes to mind is, "Why did you do this to me?" A more common response is, "I don't deserve to be treated like this or that!"

Even when we have the strength and/or insight to release a person who has treated us badly from our life, very often we hang onto the memory. We remember the first boy or man who dumped us, lied to us, failed to return our affections. We remember all the little incidents which led us to the conclusion that Mom always liked you better than me. We remember what Daddy did or did not do. One of my greatest obstacles in life was the memory of my brother's nasty habit of eating the last Oreo. It seemed as if he knew I was planning to devour it with a big glass of milk just before I went to bed. Purely to spite me, he would dash into the kitchen and get it. Needless to say, this supported my belief in the lack of Oreos and the compulsive behavior I exhibited when it looked like there was not enough of anything to go around.

You cannot accept until you forgive. You cannot trust until you forgive. You cannot build faith or discipline or obedience until you forgive yourself for all of the times you failed to accept, trust, have faith, be disciplined or be obedient to yourself for your own good. You cannot forgive anyone for treating you badly until you forgive yourself for treating you badly. You have been bad to you. You have failed to keep your promises to yourself. You have abandoned your plans and desires in order to please others. If you are a real Black woman, down to the bone, you have worked until you were senseless, abusing your body, taxing your mind, energy, and spirit. All Black women make promises to themselves which they fail to keep: "I'm going on a diet!" "I'm not going to call him anymore!" "I don't have anything to say!" You have put the priorities of others over your own priorities and standards. You have abandoned you when you needed you the most. You have worn cheap shoes and jeopardized the health, safety, and well-being of your toes and feet. Is it any wonder why people and situations continue to come into your life which cause you to feel abandoned, rejected, used, and mistreated? These external events are not the cause. They are the effects of your failure to take yourself into account and forgive yourself.

FORGIVENESS IS A MENTAL, EMOTIONAL, AND SPIRITUAL LAXATIVE!

When you forgive, you wipe the slate clean. You loosen the barnacles from your brain and allow your spirit to float freely. When you forgive, you open your mind to new insights and understanding. You give up the need to be right or in control. That is the main reason we do not forgive; we want control. If we forgive, it means we release. If we release someone or something from our minds, it may seem as if we are saying, "You were right. I was wrong." As long as we are mad with another person or because of a situation, we are in control of what people can do. We control how or if they approach us, what they can or cannot say to us. We demand an apology. If the person does not respond in the way we feel they should, we cut them out of our heart and mind. We may cut, but we do not sever. As long as we do not sever ourselves from the memories of the past, we are in control. When we forgive, we give up control.

Forgiveness allows us to see things from another perspective.

We may see that, in fact, everyone is not out to get us. Even you are not out to hurt yourself, undermine yourself. People just do what they do because of who they are and what they know. You must resist the temptation to judge, to believe that people actually mean to hurt or abuse you. You must resist the temptation to beat up on yourself when you make an unwise choice or decision. Even in those cases when you encounter people who are vicious and malicious, the choice is still up to you. The choice as to what role, what part, that person will play in your life is up to you.

At least eighty percent of the Black women I know were abused, neglected, or somehow abandoned as children. Many have a love-hate relationship with one or both parents. Others cite cousins, uncles, grandparents, or aunts who treated them harshly or cruelly. As I talk to these sisters, they reveal their belief that the people who hurt them should be punished. We are not talking here about legal punishment. We are talking about torture. Whipping. Flogging. Hanging. Burning at the stake. Vividly, my sisters recall time and time again how they were hurt, who hurt them, and what they would like to see done in vengeance to cause equal harm, pain, or destruction to these folks. When I attempt to introduce the concept of forgiveness, they shrink away in horror. "Forgiveness! Oh no, you don't understand! You don't understand what he/she did to me!" I may not understand what they have personally experienced as a result of how they were treated, but I do know that forgiveness is the only way to free your mind, spirit, and life from the past.

Black women want to see those who have victimized them suffer. They want payback. Many refuse to forgive their abusers or molesters, the ones who abandoned or rejected them. They hold on to every little tidbit of a memory their minds can digest, vowing to see the day when the ones who "done them wrong" get their due. In the meanwhile, they fail to realize they are still being abused, abandoned, rejected, and mistreated by an entirely new set of folks because of the way they think and feel. If you keep thinking and saying men are dogs, you will attract a pack of hounds. If you really believe women are sneaks who cannot be trusted, you will find yourself surrounded by conniving wenches.

With the millions and millions of people in the world, why are you attracting these people, these experiences? It has nothing to do with them; it has everything to do with you. It is not happening to you "because." It is happening because you are the cause. Forgiveness gives the divine an opportunity to create a divine cause in your life.

Now let's be honest. Everyone has done something for which they need to be forgiven. Maybe you stole quarters from your daddy's pocket. Maybe you told a lie to a teacher, or worse, your very own mother. I know everybody has a grandmother, aunt, or cousin they have killed off to get a few days' leave from work. Remember those little white lies you told to impress somebody on a first date or job interview? And let's not forget the people you have told to drop dead or go to hell. At some point in time, we have all cursed somebody or wished harm to somebody else. Yet we can convince ourselves that we are pure as snow. Honest, upright, and innocent. Conveniently we forget that somewhere in our past, we have either unconsciously or consciously said or done something to someone which has hurt them in some way. No matter how small or insignificant we may think our offense to be, when we are called on what we do or have done, we want to be forgiven. Why, then, do we find it so difficult to forgive others?

When my father made his transition, we were barely on speaking terms. I had not seen him in months. We had long ago stopped calling one another to chat, because of something he had said and done which I believed was appalling. When I got the call that he had died at home and that I should come right away, I experienced the gamut of emotions. Disbelief. Sadness. Relief. Anger. Sorrow. Upon arriving at his home, it was quite disturbing to see the man I had loved and hated all my life lifeless. Once his body was removed, the funeral plans began. We were well into how many cars we would need when someone realized my father had no insurance and that of his six children, no one had money except me. The thought of taking my hardearned money to bury this man who had created so much pain and confusion in my mind was devastating. But what do you say? I had to do what I could to make sure he got put away.

There is an African proverb which says, "The measure of the man is his children." If your children do the right thing, in the right way; if they are honorable and respectable to you and their elders; if they provide for you in your old age or infirmity, then the community will know that you have been a good person. I was not sure what the community would think, say, or know. I only knew that my father had wanted to be cremated and that it was my duty to see his wishes were fulfilled.

It made absolutely no sense that this responsibility should fall on me. My father had a wife and a woman. He had a mother and six other children. None of that mattered. He was out of cash and needed to be buried. I refused to attend or to allow my children to go to the wake. In my own little pea brain, I guess I was trying to show him something. I was just that angry at him. At the funeral I sat stiffly, looking out of one eye, listening to everything through one ear. I did not want to be in that place, having that experience. I remember being compelled to open the program we had been given. Inside, as if it had been written specifically for me, was a poem which revealed to me the healing power of forgiveness. The epigraph read as follows:

> *In our deepest hour of need, the Creator does not ask us for credentials. He accepts us exactly as we are, knowing we are His erring children. He loves us. And, He forgives us. Why can't we forgive ourselves?*

As I read it, the minister spoke it aloud. For the first time in a long time, I felt I understood what had happened between my father and me. I also understood why he had affected me so profoundly. More important, for the first time in my entire life, I felt totally connected to and loving toward him. Unfortunately, it was too late for me to tell him how I felt.

The Way Out

The Reverend Johnnie Coleman reminds her congregation frequently, "I am the thinker who thinks the thoughts that create the things." It is another way of approaching and understanding the Law of Cause and Effect. Thoughts cause effects. Karen was obviously ignorant of the law. Like many Black women, she forgot that when someone is treating us in a way we believe is unfair or unjust, we do not just sit around like abuse sponges, sopping up whatever comes our way. We are thinking, feeling, or saying something in response to what is going on. Sometimes, we do some pretty awful things in defense of ourselves. Karen, like many of the sister-friends in the world, did not realize that very often the negative experiences we have do not occur in response to what others do or have done to us, but are the effects, the karmic outgrowths, of our own being. In Karen's situation, her own thoughts and emotions came up as a dark, ugly experience with her superior, friends, and the men in her life. Unfortunately for Karen, as for so many of the rest of us, the situation came up at a time and in a manner which did not lend itself to her taking the time to figure out what was really going on.

Karen had always believed she was not good enough. Her position at work reinforced that belief. It had nothing to do with being Black, fat, or female. Her criticism of her boss and the "justifiable" trashing of the woman's character were reflected in a similar experience with her best friend. Karen never made the connection, either with her treatment of her boss or all the other people she had trashed and criticized in the past. As the youngest of five children, Karen was a whiner and a complainer. Her life experiences continuously provided her with something to whine and complain about.

Karen did not make the connection between her treatment of the callers at work and her beau's treatment and manner toward her. She also missed the fact that her hiding of documents from her supervisor at work, which she would then produce in the midst of the woman's frantic search, would eventually come up as Mitchell's hiding his attraction to her best friend's sister. Eventually he revealed that interest before the entire community. During her counseling sessions, Karen eventually realized that if the supervisor was a bat from hell who needed forgiveness, Karen herself was a rat in the corner who needed the same.

Karen had grown up in abject poverty. She had watched her mother work two jobs most of her life, wearing clothes from the Salvation Army, feeding her five children with what could barely feed one. Karen's mother repeatedly affirmed, "You work all your life, like a dog—for what? You can't eat! You can barely pay your bills! The people you work for, kill yourself for, treat you like a piece of crap, then you die!" Karen's mother was angry. She was angry at Karen's father for leaving her. She was angry at her children for needing and wanting their father. Karen's mother was angry at herself for having five children. At every opportunity she told her children just how angry she felt. Sounds like O.P.P. to me. That is exactly what it is. Another person's perspective invading Karen's life. Karen, being totally unaware of the valleys and their purpose in life, hated her mother for being angry and refused to forgive her father for abandoning her. Her own hate and anger needed to be released. They came up as the motivating factors beneath Karen's relationship with her supervisor.

When Karen's mother died of a hypertensive stroke at the age of forty-three, Karen had vowed it would not happen to her. She would not work hard. She would not die young. She would not be treated like crap. As this was what she focused her mental energy and emotions upon, this is exactly what she experienced: not working hard, feeling as though she were being treated like crap, creating a physical condition which could kill her at any moment, being angry, hateful and spiteful in response to what she perceived others were doing to her. Karen was also resistant to change. She had convinced herself that changing her perspective would not make a difference in her life. Her resistance took her on a trip to the Valley of Comeuppance with a layover in a Special Ed experience. Karen would have to be forced to change, forced to examine herself. Think about it. Who could she blame for her body being eighty pounds overweight?

Karen's situation was so chronic that she had to do the hard part first. Before she could forgive anyone, she had to learn to forgive herself. Karen learned how to forgive with visualization. She would sit for no less than ten minutes at a time, three times a day, and visualize herself talking to herself. She eventually accepted this was the only way to forgive herself for hating and to clear herself of the negative, combative, stressful energy which was forcing her blood pressure to skyrocket. Her resistance was based on her belief that to forgive meant admitting she was wrong. It took her quite some time to realize that forgiveness has nothing to do with another person. Forgiveness is the way to heal yourself from all that you have done to or allowed to be done to yourself, by yourself and others.

Karen had to forgive herself for hating her mother for being so angry, angry enough to tell her children they were not wanted or needed. She had to forgive herself for being angry with her father for leaving his wife and children, without ever returning to see how they were. Karen had to forgive herself for wishing harm on people who teased her about being too fat, too Black, too smart, or too stupid. Karen had to forgive herself for the unkind things she had said about and to other people who had reinforced her beliefs about herself. Once this was done, she realized that she had nothing to forgive her supervisor for.

Forgive yourself first. You cannot give what you do not have. If you cannot give yourself the mercy of forgiveness, you will never be able to find it in your heart to forgive anyone else. Whether or not you think you have done anything which warrants forgiveness does not matter. Do it anyway. I had to forgive myself for smoking for eighteen years and clogging my blessed lungs with nicotine. I had to forgive myself for being a slave to Pepsi, Häagen Dazs coffee ice cream, and extra mayonnaise on my white bread sandwiches. I knew that stuff was no good for me. I was abusing my body. I was real clear that my husband slapping me around was abusive. It was more difficult to see how I had abused myself. When I became aware, I stayed on a forgiveness diet for sixty days.

The blessing of forgiveness is that it does not give other people the permission to mistreat you. It makes you aware of what you will and will not accept as a fact of your life. When you release the past through forgiveness, it clears your channels of intuition. Hate, fear, anger, resentment, guilt, and shame are eliminated from your consciousness. You become extremely sensitive to what you hear, see, and experience. This sensitivity does not mean people can hurt you. It means you become sensitive to words and actions which provoke fear, hate, anger, shame, or guilt in your being. When you are aware, you are free to choose what you will accept and not accept from others in your presence. When you learn to forgive, you no longer have reasons to be angry. You see. You hear. You intuit. You forgive. You move on. It is really quite simple.

Forgiveness eliminates the negative thoughts and emotions which create negative effects in your life. It is the law in operation. If you do not think the cause, there can be no effect. Of course we all have those moments when we speak too soon, too harshly, or without complete information. Fortunately, forgiveness provides us with the strength to forgive ourselves and excuse ourselves to others without feeling ashamed or guilty. A word of caution about this powerful spiritual medicine. Forgiveness does not mean you can consciously or knowingly commit the same errors repeatedly, and then forgive yourself, only to do them again. Forgiveness is a function of awareness. Once you are aware of something, it is your responsibility to make the necessary adjustments in your behavior. These adjustments are sure to keep you out of the valley.

MEDITATION
WITH THE
MOTHER

Nature awakens in our being a feeling that we must lay at His feet that we may get the blessed approval, for we are so changeable, but God is unchanging.

—*SIX WOMEN'S SLAVE NARRATIVES*

Pray for yourself that your path shall be paved with light. Pray for yourself that your burdens shall be lightened with love. Pray for yourself that your purpose shall be revealed with clarity and exactness, that you may fulfill your mission as love in action. You the daughters must have a purpose to guide you to enlightenment if you are ever to know my true nature, which is your whole self.

Your purpose gave birth to you. It has molded and shaped who you are and what you do. Your purpose is the reason you live and breathe and move in your being as a woman. Your purpose knows you well. It knows your pains, your fears, and the misguided notions which dangle before you, pushing you further away from who you are and what you are here to do. Your purpose guides your heart, hands, and head. It is alive in you. It is there, within, that you must seek to know it and live it. Your purpose, daughters, is to use your heart, hands, and head in such loving ways that the world will come alive through the light that is woman, a reflection of the Mother.

Oh, but you fear so, daughters. You fear there is not enough to have, that there is too much to do, that you are not enough to be that which your purpose has ordained for you. You do not trust, daughters, that you are divinely guided, perfectly clear, nobly on purpose at all times, under all conditions. You pursue the rambling thoughts of your head rather than the roaring of your heart. You look to the world rather than your soul. You accept what you are told rather than what you know. You seek pleasure rather than purpose, and for this, you become lost, disconnected, or—worse—both.

I am your purpose. I am the softness in your voice, the gentleness in your spirit, the clarity in your mind before you were raped by the harshness of the world. I am your light. I show you the way to do that which you have come to do, with such exhilarating exactness that you have no time to fear. I am the love urging you to give, to serve, to be the love, peace, light, and joy that continues to elude you in the world. I am your truth. I am your strength. I am your value, worth, and honor. When you know me, not only do you have pleasure, you have it in abundance. Not only do you have love, you have it unconditionally. When you know me, you will know yourself. When you know yourself, you will know your purpose, that through which you will find all the joy, light, love, peace, and prosperity which the world has led you to believe is so difficult to acquire. Pray for yourself today to have the strength to discover and live your divine purpose.

The Valley of Purpose and Intent

8

*A*LL OF HER HIGH SCHOOL GIRL-FRIENDS HAD HUSBANDS, HOMES, AND KIDS. THEY TOOK VACATIONS EVERY summer, bought new furs every winter. She lived in a tiny apartment which had everything she wanted and needed. She took care of hundreds of children every year as a pediatric nurse. As far as she could tell, husbands were things who cluttered your clothesline with BVD's. Most of her school friends were miserable drunks or ex-drunks in therapy trying to figure out why they were so miserable. She was on purpose.

All her life she had wanted her own secretary and office. She got it. All her life she had wanted to have enough money to do what she wanted to do when she wanted to do it. She had it. All her life she had wanted a man who would love her, come at her every beck and call, and satisfy her other little needs. She had him too. There was nothing she wanted that she did not have or could not have. Still, she was absolutely miserable. So miserable, she spent every opportunity she had buying more clothes, competing to get another promotion, or sleeping with other men. She was not on purpose.

Each morning, hundreds of thousands of Black women get up, get dressed, and carry themselves off to a thing called work. It is this thing which occupies eighty to ninety percent of their waking hours, brainpower, and life force. However, if you asked the over-whelming majority of these women if they liked what they do they would say no. We work to support ourselves. We work to pay bills. We work to acquire things. We work to "never need any-body to do anything for us." Few of us work to fulfill a purpose.

While we are working, there is another group of women, an-other few hundred thousand, who do not get up or go anywhere. They are supported by husbands, parents, or the state while in their minds and bodies they search for something worthwhile and meaningful to do. When it comes to purpose, none of these women are on it either. They are alive. They are not living. A jour-ney without purpose is meaningless.

There is another group of women, a much smaller group, who awaken each morning with clarity and peace of mind. These women know who they are, what they must do, and how they must do it. They have a determination of mind which gives them focus. There is an excitement in their hearts that urges them on. They know. They are sure. They are capable, eager, and ready to meet the day and whatever it holds in store for them. These women are on purpose.

Know Your Place and Get In It!

Purpose is an activity or series of activities which enable you to use your God-given talents, gifts, and abilities to fulfill a need in the world. Purpose is not only what you do, it is what you are. As you perform your tasks, purpose—not salary, need, or desper-ation—gives those tasks meaning. Purpose is more than a goal; it is a mission—a mission born in the depths of your spirit which makes you know you must do what you do because you simply cannot do anything else. Purpose is not about money. When you are on purpose, the money and everything else you need and de-sire will come to you. There is no need to struggle or suffer.

Purpose is about knowing your place. When you are on pur-pose, your place opens up for you. Usually, you do not have to compete for it or struggle to stay in it. You do not fear losing it nor can you be removed from it. Many Black women experience discontent and unhappiness in their personal and professional relationships because they are not in their place. They are squeezing themselves into situations which are inappropriate or which they have outgrown. There are also those times when you are on purpose, in your place, and find that you are still being challenged. So what! Everything that challenges you does not have to win. When you take the focus off the people, off the challenge, and stay focused on your purpose, a challenge makes you stronger, wiser, and more determined. When you are on purpose, you are like a rock. You shall not be moved!

Purpose is not about being liked by other people, being famous, or becoming rich. It is about knowing who you are and putting that knowledge to use in a meaningful way. A way that makes someone else, as well as yourself, feel that they are better off because of who you are and what you do. A way that has a ripple effect, touching people who you may never see, never know. Who gets helped does not matter when you are on purpose. When you are on purpose, the only thing that matters to you is that you do what you are.

Purpose is a state of mind which results in clarity of vision and intent. Purpose allows us to see obstacles and challenges; however, it allows us to see a way around them. Purpose cannot be hindered or obstructed because it knows it is divine. It is born of divine intent. Purpose is willing to do whatever is necessary, whenever it is needed, without fear or hesitation. Purpose knows it is worthy and honorable, determined and capable, strong and powerful.

Purpose is a God force backed by the universal resources which are unlimited and endless. Purpose is love and light manifesting through a being in the human realm. We have been taught to work for money. To set goals in order to find success. To do and outdo others in order to have what we want in life. On this path, some of us still find purpose. Many of us do not. When the focus is on doing for money, many choose to do what promises to bring the greatest amount of money with the least amount of doing. Purpose has a much more noble intent. Purpose begins with the intent to bring into the world a service which fills a need money cannot fill. Purpose is the intent to be, do with, give of, the self without having reward or recognition as the motivating factor. Having been taught that work is the way to money, and money the means to self-satisfaction, many of us work without purpose. We educate ourselves to those tasks or careers which we believe will ultimately take us to financial security. In doing so, we spend the greater portion of our lives working while feeling unsatisfied, unfulfilled, as an individual. If you are not on purpose, the money you acquire will not help you feel better about yourself because you will not be in alignment with your soul's purpose, your spiritual journey, the reason God has given you life.

Intent Brings Alignment

What is your intent? When you get up each morning, what do you intend to do for yourself? For those with whom you will come into contact? For the world? When your only intent is to pay bills and buy things, you are headed for dissatisfaction and imbalance. Intent is the path to purpose. Intentions are the motivating factors behind your activities. When one intention is met, the mind will actively seek another. However, when intentions are hinged on the physical world, the things you can see, you embark on an endless search, a search of the world rather than the soul. In the world, facts change. There are challenges, obstacles, which threaten to block or stop your progress. The facts over which you seem powerless keep you in bondage, the bondage of wanting, needing, and not being able to acquire. The more you see, the more you want and the greater the demand from your physical senses. The things you want and cannot have become the source of your pain, the root of your dissatisfaction. Your intention becomes satisfaction of the physical senses and elimination of the pain.

Intention is the sum of what you expect to accomplish at the end of a task or deed. According to universal law, expectations always equal results. We get in life not what we say we want, but what we expect. When we expect to work hard all of our lives and to have nothing to show for it, ninety-nine percent of the time that is exactly what we get. When we expect to have a hard time in the world because we are Black or female or old or young, it is guaranteed we will get exactly that, a hard way to go. However, when our intention is to do what we love, simply because we love doing it and are good at it, the universe has a way of opening opportunities and avenues through which we can move, realizing bountiful returns and rewards.

When your intention is predicated on knowing or finding your purpose, the goals of your tasks and activities take on a different focus. There is a shift from getting to giving, from doing to being, from having to sharing. When your intention is based on purpose, you no longer work, you serve, giving the best of yourself for the sheer joy of doing, not for getting. When your intention is to use your God-given talents, gifts, and abilities, you place a greater value on yourself. You begin to realize that what you do, what you have, is a gift—a gift you can use to bring yourself and others pleasure.

Intention, when it is based on spiritual principles, brings you into alignment with your good. It brings you to your purpose. I have heard people say, over and over, "I want to help other people." My question is, Why? What is your intention? A common response is, "They need me." So, you intend to be needed. That means that whenever somebody needs you, you will be there? They never mean it like that. They mean, they want to help children. They want to end suffering. They want to fight racism. Therein lies the problem. When the intent is to do something to stop or obstruct something else, we are tied to the outcome. When we are tied to the outcome, we are tied to doing a certain thing in order to have a certain thing. If the outcome is as we expect, we are successful. If it is not, we label ourselves failures and become dissatisfied, disillusioned, and eventually burnt out. Intention is not tied to outcome. It is a function of doing. Intention is not tied to success or failure. It is the action of doing, learning, growing, and serving. Serving and service are outgrowths of purpose.

When we are not in touch with our true self or our emotional self, we will verbalize one intent, holding another in our hearts. If we say we will do one thing when in our hearts we're harboring another feeling, our true intent will manifest in the way we behave and speak. When people say things which "hurt our feelings," the intent behind the words was to do just that. When we are late or forget a commitment, it is quite possible we did not want to be involved. Our true intent was not to go. However, when we have a clearly defined intention, based on spiritual principles, our purpose is honorable and the best possible outcome is realized.

Your intention is what you feel. Your purpose is what you are. "Being purposeful" is a way of thinking to which we are rarely introduced. Our true purpose is usually couched in struggle, mediocrity, and a belief in lack and limitation. As we strive through life, we are warned and cautioned about what we cannot do, should not do, better not do. Rarely are we encouraged about the things we can do, must do, because God needs them done and has chosen us to do it. That thing you have come to life to be, which you do with all of your heart and soul, which you think about in your every waking hour, which brings joy into your heart, satisfaction into your life: that is your purpose. It may be dancing or singing or painting rocks. It may be teaching, healing, talking, or listening while serving drinks in a bar. Everybody may be doing it or nobody at all may be doing it.

You may have been trained to do it or it may come through you naturally. It is that thing which you could do for the rest of your life whether you got paid to do it or not. Somewhere, someone told you it was not possible for you to do it. You may have even been forbidden to do it. Yet it keeps coming back to you. You cannot shake it. It fills your dreams and those quiet moments when you are alone. Your purpose drives you, and at some point, you will find yourself in a situation where the desire is so great that, if only for one moment, you will forget everything you have been told, believed, or feared and step out to do what you are.

A Valley Experience

Raylene was the oldest of three children born into a highly toxic, dysfunctional family. When Raylene was three, her mother died. She and her two younger brothers were raised by a series of family relatives, in a variety of settings, ranging from abusive to neglectful. As the oldest child and the only girl, Raylene was forced to accept many responsibilities she was not emotionally or spiritually equipped to handle. She was responsible for the care of her two brothers. She was responsible for the care of her drunken aunt. She was responsible for the urges of her drunken grandfather, who frequently found pleasure in fondling her breasts and vagina. Raylene felt abandoned by her mother, abused by her grandfather, burdened by her brothers, neglected by her father. She was angry and confused.

Raylene was a brilliant child, but with so much going on at home, her schoolwork was not a priority. She found peace only when she was alone in her room, plotting and planning her revenge and her getaway. Her solitude was frequently interrupted by her aunt or uncle's physical abuse of one or both of her brothers. Many times, Raylene would not go to their defense. She would cover her head with pillows and tell herself there was nothing she could do. That did not work. After her brothers were beaten, sometimes nearly into unconsciousness, Raylene would be scolded, and often beaten, for not preventing whatever her brothers had done. By the time she was a teenager, she grew to hate her brothers along with everyone else.

A person can only handle so much hate and anger. At some point the energy will build up in the heart and mind to the breaking or bursting point. Raylene knew that to burst, to fight back, to challenge her father, aunt, or uncle, would bring down a wrath she was not prepared to handle. She had to find another way out. For Raylene, the way out was alcohol. By the time she was sixteen, Raylene was using her lunch money and all the money she could find or steal to buy liquor. She was fortunate in that there was so much liquor around her, she did not have to look for or steal money very often. Her need was fulfilled by the very situation which created the need. When Raylene had just enough to drink, she did not care who touched her, who beat her brothers, or that there was nowhere for her to go.

By the time she was seventeen, Raylene was a full-fledged alcoholic. She left home. Lived with a variety of friends and relatives who were as unconcerned about her as her primary caretakers were. She got a part-time job which she managed to keep for several years. She tried to stay in school, but they kept asking her questions. Questions about home, about the alcohol on her breath, about taking the SAT and going to college. In the first quarter of her senior year in high school, the pressure became too much. It was at about the same time that she realized that although she had left home over a year ago, no one had ever come to look for her. They had not come to school. They had not come to her friend's home to inquire about her well-being or to demand that she come home. Of course, her *brothers* had always looked for her. They wanted to, needed to, tell her about the continuing horror they lived. She would give them money or buy them pizza, and convince them they would be just fine. In the second quarter of her senior year in high school, Raylene dropped out and went to work full-time.

When you are lost, there is always a savior. Something or someone will come along at the very moment you are in need to save you from your misery and from yourself. Raylene's savior was John. He was twenty. He was working. He was the nicest person Raylene had ever met. More important, he had his own apartment in which he and Raylene could live.

She loved him. She loved him enough to want to stop drinking and join Alcoholics Anonymous. She loved him enough to have his son after she had been dry for six months. Raylene loved John so much that after they had been together three years, she began paying all the bills. It was the kind of love that silenced her when other women started calling their home. Raylene was so in love she was compelled to pay a baby-sitter so she could go out to look for John in bars and parties when he did not come home at night. She loved him so much that when she found out he had another woman and another baby, she stayed with him to try to work it out. She knew her love was not enough for John when he started to slap her around. It was at that point that she started drinking again.

Raylene was brilliant, intelligent, and especially good with people. She had become the manager of the shoe store at which she worked in four short years. She was not happy there, but it was the only way she knew of to take care of her son and still have a little bit to share with her brothers. Raylene was now so good at her job that she could work all day, drink half the night, and still get up to go to work the next morning. When she was not working or drinking, Raylene dreamed about going back to school and getting her diploma so she could go to college and become a math teacher. That was her secret dream, to be a math teacher. She loved children and she loved numbers. It made her an excellent manager in the children's shoe store, but it did not save her relationship with John. Three days before the eighth anniversary of their being together, John packed his bags and left.

When one door closes . . . Before Raylene could get into a serious depression about John, she received a notice that she had been accepted for a better paying job with city government. She knew this meant she would have to stop or at least cut back on her drinking. She was relieved to know she would have more money and some security, but she also knew it meant she would have to go back to A.A. We do what we must when we are forced. Six months into her new job, Raylene was informed that if she did not get her high school diploma, she would be terminated. Her A.A. mentor told her it was about time, anyway. He would help her study for her G.E.D. and she would pass. Which she did. The amazing part was, she hardly studied. She got a perfect score on the math portion, and the lowest grade she got on any other part was four points below perfect. When the scores came in, her mentor begged her to go to college at night. But Raylene figured it did not matter. Who would care anyway? No one in her family had gone to college and she believed she was destined to end up like most of them, drunk and broke.

With John gone just long enough to show up again when Raylene thought she was over him, she had very little time or energy for another relationship. She spent most of her time working overtime; first, so that she would not drink; and second, to take care of her son's ever-growing needs. Her brothers still came around now and then, but they were in about the same shape as she was—lost and angry. Although Raylene and John had supposedly been separated for two years, he would still pass through every other week or so for sex. He had introduced Raylene to the art of snorting cocaine. They were quite high and very naked the night he announced he was getting married. In her anger, Raylene doused him with the glass of Seven-Up at the side of the bed, locked herself in the bathroom, and snorted all of his coke. He left vowing never to set foot in her house again. He never did. He died of an overdose three weeks after he married his drug counselor.

Raylene needed someone to talk to, someone to love. A series of disappointing relationships had led her to believe that it was not going to happen. All of the men she met were into the same thing as she was—getting high and giving up. Raylene had been seeing Gary on and off for about a year. He almost fit the bill except that he would not hang around anytime Raylene got high. He did not understand that she had to get high to ease the pain and simmer down the anger. He had become more like a counselor than a lover. He would listen to Raylene, but he always warned her about her behavior, just like her mentor. Her A.A. mentor had become a real pain in the butt. He called her at work, showed up at her door unannounced, and kept sending her college catalogs in the mail. He just wouldn't quit. So Raylene moved and left no forwarding address. She told her supervisor at work that an ex-beau was threatening her by telephone, in order to have her work extension changed. Finally Raylene was free to snort cocaine, drink liquor, and sleep around to her pleasure. All within moderation, of course.

As divine order would have it, drug screening became a requirement at Raylene's job. She stayed clean for three whole days, submitted to the test, and still got a positive result. Raylene was told that if she did not enter a drug program, she would be terminated. She told them she did not have a drug problem, she had a cold. She was taking cold medication. When she was over the cold, she would retake the test. That was not good enough. She was suspended for thirty days. If during that time she entered a drug program and submitted proof, she would be given one year's leave at two-thirds pay. At the end of that time, she would be reinstated. How dare they accuse her! They could take their job and shove it. So they did.

Raylene stayed with Gary for a while. When he got on her nerves, she stayed with Carlton. He was getting high so much that she left him and stayed with David. When he suggested that she sell his friends certain sexual favors, she left and went to stay with her younger brother, his wife, and their three children. Her brother and his wife both worked in the day and were going to college at night. Raylene was a blessing to them because she would cook and watch the children in return for room and board. Raylene loved children. She actually loved doing the little things around the house, like cooking and the laundry, but since no one, particularly John, had ever seemed to appreciate it, she had never bothered much before. Her brother and sister-in-law were really cool. They didn't bother her about getting high. Actually, they didn't know since she only did it on the weekends and never in their home. They saw to it that she had a few dollars of her own, and for the first time in her life, she felt like she was part of a real family. At night, Raylene would wish she had a home for her son. He was fourteen now, and living with his father's mother. Raylene missed him, but she knew he was better off without her.

A year passes by quickly when you have nothing to do. Raylene's brother was about to graduate from college and was talking about moving. The children had become very attached to her, but she knew her days were numbered. Her brother suggested that she keep the apartment after they moved. He thought she should go back to school. He could get her a part-time job at his job and she could go to school at night. Raylene took him up on the job offer but nixed the school thing. The job worked out well, for a while. The work was easy, but the people were another story. Raylene was just a clerk. People do not treat their clerks very well. Raylene found herself being blamed for anything and everything that went wrong. She was never given an opportunity to explain. Instead, she was scolded as if she were a child. Her bosses reminded her of the aunts and uncles she had grown up with. She decided she was not going to put up with it. One day she went to lunch, bought a bus ticket to South Carolina, and went to live with Gary. He was shocked and excited. He was happy and unprepared. But he loved Raylene enough to give it a go. They lived together for two years.

When Raylene got the call that her father had died, she was relieved. Then she got angry. This man who she believed was at the root of her suffering had died before she got the opportunity to spit in his face. She went back home for the funeral. It was a real zoo. All her father's women came out of the woodwork. They were arguing and fighting about who he had been with the longest, and who had the money to pay for the funeral. Raylene's youngest brother paid for everything and shut everyone's mouth. Throughout the week's festivities, everyone who laid eyes on Raylene would tell her how much she looked like her father. Her mannerisms were like her father's, her smile was like her father's, even her habit of holding her chin in her hand reminded everyone of her father, her dead father, whom she hated with a passion.

After the funeral, Raylene stayed in her hometown. She got a job in a children's group home. Gary came back home too. They saw each other on and off, but Gary was on Raylene about her drinking and drugging. After her son got arrested and sent to prison for five years, Raylene really started bingeing. Gary tried to talk to her, but she would not listen. When she was high or drunk, she would call him or her younger brother and cry about how bad her life had been. She would relive her childhood. That always made her feel worse. Several of her close childhood friends had already died from overdoses, drunk driving, and bad living. Raylene was convinced that, unlike them, she was invincible. She was not an addict or a drunk. She was troubled and alcohol made her feel better. Gary told her that if she would stop drinking, they would get married. Raylene thought it might be her last chance at happiness. So she did and they did.

Things were fine for the first year or so. Raylene loved Gary even when he was bugging her about going back to school. Gary was the only person Raylene could remember who had ever told her that she was pretty or smart or that she had the ability to do anything she wanted to do. Gary was also the only man she'd met who could occasionally get high and still live like a "normal" person. But like her, Gary was defective. He had big issues with his father too. He had never finished college or done any of the things he kept telling Raylene to do. What Gary had was a big, fat paycheck from his job with the state. He was a probation officer. He had been one for almost twelve years. He had worked in several different states and was about to become a training supervisor. Still, he was as defective as Raylene. What she did not realize was that just because a person is defective, it does not mean they cannot see your defects.

Besides Gary, Raylene had her job. She loved her job. It did not make her completely happy or give her a reason to stop drinking completely, but she loved being with the children. By now, Raylene figured she was too old to go to college or to ever become a math teacher. She satisfied herself helping the children in the group home with their homework. If one of the teachers were absent, Raylene would volunteer to take her class. The children always responded to her. She could get them to do what others could not. Her ability to communicate with children was like a gift to her. A gift she had never really developed.

When Gary first started going to church, Raylene thought it was a joke. He would ask her to come, but she would refuse. What the hell could God do for her now that He had refused to do all of her life? Gary became very annoyed when she spoke in that manner. He told her he would pray for her anyway. In his absence, Raylene found the prime opportunity to snort a little coke and feel sorry for herself. Since Gary had stopped getting high, he forbade her to do it in the house. She had to wait for him to go out, which he did more often since he had joined the church. When she was high, Raylene would call her baby brother. He would always listen to her stories and commiserate with her. This Sunday, for some reason, her brother tried to switch up on her. When she called him, he told her he was tired of hearing her whine and complain. He asked her why she did not forget the past and move on. Oh, he didn't understand. Had he forgotten how badly they were treated as children? Had he forgotten what an SOB their father was? He didn't know how John had treated her and how she had stayed with him so long just to be able to take care of her son. Had he forgotten all the money she had given him? Things she had bought him when they were younger? No, he had not forgotten, he was just tired of hearing it. He was tired of watching his sister destroy herself over people and things that no longer mattered. He was tired of waiting for the telephone to ring with someone on the other end telling him his sister was dead. He was tired of watching her wallow in self-pity and he wished to God that she would get her head together and get on with her life.

Furious, Raylene hung up on her brother. It was too late. Gary had come back from church and found the remnants of cocaine in the bathroom. For several very long, very silent moments, Gary stared at Raylene. It made her nervous. He didn't scream. He didn't even seem angry. If anything, he looked hurt. No, lost is a better description. Without ever opening his mouth, he dropped down on his knees right next to the toilet and began to pray. He asked God to save his wife from the demons in her soul. He asked that she have peace of mind. He asked God to show her the way to forgiveness. He asked God to forgive her for being so angry, for so long, that she could not find her way to Him. He asked God to give his wife meaning and a purpose beyond her flesh and blood. He told God how much he loved her. Then, he asked God to give him the strength to do what he needed to do. When he stopped praying, he started crying.

Raylene was helpless. She had never seen Gary—or any man, for that matter—cry. She didn't know what to say, to do. She tried to apologize. Gary kept crying. Through all the years, Raylene had stayed in pretty good shape. She had a few pouches here and there, but miraculously, she was still a decent-looking woman. She tried to seduce Gary. It didn't work. He was adamant. He would no longer live with a drug addict. He could not carry her emotional weight any longer. Either she checked in for treatment today or he would leave. But Raylene was not addicted. She got high because she wanted to. With that statement, Gary got off his knees, packed an overnight bag, and walked toward the door.

When he was on the other side of it, he told her he would call her and let her know when he would pick up the rest of his things.

The words of Gary's prayer kept ringing in her ears. Forgive! What did she need to be forgiven for? She had never done anything to anyone, except maybe her son. Everything had been done to her. That is why she didn't have peace of mind. The only demons in her life were the people who raised her. The people who supposedly loved her, who had abused her and left her. Raylene got the scotch she had hidden in the laundry basket. Gary wasn't the first man to leave her and he wouldn't be the last. Raylene felt pretty sure that he would come back, eventually. As soon as he cooled off a little, he would come back. She took a drink.

Suppose he didn't. Suppose this time Gary did not come back. Raylene thought of being alone, and panicked. It had been quite a while since she had been alone. She took another drink. What the hell difference did it make? She had been alone most of her life anyway. Gary was just like everyone else. Stay awhile and then leave. It made her mad. She took another drink. As her head began to get lighter, Raylene thought of John. She thought of how much she had loved him and how he had treated her. This time she took a long swig from the bottle. Against her will, she thought about her grandfather, how he used to touch her, how it felt when he put his hand or his mouth between her legs. She stopped that thought in midstream, threw the bottle on the floor, and searched for the last package of cocaine she had hidden.

As she was searching, she came across an old picture of her mother. *Bitch! She just up and died on me.* She thought about the days and nights she had wished for, cried for, her mother. She couldn't find the damn cocaine. Then she thought about her father. She hadn't cried at his funeral, but for some reason she now felt sad to know that both her parents had died without ever telling her they loved her. Frantically ripping the clothes out of the drawers, she was about to conclude that Gary had found it when she saw the glassine bag stuck between a bra hook. *Move on! Move on!* Her brother's words were coming back to her now. Her sweet little baby brother. He didn't know what he was talking about. Raylene went to her usual get-high spot on the side of the bathtub.

As soon as she opened the bag, her ears were filled with the sound of Gary's sobbing. Startled, she jumped. He was back. She folded the bag and stuck it in her bosom. The apartment was empty. *Oh Lord! I'm losing my mind.* She started back to the tub. This time she could hear him crying and praying as soon as she set foot in the bathroom. This was weird. Raylene could hear Gary crying and praying as if he were right there. *Teach her to forgive. Show her the way!* Now she could hear children laughing. She thought about the children at the home. How much she loved them, and the fact that she knew they loved her. So many of them came from situations worse than hers. So many of them were angry and frightened just like her. Still, Raylene knew that her life was for the children. Even though she felt she had failed with her own child, she knew she could help a child somehow, someway.

Raylene reached in her bra and retrieved the glassine bag of cocaine. Standing over the toilet, she toyed with the idea of dumping it. Now that Gary was gone, who would help her get clean and stay clean? She did not have the strength to do it alone. Could God, would God, really forgive her? She was so pissed off with Him, maybe He wanted nothing else to do with her. Well, the feeling was mutual. Still holding the bag of cocaine, Raylene felt the hot tears begin to roll down her face. These were not her usual drunken tears. These were big, hot, salty tears which came up from her feet, through her legs, up her spine, to and through her heart, up her throat, and out of her eyes. She dropped the entire bag in the toilet. Now her tears were accompanied by a loud sobbing. She fell to her knees. The scotch and her crying were not mixing too well today. She had an overwhelming urge to throw up. Before she did, she flushed the toilet. Then she put her face all the way in the toilet and cried. She was still crying an hour later when Gary came back. He pried her from the toilet, held her in his arms. When he asked her if she was ready to go into treatment, she nodded her head. She could not speak. He told her the only reason he had come back was to get his Bible and other prayer books. He had left them on the kitchen table. Gary held on to Raylene all the way to the entrance of the Valley of Purpose and Intent. She took the final, most crucial step on her own.

The Law of Compensation

If what we have come to life to do were just handed to us on a silver platter, we would probably ignore it because it would be too easy. If we had nothing to work through, overcome, or figure out, we would make something up. We seem to need challenges and difficulties to keep us alert. Some of us need more than others, but we all need something to look back on and wonder "how I got over." The universe is so wonderful. It always gives us exactly what we ask for. It may not give it to us the way we want it, but we always get it the way we need it.

Some of us need more time than others. Others need more drama, more pain. There are even those of us who need to go so low, so painfully low, that it takes a miracle to bring us back up. A few of us can catch ourselves on the way down. We recognize and realize the problem right away. Unfortunately, we do not recognize the solution, the way up or out. Life is strange like that. You would think that the universe of life would be more merciful and understanding. You would think that life would save us from ourselves and the other people in our lives who understand no more than we do. Well, even when we do not recognize it, life is good. Life keeps us alive at the very core of our being, that which we are born to be. No matter what happens in our lives, the mission, the purpose, does not change. Our path to it may be altered, but the lesson we need to find, purpose, does not change. Life only gives us what we need to grow, to fully understand; and it gives it to us according to what we think, say, do, and believe. It is called the Law of Compensation.

What habits keep us in bondage? Suffering? Limitation? Poverty? Is it our responsibility to accept the limitations handed down to us by our family? Many of our ancestors believed they were duty bound to suffer in this life because they would receive their rewards in heaven. As a result, many of us are so heavenly bound, we are no earthly good. We have missed the point. We suffer needlessly because we do not know the law. In the Valley of Purpose and Intent, the governing Law of Compensation says:

> *As above, so below. As you think, do, and*
> *give, so shall it be done unto you.*

This law is the first cousin to the Law of Belief, where what you believe creates what you experience. The difference being, compensation gives you exactly what you give. What you are thinking above your neck determines what you do and experience below your neck. With belief, that is all you have to do. With compensation, an action is also required.

The Law of Compensation, when used properly, provides us with the opportunity to lift ourselves from where we are to where we rightfully belong. It hinges on intent. What do you intend to do about where you are? How do you intend to do it? In order to comply with this law, you must act. Think right. Order your life. Act right. Take for example Algebra 101. You are given a formula and expected to work out a problem. In the beginning, you will make many mistakes. You may apply the improper formula, apply the correct formula in an incorrect way, or you may not carry out the operations to their fullest extent. Your mistakes do not always result from not having correct information. They are also the result of your miscalculations. If you continue doing the same thing, you will be compensated with the incorrect solution to your problem. You cannot change the formula, the way to the solution. You can, however, change how you apply the formula to the problem which confronts you. The formula always works. The issue is how you apply it. Your purpose is always in you. The issue is how to work through the challenges to get to it.

The Law of Compensation does not imply that we are to ignore the wrongs we experience in life. We cannot pretend we do not have empty places in our hearts. We must admit when we have been underdeveloped in certain areas. What the law requires of us is to not act as if we are fully developed. We must ask and wait for guidance and support. In doing so, we are ex-

pected to think beyond the dark spots into the light, always acting in a manner that will ensure that we move through the darkness. In his book *Working the Law,* Raymond Holliwell suggests:

> *Crowd out all inferior thoughts by superior*
> *thoughts, evil thoughts by good thoughts, ugly*
> *thoughts by beautiful thoughts . . . In other words,*
> *learn to think constructively of all persons, all*
> *things and events, and all circumstances.*

The key is intent. When we intend to move beyond wherever we
are, we will move. Our actions will become aligned with our
deepest desire and the way will be made. However, when we
have no intent, when we become stuck where we are, or when
our behavior is an inappropriate formula to escape the situation
in which we find ourselves, it will be virtually impossible to find
the solution.

What does this have to do with purpose? Remember, intent is
the path to purpose. When you have an intent in your heart that
is in alignment with the universal laws and your spiritual mission,
you will move beyond all difficulties to your purpose. The Law of
Compensation helps those who help themselves. When you strike
out to overcome the challenges and obstacles, eliminating all mal-
ice from your heart, keeping your intent pure through honest desire, the universe will support you. When you live as if the world
owes you a living and the people in the world owe you an apology, your intent is not to move beyond where you are. Your intent is to be right. Somebody was wrong and you want to be
right. Somebody hurt you and you want to see them hurt. You
are putting out thoughts which will reap you returns. You are be-
having in an inappropriate manner and you will be compensated.
Only when we cease to acknowledge a situation will we cease to
attract it. The law says, put your house in order, your mind and
your life. Then you can and will realize an orderly flow of events
in and through your life.

The law is exact. We always reap what we sow. When we
attract unpleasant experiences, it is often because there is a dormant or undeveloped part of our nature which requires awaken-

ing. That is the issue being challenged by a given experience. Our experiences do not come to make us suffer. We attract what we need to grow, to awaken our spiritual nature. That part of our nature is more often than not directly linked to our purpose. Whatever we attract, no matter how difficult, we need in order to grow and learn. Whatever we attract or experience, we can work through if we know the law.

What you are, you must give. What you give, you get. With regard to purpose, when you give of yourself the thing you know yourself to be, you will be rewarded in kind. If you know you are a dancer and you give a hundred percent of yourself to that art, the universe will reward you with greater opportunities to share your gift. If you know you are a healer, share your healing gift. In return, you will be adequately provided for in life. If you are a teacher, teach. If you are a plumber, fix pipes. Follow the urging of your heart and do what you are. We get thrown off track when we listen to the opinions of others who may believe what we are good at will not bring us bountiful rewards. We are thrown off course when we get stuck in the drama, pain, or shame of our life's experiences. The most common deterrent to the pursuit of purpose is the belief that the thing we want is not right, not good enough, or not what spirit wants us to do. We are always questioning whether or not we are doing the right thing. When what we are doing does not appear to bring us the prosperity and abundance we want, our immediate thought is that we are doing the wrong thing.

Remember the formula? It may not be that you are doing the wrong thing. It may be that you are doing it in the wrong way. With the wrong intent. If the thing you want in your heart is the thing spirit wants for you, why would spirit not want you to do what makes you happy? If you're doing what you love, giving it a hundred percent of your energy and attention, and still you are not receiving prosperous returns, the problem is in your mind, not in your actions. Prosperity is a state of consciousness. It is not a reflection of what you do. What you give, you get. If you are thinking "I can't make money doing this" or "I'm not doing the right thing," you will be compensated for your thoughts. You will not make money. You will not execute your tasks with the level of excellence and commitment which will bring you ample returns.

When you are on purpose, when you are doing exactly what you were born to do, you must be compensated justly! When you give what you have—whether that is a musical or mechanical talent; an ability to see, hear, or speak; the patience to sit; or the strength to lift—you will get all that you need and desire to enable you to continue to give and grow. This does not mean you will not be challenged. Nor does it mean you will not have your valley experiences. What it does mean is that your outlook, your perceptions, and your reactions to the things around you will be different. You will not be so easily knocked down or thrown off course. When you are on purpose, you understand your mission. When you have a mission, you are focused on what you are doing. When you have focus, that vision is like a razor, cutting through difficulties, paving a path for you to follow.

Purpose is much broader than goals. When we set goals, we set a prescribed way of doing a thing, within a specific frame of time and activities. Unfortunately, goals are usually limited to our perceptions and judgments. We set goals based on what we know, what we can see, what we fear, and what we think may or may not happen. Very often, when we set goals, we do so in response to our perceived limitations and those of the world. Purpose is different. When we are on purpose, we allow spirit to guide us and provide for us. Our concern is not with the world, what we see or what we know. When we are on purpose, we may set levels of achievement, but we are not fixed to a prescribed way. We are open to our inner guidance. Our desired outcome is not tied to money, fame, or recognition. We are doing what we do because it is a part of us we must give.

Since life is set up to teach us lessons, to provide us with the opportunity to learn and embrace spiritual virtues and to broaden our sense of self, our purpose is usually hidden beneath a barrage of challenging experiences. The most difficult experiences in your life are designed to teach you the most valuable lessons. Ninety-nine-point-nine percent of the time, those lessons are attached to your purpose. Take for example Ray Charles. His purpose is to give music, to play the piano. Rest assured, the process of learning how to play was much more difficult for him than for a person with vision. Yet from somewhere in his soul, he found the strength to work at it and learn. He not only had to play the piano, he had to write music. He not only had to write the music, he had to communicate it to sighted people. Ray was on purpose. The clue was that he had a singing voice. You will always have a natural propensity to do your purpose. The spirit of life provides you with exactly what you need. Your job in life is to trust yourself to do what you love. Develop enough faith in yourself and the process of life to provide you with what you need. Above all else, the lesson we come into the Valley of Purpose and Intent to learn is commitment. Commitment is the stuff that dreams are made of.

The Lesson

In addition to being angry and wanting to escape, Raylene had no commitment. She was not committed to her brothers, her son, or herself. She was committed to John, and when he betrayed her, she lost her sense of commitment. She was not committed to finding a way out of the pain she had experienced in life. Raylene's commitment was to escape. She wanted to escape the pain and disappointment of her life. She did so by blaming others, using alcohol and drugs, and living in denial. Throughout it all, her purpose continued to come up. Go to school. She loved children and numbers. She wanted to be a math teacher. She never forgot the dream. Unfortunately, she was not committed enough to pursue it. She had the right formula—escape. She simply applied it in the wrong way.

When I was growing up, I was constantly told I was stupid and I talked too much. My family was completely unaware that they were destroying my commitment to my purpose. My brother told me I was stupid. My caretakers frequently asked me how I could be so stupid. It seemed as if everyone took the opportunity to tell me how stupid I looked, sounded, or behaved. When I was not being told how stupid I was, I was being told to shut up because I talked too much. I grew up believing I could not think my way out of a paper bag and that if I could think, I better not talk about it.

Your purpose is going to be challenged. Some of the wealthiest people in the world grew up in abject poverty. Some of the most loving people in the world were raised in abusive situations. Some of the most talented, gifted musicians, artists, teachers, and doctors grew up in situations which, had they succumbed to them, would have taken them off purpose. You must earn what you have. Life does not give you anything. You must give in order to get. You must stand up to the very thing that challenges you, look it in the face, get clear about your intention, order your thoughts and your life, and proceed without fear or hesitation. Life is not unfair. Along the way, you will always find bits of information and support to guide you to purpose. People, sometimes strangers, will support you in doing the very thing you have been told not to do. At seemingly inopportune, inconvenient moments, you will be urged or supported to get on purpose. When you have a clear intent and commitment, you will find your way.

Raylene had many opportunities along the way to get on purpose. When she worked for the city and was mandated to get a high school diploma, the ease with which she took the test was a sign. Her A.A. mentor encouraged her. The undying love for numbers and children was another clue. Raylene, like many of us, was stuck in her past pains and hurt. Her intent was to survive, not flourish. At the core was the issue of belief and thoughts. Raylene did not believe she could flourish. Her thoughts were confined to her negative experiences, which produced hate, fear, and a lack of trust. In my own life, my family's affirmations of my stupidity and loquaciousness were counteracted by the praises of my teachers and friends who constantly told me how smart I was. Did I listen? Of course not! Human nature is to cling to the not so good and ignore the good. I was unconsciously eager to accept what others said was not good about me and ignored the support and encouragement I received.

If we go out to a party, we may find everything in perfect order. The host and hostess are gracious, well dressed, and accommodating. The food is beautifully presented, tastefully prepared. The music is jamming. The guests are friendly, a real party crowd. We enjoy ourselves, get home at a reasonable hour, still humming and patting our feet. The next day when a friend asks, "How was the party?," our response is, "Everything was nice, but the beans were salty!" We find the one thing that was out of sync and dwell on that rather than reinforcing all the good. The issue of picking the scabs comes up when we are examining ourselves or our lives. We get stuck on those things which bring us pain and discomfort while ignoring the support and help we receive from any number of sources.

How do we know Raylene is in the Valley of Purpose and not that of O.P.P., Light, or any of the others? She had no commitment. Raylene was not committed to anyone or anything. She took whatever came along rather than using her time, energy, and talent to create what she wanted or needed. The big clue was that she had a talent, a gift, which continued to surface. She did not make the necessary effort to put that gift to work for herself, but she never lost it. We cannot look at the situations and experiences which took Raylene off track. We must look at her response to them. In spite of all of the hardships she experienced, the one thing she loved, the thing she was good at, was the thing she resisted the most. Nothing she experienced made her any less fond of children or dissipated her talent to work with numbers. In addition, she openly resisted all opportunities to go to college. She bought into her negative experiences by remaining angry about them and refusing to confront them. Finally, at key points in her life experience, Raylene was being encouraged to pursue her purpose.

"You got to have a dream/If you don't have a dream/How you gonna have a dream come true?" That song from *South Pacific* is the purpose theme song. All people need a dream, something they can look forward to, something they live to see materialize. When we dream, we transcend all external experiences and go right to the end, the experience we desire. When that experience is tied to the thing we are good at or the thing we love to do, we set up an energy to which the universe must respond. When we can take small steps toward the dream, when we keep a commitment to manifesting the dream in our hearts and minds, we will find just the right opportunities at just the right time to push us forward.

When you have a dream and realize that dream is your purpose, your place in life will open up for you! The little girl in you becomes excited. The virgin in your consciousness, innocent and trusting, wants to explore the available opportunities. The mother in your soul will order your life, protect you, and support you with the right thoughts and emotions. The crone, the wisewoman, will at every turn tell you exactly what to do. Your job is to listen. No matter what others are doing, no matter how they are doing it, no one can do what you were born to do the way you were born to do it. Your purpose is you. If you get stuck in drama, trauma, pain, and hate, you close the door of possibility to purpose. If you buy into the negative affirmations and experiences of your home or the world, you lower your sense of self to the breaking point. Once it breaks, you may believe you are not worthy of doing better or being better. Your purpose does not care what you look like, how you grew up, what you have and do not have. Your purpose is waiting for you to bring it to life, much in the same manner it brought you to life.

The Way Out

Do not make the mistake of believing that everything in your world will be put on hold while you search for your purpose. Chances are, your life will continue to revolve at its whirlwind pace. You must be able to recognize your own growing discontent, inharmonious relationships, and superficial distractions. It will be up to you to decide to detach, pull back. Identify and release all nonessential activities and commitments. Cease all nonmeaningful, unnecessary conversations. Execute your required duties at home or at work while making time for periods of silence when you can ask yourself and answer for yourself, "What is my purpose? What is my dream?"

When you are in pursuit of purpose, the Valley of Light is a good place to go. Spend time alone. Pay attention to what you are feeling. Investigate your thoughts. Examine your activities. Do not judge, condemn, or criticize anything you are doing or have done. Postpone making decisions and pronouncements until you are clear and peaceful within. Consciously, patiently, unwind yourself from the day-to-day affairs of the world. Avoid the temptation to read newspapers, listen to the radio, or watch television. From those sources you will hear how bad things are, how terrible it is, which is sure to reinforce any negative thoughts or emotions you may be having. What is going on in the world is not your truth! Your truth is within you. Your purpose is couched in your truth.

When you are searching for purpose, music always helps. Find some slow-paced, melodic music to suit your mood. If you feel stuck, you may want to dance. Play something with drums. If you are not sure what you feel, play some soul-stirring jazz. If there is a particular quality you want to invoke, try gospels or spiritual music. Music, dancing, and singing raise energy vibrations, internally and externally. Do not think of purpose or finding it as work. Finding your purpose is a process of extrapolating from the inside to the outside what it is you have come to life to do. That must not be seen as a task or a chore. It can be an exciting, fun-filled journey. If you reduce the process to a tedious, desperate chore, you will discourage yourself and opt out for what you are already doing.

Many of us will think the steps toward finding purpose are impossible if we have children, mates, and other family members around. Know that they are not. Children are your greatest allies and support. Each day, make a sincere effort to tenderly embrace and adore the children around you. That will help to nurture the child in you. Say to your children the things you need or wish to have said to you. Spend five quality minutes with them and tenderly ask them to help you. Tell them you are trying to figure something out and you need to be alone. Ask them to play quietly, stay in their room, or find something to do. When you speak to the children, look at them, look directly into their eyes. Talk to their spirit, their soul, not their mind. Elicit a promise from them to help you and hold them to their promise. When they forget, get noisy, or come banging on the door, remind them of what they promised to do.

Toddlers are going to challenge you. They will keep coming back. Simply repeat your need for space and their promise to be still. Repetition is the mother of skill. If you repeat the process often enough, you and they will master it. Male children are the best support you can have. Hug the little male children. Hold them in your arms, nestle them close to your breast, stroke their heads and rock them. They are children, but they are still representations of male energy. Their energy will help to balance your energy. Nurturing the male energy will help bring your feminine energy into focus.

When possible, give the older children charge over the younger ones. Give them an assignment like folding the linen, shining the silverware, organizing the pots, picking lint balls—anything to keep their little minds occupied for ten or fifteen minutes at a time. That is all you will need at regular intervals to get still and get in touch with yourself. Husbands, boyfriends, live-in mates, and family are equally easy to handle. They may become frightened or concerned by your need for silence and withdrawal. Tenderness is the key. Do not tell them you do not feel good or that you have a problem. Their response will be to want to help you. They will feel guilty. They may want to encourage you to dismiss the situation. Tell the truth: it will set you free. *I need some space alone.* If you say "time alone," they will want to know how much time. Let them know that space is personal and personally defined. Reassure them that absolutely nothing is wrong. Elicit their support in keeping the children quiet, occupied, or otherwise engaged. Perhaps you can get your mate to cook or do the housework while you take a walk or just sit.

Laundry is a great way to get them out of the house or yourself out of the house. People regard the laundry as an unpleasant task; however, have you ever noticed how quiet the Laundromat is? People rarely talk to one another. Everyone is focused on getting the clothes done and getting out. The Laundromat, like the laundry room, is an excellent place to find peace and solitude.

One advantage is that no one will question why you are spending so much time with the laundry. If you withdraw, you are bound to be grilled with questions like, "What's wrong with you?"

When you are searching for purpose, trying to detach, the telephone will be your greatest challenge. Should you answer it? Should you use it? Will the machine hold all your messages as you withdraw and seek refuge within? If it rings, you may become annoyed. If it does not ring, you may wonder why. It may be worthwhile to unplug it and the answering machine. If you only unplug the telephone, you will be tempted to answer certain people when they call. If both are disconnected, you will get the news when you get it. Partial detachment is an effort to maintain control. You must detach completely for intervals of time in order to hear and feel what is going on within.

How long? How long does it take to detach? How long does it take to find purpose? It takes as long as it takes. For some, clarity comes right away. Others need hours, days, weeks, or years. Whatever you need will be determined by your desire, intent, and willingness to know what it is you have come to do and be. Trust yourself to know and you will know. Allow yourself to get still, to sift through and sort out the events and activities of your life. Ask yourself the hard-core questions: What do I want to do? What do I like to do? What must I do to be in service to spirit? The goal here is not to drop out of sight or life. It is to become still, to listen and reflect in order to gain clarity and direction. You can do this ritually every day or once a week. You can do it consciously as you move through your day. Or, as suggested here, when the events of your life collide and/or crash, leaving you feeling lost or hopeless, you can make a concentrated effort to pull back. Take your time. You cannot lose your purpose; it is waiting for you to seek and find.

There is another group of purpose seekers we must recognize. This is the group of people who already know their purpose— they know exactly what they have come to do in life and they are willing to do it. Some may even be working at their purpose. The issue for them is how to make it pay off. How can you live your purpose and still enjoy a good life? This is a particularly pressing issue for artistic and creative people. The dancers, artists, writers, etc., whose skills and talents are not considered among the important priorities in a capitalist society. These are the people who spend year upon year training and trying to earn a living at what they do. They are on purpose but they are starving to death.

The key is commitment. Many people treat their purpose as a hobby and their job as a way of life. Only when your purpose becomes the priority will it treat you like you treat it, royally. You must be committed to your purpose even when it does not pay well. Each day, you must commit a certain amount of time to your purpose, your talent. You must have a dream. Be able to see how what you do can be, will be, of value to the world. That dream should not hinge on making money. It should hinge on your love of what you do and your willingness to give of yourself doing it, not on whether or not you get paid. Everyone may not have the opportunity to be the lead dancer in the Dance Theatre of Harlem, or a drummer on "The Tonight Show." What each and every one of us does have is the opportunity to spend some part of every day giving of ourselves to the thing we love.

I have many friends who are musicians. Quite often they become frustrated and discouraged in their music making: they don't have a record deal, they don't have the money to go into the studio. I ask them, Is your intent to go into the studio or is your intent to make music? Most of them want to make music in the studio so they can make money. Wrong! Just make the music. Live your life committed to making music. Play where you can for whoever you can, in the right way, the divine way; when it is time for you to go into the studio to make a recording, you will go. Nothing can stop your purpose. Maybe it is not your purpose to be a recording artist. Your purpose may be to teach music or simply to play it to discipline yourself. Perhaps your love of music will open your heart to the divine love of the universe. Still, if the desire is in your heart to record, you will record. You play the music and let the universe take care of the details.

Purpose is about being and giving, not doing and having. If you are a musician, be a musician. You may work in the post office, but be a musician. Do everything in your power to perfect your skill while you are supporting yourself. If you are a nurse, be a nurse. Be health-conscious, health-minded, live every single day of your life as if you are a health-care professional or practitioner. It does not matter whether or not you have your degree. Do not be concerned if you work as a secretary during the day while going to nursing school at night. Be a nurse right where you are at all times. When you live your purpose, you develop commitment to it. You begin to embody all that which encompasses what your purpose requires. Get clear about exactly what your purpose is, because you can get confused. When people ask me, "Are you a writer?," I say, "No, I am a teacher." My purpose in life is to teach through my speaking and writing ability. I happen to be a teacher who has the ability to write. I write. I am not a writer. I am very clear about the fact that I am a teacher on a mission of healing. It may manifest in various ways at various times, but I am on purpose.

It may be necessary for you to expand your definition of what you now do in order to get clarity on your purpose. When we think of teachers, we think only of schools and classrooms. Teachers are also facilitators, trainers, housewives, all sorts of people in all sorts of environments. Doctors are not only those people who have medical degrees. Doctors bring healing to the mind, body, and spirit. A counselor is a doctor of sorts. A beautician is a doctor of another kind. Barmaids are doctors. Each of these people in his or her own environment brings forth some sort of healing. Labels restrict us. Definitions which we have created for ourselves keep us in bondage to O.P.P. and the limitations of others. When you expand your view of yourself, you will undoubtedly know the concept of your purpose. In his book *You Can Have It All,* Arnold Patent reveals the perfect formula for finding purpose and making it pay off. You can do what you love, what you are good at, while providing a needed service to the world, the world community, and the world of your local community, and at the same time, realize personal fulfillment and material satisfaction. The keys are intent, trust, faith, clarity, and commitment—all of the lessons the Valley of Purpose and Intent is designed to teach.

MEDITATION WITH THE MOTHER

*Ahhh. Satan was happy with these people. Hate is
so helpful in things he likes to do!*
   —J. CALIFORNIA COOPER, *IN SEARCH OF SATISFACTION*

*Where is the Mother when the daughters are in pain? She is there,
waiting for them to surrender. Where is the Mother when the
daughters spill their blood, their life force, on unworthy flights of
fancy? She is there, waiting for them to surrender. Where is the
Mother when the daughters cry, burdened and broken down from
the weight of this life? There she is. She is waiting for them to surrender.*

*Where is the Mother when the daughters want to surrender but
cannot, do not, in fear that no one will be there to save them? She
is there, waiting, praying, that they will surrender. For when they
do, she will not only catch them, save them, heal them, she will
open their minds to their true salvation—the undying salvation of
a mother's love, which is the only thing that can save them from
themselves.*

The Valley of Non- resistance 9

*H*E WAS SIX-FOOT-TWO AND WEIGHED 223 POUNDS. I WAS FIVE-FOOT-FIVE AND WEIGHED 137 POUNDS. The hallway was nine feet long and five feet wide. It was a long, narrow hallway. I was on the bottom. He was on the top. His hands were around my throat. He was choking me—to death, I thought. With every fiber of my being I fought him. Clutching at his hands. Scratching at his eyes. Twisting my body, trying to knee him in the groin. It was not working. He was still calling me a bitch. Still choking me.

This was getting serious. My thoughts were getting fuzzy. I could feel the strength waning from my legs and arms. Every few minutes, he would let me go just long enough—long enough to get enough oxygen, to gain enough strength to wiggle, wrestle, and fight some more. It dawned on me: "He likes it. He likes to see me squirming and fighting." I really didn't believe he wanted to kill me. Hell, he wasn't even as mad this time as he was the time he hit me in the head with the bed slat. He just liked to fight and watch me fight back as he beat me, slapped me, or like now, choked me. Well, he wasn't going to get his rocks off on me to-day! In the midst of the next fuzzy-head spell, I stopped. I let my hands fall limp at my side, my legs slide to the floor. I just stopped fighting him. I focused my eyes squarely on his eyes

248

then on his twisted, writhing mouth, and I just stared. With both hands firmly around my burning neck, he gave one last push, as if to expel the air out of my body. And then, he got up.

I once read in a magazine article that when a person gets electrocuted, nine times out of ten it is not the electricity that kills them, but their resistance. When the voltage of a kitchen light passes through the human body, it is not powerful or dangerous enough to kill you. But when the person feels that shock, immediately the body goes into fear. It stiffens with the impulse to pull away. Unfortunately, the brain works faster than the body can interpret. Rather than pull, the body's impulse is to push against the very source that created the shock. In fear and the attempt to get away, you give power to the thing. I guess it would take pretty quick thinking to relax and let the current flow through your body, which according to the article, would not kill you. Human beings, however, are programmed to resist that which they fear, that which they cannot control. In the end, fear and resistance knock you flat on your behind.

A Valley Experience

Sharon is a beautiful sister. She has the body of life and the face to match. She is, however, the ugly duckling in her family. She grew up in a family where there was little support, even less encouragement, and many, many secrets. Sharon learned early that she was to do what was expected of her and make as little trouble as possible. Sharon's father, a wealthy businessman, was an alcoholic who openly kept a mistress. Her mother, the perfect homemaker, was often brutally beaten by her father. Sharon and her sisters grew up in a beautiful home, wore expensive clothing, went to private school, and lived in total terror.

Sharon was blessed and cursed to be the rebel. She was always the first to jump to her mother's defense, for which her father would beat her and her mother would scold her. She persistently questioned the inconsistencies she lived at home: the immaculate house, fraught on the inside with violence, provided a loving-family image even though its inhabitants rarely spoke to one another. At age thirteen, Sharon was labeled disturbed and sent to therapy. When she told her therapist how she felt about her mother and her father's mistress, therapy ended and she spent two weeks alone in her room on punishment. When she was eighteen, Sharon was sent away to an Ivy League college. She was relieved to be away from home.

Sharon immediately joined every militant group on campus. She spent most of her time in rallies and meetings. Her grades were deplorable in every class except art. Sharon loved art, but she knew, as her mother had told her, "You cannot make a living drawing pictures." At the end of her sophomore year, her parents called her on the carpet and refused to continue paying tuition for her to fail. Sharon didn't care. She'd come home and work. Fine, her parents told her. You'll work and you'll pay rent. They had to be crazy! She would not pay rent to them. They were supposed to take care of her. She refused. They refused. Sharon moved in with her boyfriend, Richard, who lived in his mother's basement.

Several months of playing house with Richard rendered Sharon very pregnant. They decided to get married. Both sets of parents were skeptical, but they helped out by splitting the bill for the apartment and furniture. Sharon had the baby and went to work for a local art museum. Richard stayed home with the baby to try to figure out what he wanted to do with his life. When he hadn't figured it out after two years, Sharon took the baby and left.

All the parents were in an uproar. Where will you go? What will you do? We'll keep the baby. Sharon would hear or have none of it. She found a small apartment and kept working. She would show them what she was capable of. Shortly after her separation, Sharon was offered a job out of state. It paid a great deal more money than she was making and had some pretty nice perks. When Sharon told her parents and her husband, they all had the same response: "You can't go and take the baby away from us." Sharon left within ten days of receiving the offer.

The job was great. She found a lovely studio apartment. Her salary adequately covered her expenses and all seemed to be going her way for the first time in a long time. Unfortunately, Sharon could not enjoy her newfound freedom and sense of self. She was still very angry at her parents and very lonely. Toward the end of the first year in her new home, Sharon met a man—a married man who seemed to be madly in love with her. He took her and her son on wonderful trips. He was very generous and bought her nice things, including a car. Sharon could talk to him and he would listen, because he liked the things she liked. There were times when Sharon was uncomfortable about being in a relationship with a married man, but she learned to overcome those moments. Her new beau encouraged her to pursue her art, even to return to school. He said he would help pay for it. Things were looking pretty good, until Sharon met the man's wife.

Sharon arrived home from work one evening to find a woman and a dog seated on her front steps. As she approached them, the woman called her name. She introduced herself as the man's wife. Sharon almost fainted. The woman looked to be about thirty years older than her beau and she was blind. She explained to Sharon that the man had married her for her money. He had made a deal with her father to marry her, and have children with her, in return for the inheritance of her father's business. He had always kept a mistress, which the wife said she didn't mind as long as things didn't get too serious. Things between him and Sharon were getting to the point where he was talking about divorce. Sharon needed to know that if he divorced her, he would be without a dime and a few other vital parts of his anatomy. It would be best for Sharon to leave town quietly, before she too lost a few parts of her anatomy. Sharon tried to reach her beau and could not. She left town two weeks after the visit. She ended up back home, paying rent.

Things had really disintegrated between her parents. They hardly spoke, partly because her father rarely came home. With all of the children gone, he stayed out most of the time. After thirty-two years of marriage, Sharon's father sent her mother by mail a notice of intent to file for divorce. Sharon's mother fell completely to pieces, although it wasn't as if she hadn't known it would happen sooner or later. During the divorce, Sharon was glad to be home, to be a source of support for her mother. Her father had entered A.A. and stopped drinking. His business was doing great. He soon married his longtime mistress and bought a home in a very exclusive part of town.

Sharon stayed home with her mom for a year. For the first time in her life, Sharon felt a sense of closeness with her mother. They laughed and talked together. At last she felt that her mother loved and respected her. Things were fine until Mom began to criticize her every move. Why did she insist on chasing that art crap? Why did Sharon refuse to get a real job? Why didn't she go back to Richard? Why did she keep cutting her hair off? Eventually, Sharon left home again, divorced Richard, took another low paying job and moved into another small studio with her son. She tried to figure out what to do. Before she could get it clear, she met Victor. Victor worked with her, respected her, seemed to have his stuff together, and had the body of life! Victor stated early on his desire to marry Sharon and make a home for her son. Sharon agreed that would be best. They bought a house. They got married. They had two children in two years and Victor lost his mind.

They had always had volatile arguments. Victor was a real man and he wanted a real woman. Sharon was to cook and clean and serve at his every beck and call. He was to drink, snort cocaine, and have as many women as he wanted. If Sharon did not like it, he would smack her in the face or punch her in the mouth, or throw her down the stairs. Things got worse when he began to throw the children around. Sharon was frantic. She didn't know what to do. She couldn't go home, but she had to get away. The day Victor broke her son's arm, she knew she had to figure it out.

Sharon sent her oldest son to live with her father. She took the two smaller children with her, back into a studio apartment. For two years Sharon struggled to make ends meet, only to eventually be evicted. She found another apartment. One year later, she was evicted again. She had been seeing a man for a short while. He offered to put her in an apartment. She accepted. He moved in. He beat her. She moved out. She got another apartment. She got evicted again.

Sharon's family watched her critically, hopelessly and help-lessly shaking their heads. They all knew her problem. Her parents and siblings never missed an opportunity to tell her what was wrong with her. She was irresponsible. She was inconsiderate. She was immature. She was an embarrassment to the entire family, all of whom were financially and emotionally secure. Something, they said, was wrong with Sharon. None of it was new. She had heard it all growing up. It just had a different sting to it now. They reminded her of all the mistakes she had made, like leaving Richard who had become a successful attorney. He was prospering and stable. He had also been watching, and at her lowest ebb, decided to sue Sharon for custody of their son. It sent shock waves through her body.

Sharon was devastated. She felt totally alone and vulnerable. She felt that everyone was picking on her and against her. She was defensive and wounded. With the help of a few friends, Sharon found the money to defend herself in the custody battle and rent a new apartment. She was promoted on her job. She set up a lovely home environment for her children. Her oldest son was now fifteen. He did not want to come home to live with her. She was poor. She could handle her family coming down on her, but not her son. She begged and pleaded with him and finally put her foot down. He came home and the wolves really came after Sharon.

Her mother told her she was unfit and could not handle it. Her father told her she was an ingrate who had broken his heart. Her first husband vowed to drag her through every court in the system. Her most recent husband refused to pay child support and took every opportunity to stalk and threaten her. Sharon had a really hard time at work. She was continuously in a controversy, argument, or dispute with management and co-workers. She was deeply in debt and her salary barely covered expenses. She felt tired. She looked old. She could not afford a new dress or a dinner out. She had not been sexually active in two years. This was a bit much for a girl to handle.

Sharon had just about reached her wits' end when she got the telephone call. A prestigious art gallery in another state had heard about her and wanted to hire her. Would she be interested? She borrowed some money and bought a new outfit. She went to two interviews before they offered to double her current salary. Sharon knew that meant leaving her hometown again. She knew it meant uprooting her children again. She knew it meant being alone, more alone than she was now. She turned them down. A few weeks later, they called her back. They would give her two and a half times more than she was making now. She said no thank you.

Sharon confided in a friend about her situation. The friend told her this was an opportunity for a new start and that she should not let fear control her. Sure, it meant change, but change is always good. How would she get to and from work? Commute until the end of the school year and then move. Who would take care of the children while she was away? With the kind of money she'd be making, she could hire someone. Where would she live in a new city? Rent a room until you find a house. What would her parents say? Don't tell them until you're gone. Sharon was still wavering when the third call came. The new employer offered to pay her at the top of the line for the first six months. After her review they would shift her to another line where there would be annual increases of fifteen percent. Her starting salary would be four times more than she was now earning. Sharon hung up and started packing.

The baby-sitter came. A reliable vehicle came so that she could commute. Friends rallied around her. The family was skeptical but quiet. Sharon started the new job. It was tough the first couple of weeks, but she got the hang of it. The commute was rough, but the money was great. Then came the new boyfriend. He had no job, no money, but he was great with the children and great to Sharon. He was gentle, kind, and extremely supportive. He had the baggage of an ex-wife, several do-nothing adult children, and a rip-roaring case of confusion, but he was a nice guy.

They got rid of the baby-sitter because they suspected she was stealing. He moved in and became a househusband. Sharon became the sole support of the family. One of his sons and a grandchild came to live with them. They moved into a bigger house, closer to Sharon's job. Six months into the relationship, there were seven people living in the house, Sharon was the only one working, and she was five months pregnant.

One bright, sunny morning, Sharon sat down and took an inventory of her life. She immediately came to the conclusion that she was not a happy camper. There was so much going on in her life and she couldn't figure out how it had happened. Things seemed to be fine on the outside. Things were going smoothly, but she had a gnawing feeling in the pit of her stomach that something was about to blow up in her face. Of course it did. Her new beau had not been faithful. He could not be faithful because he was in love with another woman. He loved Sharon, but this other thing was something else. He did not want to leave, but would Sharon please help him work through this? Sharon looked at him in total disbelief. She knew what he was saying to her, but she could not believe it. The man she had been supporting financially, a man who had lied to her, who had betrayed her, now wanted her to be his therapist. She was incensed, but she was also pregnant. She was afraid of being left with four children to raise alone. Against her better judgment, almost against her will, she promised her weeping lover she would not leave him. They would work it out. In her sacrifice of her own needs to heal her wayward lover, Sharon took the final plunge into the Valley of Nonresistance.

The Law of Nonresistance

When something is in our way, stands in opposition to what we want, what we think, or what we are doing, the natural inclination is to fight it. To use all of our mental and physical power to remove the thing. To do away with it. We resist that which opposes us. We resist to the point of exhaustion, which inevitably allows the thing to overtake us. It is a funny thing about resistance. When we see those food commercials on television, or sale circulars promising to give us everything under the sun for half price, we do not resist. We take our pennies, dollars, and credit cards right down to the nearest store, spending uncontrollably because no one can resist another piece of pie, chocolate, fried chicken, a good sale. Yet when it comes to the bigger issues in life, making hard decisions, definitive moves which would propel us into a new state of consciousness, we resist.

Resistance causes friction. Friction causes irritation. Friction in the form of opposition and resistance wears down the life force of the mind, the body, and eventually, the spirit. When you go through life fighting opposition, resisting the things and people who oppose you, you will eventually lose sight of the real objective of life: to live in peace, harmony, and freedom. The Law of Nonresistance states:

> *The wise ones will not fight the obstacles, but bless them and go on. As they go on with faith and assurance, they grow stronger. Their course becomes more direct, their understanding is of greater depth than the mighty ocean, their ultimate objective is not far from them.*

In other words, as a dear friend of mine would say, "I don't know what you are doing! I know what I am doing and I am doing it!" We do not need to stop what we are doing because of anything anyone else is doing. Obstacles, challenges, differing views and opinions are an active part of life. When we resist and fight against difference, we allow ourselves to be taken off course, stopped in our tracks, and beaten down.

The need to be right and in control is the steady diet of resistance. When we meet up with people or situations which threaten what we believe or want, immediately we become resistant. We label them, we fight them, we dilute our energy. "Bless them that curse you; do good to them that hate you; pray for them that despitefully use you," is the way the Bible states the law of nonresistance. When we hate, rebel against, wish ill toward people, we set into motion the energy of resistance. When we can bless a thing, look for and affirm the good in it, it alters our perception and declaws the cat we believe is out to scratch us. When you pray for or wish good unto the very thing that threatens to harm you, you increase your own vibration. You call forth the good in yourself. You take the emphasis off of what might happen and generate the power in yourself to make what you want to happen, happen. What you give, you get. That is the law. When you send out good, you must receive good.

FLOW WITH THE FLOW!

Throughout life, we develop ideas of how others should be, how they should behave, and how they should treat us. When things are not as we think they should be, we resist. These "shoulds" are judgments by which we measure our experiences. Parents should be loving to their children. Parents should behave honorably in front of their children. Parents should be nurturing towards their children. Judgments have nothing to do with the truth. Judgments are based on facts which can be altered. Truth is constant.

The truth is, some parents do not know how to love and nurture, often because they were not nurtured or shown love. The truth is, parents have lessons to learn and issues to work through. Before they were our parents, they were people living in situations and conditions they resisted and often rebelled against. The truth is, different people have different ideas of what love "looks" like. My husband's idea of love was me doing whatever he said. When I resisted, he loved me enough to smack me around, whip me into shape. One person's idea being in conflict with another person's idea does not make either a "bad" person. Remember, we do what we do based on who we are, what we have experienced, and the information we have at the time. It is not right. It is not wrong. It simply is!

It may not seem fair, but children do get caught in the middle of adult confusion. As children, we are helpless and defenseless: expecting the best, but accepting whatever is offered. The best the child can do is go with the flow. The flow within the home, the conditions in which we grow up, create the experiences we need to learn our lessons. As adults, we can make alterations by discarding and amending the information, the facts, we have received. This does not mean we resist by being angry, frightened, or rebellious. It means we must detach from the emotion of a situation, discern the truth of it, integrate what we can use, and discard the rest. Parents are meant to be role models. However, they can only model what they know. As children, it is not our job to judge. If and when we do, we become the sacrificial lambs of the wounds of our parents by resisting and rebelling against what they have done.

By resisting her parents' instructions, Sharon sacrificed herself to her parents' wounded behavior. Her fear of becoming like her mother and her anger toward her father kept her in bondage to their issues. It was her thoughts which drew her into toxic and abusive relationships. Her fear which attracted her to unfaithful men. Her anger which made it difficult for her to provide a loving, stable home for her own children. Sharon's resistance and anger led her to make unproductive choices and kept her embroiled in controversy with those around her. It was her resistance to *other people's stuff* which she eventually adopted as her own. It was her own thoughts, which she obeyed in deed, that drove her to re-create in her own life the same experiences she had lived as a child.

At last report, Sharon did not know if she was ready to end her relationship with the man who loved another woman. She felt the man had some very redeeming qualities and there were certain conveniences she was not ready to give up. She decided to wait until after the baby was born and then try to figure out what to do. In some ways, Sharon had given up. She was tired of fighting, tired of being hurt, tired of being alone. She did what so many of us do when we do not know the law: she gave in. The Law of Nonresistance does not teach us to cave in, give in, or give up. The experiences of this valley are designed to teach us the ultimate act of nonresistance, surrender, which has a completely different meaning and outcome.

The Value of Surrender

I always want to know what is going to happen. Many of the most difficult decisions I face are not difficult at all. I make them difficult when my mind begins to race, trying to explore every possible option, every feasible outcome, in search of the one which will bring me the greatest amount of pleasure—or the least amount of pain. In the process of trying to make a decision, I drive myself crazy, resisting the things I do not want, trying to control what I do want. At some point, I become so stressed out, so frustrated, I have no choice but to surrender. I do not give up—I give the situation to the Father/Mother God and trust that the best will happen.

I lived in New York for the first thirty-three years of my life. I lived in apartment buildings in some of the best and worst neighborhoods Brooklyn has to offer. When I left New York to move to Philadelphia, I promised myself and my children we would live in a house. I started my search with absolutely no idea of what I wanted—I simply wanted a house. The first few weeks of my search were fruitless. The houses I wanted I could not afford. The houses I could afford were like apartments without the surrounding doors. I ran up and down the New Jersey Turnpike like a madwoman, determined to find a house. I was just about to give up when a friend told me to surrender.

I was ranting and raving about homeowners not wanting children and pets. I suspected I had been refused most of the nice places because I was Black. I did not know Philadelphia, so I did not know where I should be looking. I was furiously determined that I would give my children something my parents never gave me: a home, with a front door that had a mail slot. My friend asked me if I had a picture in my mind of what the house would look like. I had kind of an idea. She asked me how many rooms I wanted. I wanted whatever was available. She then told me to sit down and create a picture in my mind of exactly what I wanted. The size of the house, the number of rooms, the color of my kitchen—everything down to the most intimate detail had to be clear in my mind. She told me to look through magazines, books, anything that would give me a clearer picture of my divine, ideal home. Once I had that done, I was to thank God for it and stop looking.

I was fine with everything except the "stop looking" part. How was I supposed to find a house if I didn't look for it? She told me to surrender it to God. To trust God to bring into manifestation the very thing I wanted and needed. She explained that surrender does not mean we give up. It means we give over to the perfecting presence of God in our lives. This was new to me, but my 1977 Fiat could not take another trip down the road to Philly. I did just as she told me.

Skeptically, I worked with the concept for about a week. It was a

Tuesday night when the picture of the house became vividly clear. As instructed, I surrendered my house to God. At 9:45 Wednesday morning, I got a call from the Public Defender's office in Philadelphia. They wanted to offer me a position. Could I come back to Philadelphia to meet the head of the office? I would be there Friday morning. At 7:30 Wednesday night, I told God I would not take the job unless I had a house for myself and my children. I tempered it by saying, "Please, God. If you help me out this time, I will never ask you for anything else. And this time, I really mean it." At 7:15 Thursday morning, I got a second telephone call from Philadelphia.

"Hello, you don't know me, but I am a friend of Sandy's. She says you want to move to Philadelphia. I have a house for you if you are interested."

I dropped the telephone.

When I walked in the door of the house, I fought to hold back the tears. Everything in the house was exactly as I had seen it in my mind. The staircase leading upstairs was on the same side of the room as I had seen it. The kitchen had a window in the exact same place as I had seen it. The most humbling fact was, the rent was a hundred dollars less than the nicest house I had seen, which I had been refused. When you surrender, you allow the creative force of the universe to work in its own way, to bring to you exactly what you need. It is easy and effortless—a process you cannot see, probably would never even think of, and that usually reaps better results than what you had planned.

Surrender your thoughts, your anger, your fear, your resistance to not knowing, not being in control. Do not tell yourself you do not feel what you feel. Simply surrender it to your God self asking that your thoughts and emotions be harmonized, brought into alignment with your highest and greatest good. From that point on, do not think about the situation, unless you can see it in your mind exactly as you want it to be. If the thought should pop into your mind, if you find yourself going into fear or panic about the situation, breathe and affirm, "I surrender this very thought to the spirit of God in me. I trust God to perfect this situation right here and right now. Thank you, God!" Give your concerns to the greatest power there is, the almighty, all-knowing power of good.

Black women expect too little for themselves. We ask for only what we need today, the transitory need of the moment. We do not realize there are far greater possibilities, things which we cannot see or imagine waiting for us. We get stuck in anger, lack, fear, and limitation. We are overcome with trying not to do what has been done and trying to get away from what is being done. As human beings, we cannot conceive the goodness of God. We hold on to the past, we fight against the now. In doing so, in resisting, we hold ourselves back. Far too many Black women mouth a belief in God. We sing beautiful songs, offer beautiful prayers. Yet our belief in wrong, in "shoulds," in evil and evildoers, rises to the top in the final hour. We go back to our controlling behavior, resisting our opposition and blocking God's way. Surrender is the key.

It is hard to admit that we do not know everything. We cannot see five miles down the block, around the corner, and under the bush. We want to, but we cannot. Because we cannot, we respond or react to everything that stands between us and the corner, the corner and the bush. We are resisting the truth—the truth that we do not know. We do not know what will happen, how it will happen, and in some cases, if it will happen. Because we do not know, we perceive and judge, which takes us into fear, anger, guilt, shame—the entire gamut of negative emotions which create resistance. If you resist a thing, it will persist. The harder you resist, the greater will be the persistence of the thing which opposes you. When you surrender, you allow whatever it is to exist in its own way, having its own space, while you pursue your objective without fear, anger, or distraction.

The value of surrender is that you do all you can do to the best of your abilities. When you get to that point, you let go. It is a hard, cold fact of life that there are things you simply cannot do anything about. This does not mean you are powerless or helpless. It means that when you run out of ability, you must rely on a greater ability than yours: the ability of the universal power of spirit. Surrender means to allow the universal power of spirit to take control of the situation, knowing that the goal of the universe is your greatest good. It may not always look or feel that way, but the law is very exact.

What Sharon's mother did was give up and give in to her environment. She could not see a way out. She misinterpreted her level of responsibility to her husband and her children. It is also quite possible that she was too afraid or too beaten down to look for a way out. That is not surrender. You are never required to surrender yourself into or because of a situation which is harmful or dangerous to your well-being. In her case, surrender would have been a willingness to surrender the marriage, stop trying to fix it or make it work. To have the husband removed from the home, while surrendering the fear of not being able to make it without him. Or to leave the home, while surrendering the fear of possibly having nowhere to go. In order to surrender, you must first be willing to admit you do not know what to do, you have done all you can, and you now invite the holy presence of spirit to take over. You then allow it to do so, remembering, "I shall fear no evil!"

What Sharon did was rebel against what she could see. Judging her parents wrong, she resisted their guidance. Her rebellion and resistance created the friction between Sharon and her parents which ultimately directed the tides in her life. As a young adult, Sharon needed to be guided to surrender her judgments and anger, to allow her parents to live their lives while she developed her own goals and dreams. This would have been no easy feat for a young woman. However, as an adult, Sharon continued to make the error we commonly make when we do not know how to surrender: she wanted to tell her parents how to live, but did not want them to tell her how to live.

So often, we know that situations and people are not productive or wanted energies in our lives. We proclaim our desire to be away from or rid of them. At the same time, we allow these people to encroach on our lives by accepting their favors, because it is easy or convenient for us to do so. We forget their negative influence when we need them or want them to do something for us. We want their time, money, or assistance, but not their guidance, comments, or suggestions. Remember, everything comes with a price. You must always give up in order to get. When you accept favors from unproductive energy, you give up a part of yourself to that which is unproductive. That is the law! In the valley of nonresistance, knowing the law is critical to your survival and evolution. You must know in your mind, heart, and soul that if you are on the right side of the law, all will be perfected in your favor. In order to know, you must also master the lesson of this valley: trust.

The Lesson

Belief or insistence that a particular way is the only way we can be satisfied indicates that we do not know the true meaning of surrender. To truly surrender, we must know that the outcome of a situation will be in divine order. Even when the outcome does not look like we thought it would look, we must know it is divine. When we say it "should" be this way or that, we are questioning God's wisdom, the universal wisdom, and enforcing our own limited beliefs and perceptions. In order to move beyond resistance, to surrender and allow God's wisdom to prevail, we must detach ourselves from the outcome. In order to detach, we must learn to trust.

Trust is recognition that we are not in control, we cannot see all the possibilities. If we resist or fear what is happening or not happening by staying attached to a particular outcome, we may in fact be limiting ourselves and God's perfect plan. Desire, pure intent, obedience, patience, detachment from the outcome, and trust are the ingredients of total surrender.

Marilyn and Tony separated. She went home to her mother in Texas. He stayed in their apartment in New York. Their two years of marriage had been fraught with disappointments and stress due to financial pressures and Tony's propensity to "stray" from the marriage, fostering Marilyn's decision to leave. They loved one another, but Marilyn wanted a stronger commitment. Tony needed to feel free, uncontrolled. It was time to surrender the marriage.

Marilyn understood all the principles of surrender. Putting them into practice was a different story altogether. The first two weeks were pure torture. Marilyn prayed for guidance, being conscious not to ask for salvation of the marriage. Her quest was for peace; whatever would bring it to her was fine. She praised her spirit for guiding her and her husband so they would know exactly what to do. Anytime she had an overwhelming desire to call Tony, she would surrender the feeling and pray for strength. Marilyn knew they both needed time and space to get clear about what to do. But at the end of two weeks without Tony, her fears kicked into high gear.

In examining her willingness to surrender the marriage, Marilyn realized she was afraid. She was afraid she might lose him. She started telling herself all the things he should be doing if he really loved her and wanted to save the marriage. Spiritually, Marilyn knew that if she surrendered the marriage and Tony was not her divine right mate, he would go away. Secretly, she wanted Tony to stop running around, start saving money, and make a commitment to her. This was not surrender. This was attachment to her way.

The process of surrender and detachment, which is based on trust, is recognizing that whatever happens, happens in the manner in which it is divinely ordained to happen. The minute you start giving demands and creating pictures of what should be, you are in resistance, not surrender. When you are looking for signs that what you hope to happen is actually happening, you are resisting, not trusting. Hope that can be seen is not hope. Surrender is knowing, based on trust, laced with faith, that you will survive no matter what. Since most of our wants are constructs of our fears, what we want may not be what is divinely ordained for us. Marilyn "wanted" to stay married to Tony not only because she loved him, but because she "did not want" to be alone. She "did not want" to admit she could have been wrong about this Mr. Right. She "did not want" to feel the pain of a broken heart. She "did not want" to admit failure or face loss. She was resisting the natural flow of events and thereby possibly postponing something better. At the end of the first month, Marilyn realized that if Tony did not get it together and come for her, she would be forced to face all of her fears. The thought of it was so traumatic that she threw trust, faith, and detachment out the window, broke down, and begged God to save her marriage.

"When one door closes, another door opens." Everyone must walk through the door in her own way, at her own pace. You cannot create a door for someone. You cannot hold the door open for her. You cannot push her through the door unless she is willing to enter. When we find ourselves alone and approaching a closed door, many times we panic. When jiggling the knob, knocking on the door, calling out for help does not cause the door to fly open, we shift into pissosity: fear laced with anger. Now we bang on the door. Using a bit more force, we rattle the door-knob. If we are particularly pissed, we may even kick the door. To no avail. The door is closed and we cannot get in, period.

If we do not know how to surrender, we will walk away from the closed door angry, vowing never to trust again. Remembering what we were told that brought us to the door, what we were promised if we came to the door, what we went through to get to the door, we conclude a closed door is our failure to realize something we hoped for. In some instances, we call a closed door betrayal, rejection, or abandonment. Our sensibilities are offended. The thing we fear is about to be realized. We become obsessed with getting the door open, without stopping to realize the door may be closed for our own good. We are resisting the lesson. Eventually we will be forced to make a choice: to stay in angry hysteria or surrender.

Tony did call Marilyn, three months after they separated, six weeks after he entered a drug rehabilitation center. He wanted her to wait for him. He loved her and was sorry. He wanted forgiveness and vowed to get himself together for them. He wanted children and a home. He needed underwear, some cigarettes, and a few dollars. Marilyn listened intently. Something, she was not sure what, had changed. She did not resist. She did not make any decisions or commitments. She surrendered. She told him she was not ready to see him but she would send what he needed. In total surrender and trust, Marilyn knew she would know what to do when the time came. Until then, she would stay in peaceful, trusting prayer and surrender.

The Way Out

There are many Black women who do live guided by their thoughts, dreams, visions, and intuitive, introspective knowings.

Yet there are those moments, those situations, when they forget to trust what they know and are maneuvered into fear. In fear, resistance rises. Resistant fear colors and eventually erodes what you know, what you can trust. Without trust, you cannot be sure that what you are doing at any moment is part of your divine plan. You experience weakness. You are on guard. You prepare yourself to do battle with the enemy, the opposition. The battle for which you are preparing is not a physical battle. It is a spiritual one. In order to emerge victoriously, you must have on your spiritual armor.

Nonresistance does not mean you roll over and prepare for physical death. It means that you give up your way, the limited human way, as you ask for and allow yourself to be shown "the way." Surrender does not mean going along or giving in to demoralization, destruction, or degradation. It means standing up and standing on solid ground, spiritual ground, the ground that does not shake or crack beneath the threat of human undoing. Trusting does not mean you do not fight for what you want. It means you do not struggle, you do not worry. You do not wrestle with "powers and principalities." You fight, but you do not use physical weapons. You use spiritual weapons. You do not tell people who you are and what you are going to do. You show them. You do not prove to them, compete with them, or challenge them. You let them do whatever they are doing as you move trustfully, knowingly, toward the objective of your heart.

PUT ON YOUR SPIRITUAL ARMOR!

As a Black woman, one of the most powerful instruments of my resistance was my mouth. I always had something to say. I had an opinion about everything and everyone. I was compelled to tell people what I was planning to do, how I was going to do it, and why. Painfully, I learned that talking creates great opposition and great friction. Talking creates energy which when unleashed into the world, fraught with negative emotions and unconscious implications, yields unnecessary challenges and misunderstandings. As you surrender and become more trusting of the spirit within you and the spirit in the universe, you find you have less of a need to tell everyone everything.

Silence is a spiritual weapon of nonresistance. When you are silent, you can hear yourself think. When you are silent, you can hear the great spirit of power speaking in you and through you. When you are silent, you can listen. When you are listening and obediently following your inner authority, the guidance of your spirit, you have no need to fight difference, attack problems, or fight for solutions. When you are obedient, you can move with courage, trusting yourself, knowing the universe is supporting you. In this state of consciousness, you can detach from the outcome and move in peace.

Did you hear the moon come out last night? Did you hear the sun come out this morning? Did you hear the sperm converge with the egg to create the miracle we call life? The most powerful forces in the universe are silent. They do not have opinions. They do not battle opposition. They do not have anything to say about anyone. They rise and set, join and create, bring forth and control the flow of life, silently, without resistance, without hesitation. In silence, we develop the faith to surrender, the wisdom to trust, and the insight to move beyond anything or anyone which could in any way stand in opposition to the divine plan for our lives.

Prayer is a spiritual weapon of nonresistance. You cannot surrender or trust if you cannot pray. When you surrender, you must pray moment to moment. The enemy thoughts and emotions will besiege you. They cannot be seen with the naked eye. No one but you can hear their threats. You cannot outrun them. You cannot slay them with bullets or knives. Prayer is the only way to subdue and conquer the enemy which will rise up from the crevices of your mind and heart when you place yourself in spirit's hands. When you surrender, you must know how to "pray without ceasing." As you pray, you fortify your spiritual armor and eliminate the need to spill your life on the battleground.

Gratitude is a spiritual weapon of nonresistance. Whatever you are challenged by, be grateful. There is a lesson to be learned. Millions of Black women did not make it through their lesson. Be grateful you are alive, being given the opportunity to grow, learn, and conquer yourself. The old wisewomen say, "When the praise goes up, the blessings come down!" Be grateful that you have made it through those tight spots you thought you would not make it through. Be grateful there's a challenging experience upon you now, knowing you are equipped to handle it. When people do not care about you, they leave you alone. When you are loved by them, they want to be in your face. God loves you. God has not left you alone. You are being challenged to grow. Challenged to surrender. Challenged to develop your trusting faith that the presence of God through the spirit in you is in your face as a sustaining power. Be grateful for every little thing in your life.

The most powerful weapon of spiritual warfare and nonresistance is love. Love not only makes the world go around, love will make any unloving thing jump out of your life. Spiritual love is not mental or emotional. It is the ultimate act of surrender and trust. When we "make love," we remove all of our outer clothing, strip ourselves to the state of our birth, nakedness, close our eyes, and surrender our entire being to another being. You are naked, you cannot run away. Your eyes are closed. You cannot see what is going on. You open your heart and body to receive the life force of another being, without resistance or fear. In this state of humble nakedness and surrender, we seek what we call love.

When we are challenged in life, we must exhibit this same humble surrender we call lovemaking. We must take off the outer garment of pride and ego. We must shut our eyes to the past and the future. We must bring ourselves fully into the moment, allow ourselves to see and feel the naked truth, and then, without judgment or fear, trust ourselves enough to know that whatever is about to take place will be good.

When you can look at people and things squarely, knowing that no matter how negative they may appear they have come to help you grow and learn, you must love them. Love them for what they are bringing you. Love them for what they are taking away from you. Love them because the spirit of life determined that you were worthy of the blessed opportunity to evolve to a higher state of consciousness.

MEDITATION WITH THE MOTHER

"Many are called, few are chosen," should be,
"All are called, few choose to listen."
—*A COURSE IN MIRACLES*

You start and stop, start and refuse to complete, because you are not sure. What would it take, daughters, to assure you that you are worthy enough to undertake the task? Capable enough to complete the task? Valuable enough to receive the rewards that completion of the task would bring? You wonder and worry, doubt and fear, because "they" say you cannot, must not, do what has been ordained for you. What would it take, my dearest ones, to make my voice louder than theirs? To make my blessed assurances stronger than "their" weak denials? To bring your heart and mind into direct contact with my perfection for you, when all around you see their destruction of you? It is really very simple. It would take "you" being willing to do the very thing "they" say you cannot do.

This life is such a precious gift. It is a gift that blesses both the giver and the receiver. The One who has given you life is blessed when you use life to its fullest capacity, giving and sharing as you grow through life's activities. Those who receive that which you do with your life are blessed, for they then become stronger, better able to grow in their lives, using themselves to their full capacity. The gift is not returnable or refundable. It is yours to keep, to do with as you choose. What you choose determines the value of the gift. This gift of life is worth more than doing and not doing, having and not having. Life becomes a valuable event, a worthy gift, when all who have come to partake of it give and receive, share and grow, live and do all they are able to support the living of others.

Do you stop in the middle of opening a gift? Of course not. You proceed with eager anticipation, knowing that whatever you receive is only a symbolic representation of all that is available to you. Do you pile your gifts in the corner, allowing them to lie dormant, unused, fearing the gift is not right for you? No. You do what is honorable. Receive and accept with gratitude, using what you can and distributing the rest to be used by others. If you can find some use for the things "they" give you—sweaters and pots, glasses and boxes—why is it so difficult, challenging, frightening, for you to find ways to put the gift of your life to valuable use?

The
Valley of 10
Success

ℒET'S FACE IT, ALL OF US ARE NOT
BORN POOR, DESPERATE, AND DYSFUNCTIONAL. THERE ARE A LARGE NUMBER
of Black women born into well-to-do families with many resources. They are raised in a loving, nurturing environment, with
many advantages in life. The average person would think these
women are born into success. It would appear they have no reason to complain and that they cannot or should not fail. Some of
these women go through life and do very well. They are refined,
educated, professionally and personally successful. They do not
know what it is to want or need any material thing. They marry
well and continue the traditions of a well-established family and
social lifestyle. A few of these women stumble or fall from grace,
throwing away all they have been given. They feel lonely, desperate, crazy, and even worse, unloved and unwanted. They worry
and fear more than those who, it would seem, really have things
to worry about and be frightened of. However, all so-called successful women, just like the rest of us, at some time or another
find themselves in one of the valleys.

Remember, a valley is an experience. It is an experience designed for your growth. It is not a condition of birth. It is not an
outgrowth of your economic, social, or political resources. A valley is the result of what we do and do not do to violate nature's

laws and universal principles. Money cannot save you from a valley experience. A good education will not save you from the valley. Having a mother who baked cookies for you and a father who tucked you in at night will not save you when your time comes to grow and learn a spiritual lesson. From a spiritual perspective, success in life, or lack of it, has nothing to do with where you live or where you grew up. Spiritual success, that which the valleys are designed to promote, is the ability to live life with a sense of freedom and peace, doing what makes you feel good, that which is good for you, while you face challenges and obstacles with strength and tenacity, knowing that no matter what happens, you will be just fine. Success, like the valley experiences, is not one-size-fits-all. Success is personal, born of the deepest desires in our heart and our ability to feel good about who and what we are, no matter where we are and what we have at any given time.

Starting at the Bottom Does Not Mean the Top Is Further Away

I grew up on the lower end of the economic ladder. We had a roof over our heads, food on the table, but I never had the frills and lace that many of my friends had. There were many things I could not do as a child because we could not afford it. In my very family-oriented neighborhood, where most homes had two parents, I watched my friends get dressed in their very nice clothes, go on family trips and outings, and enjoy the many amenities of life that money enables you to enjoy. I hated them! I mean I liked them, but I hated the fact that they were able to do things my family could not afford to do. As I grew into adolescence, I realized all of us had the same problems at the same time! We all worried about our breasts being too big or small. We all agonized over zits, cramps, and the new girl in the class looking at the boy we planned to marry. We all cried when we got dumped or failed a test. We all laughed when the new girl, who stole our boyfriend, slipped down the stairs or tucked her skirt in her panties and came out of the bathroom with her behind exposed.

In the things that really mattered, having or not having money did not save you. The zit on the face of a well-to-do girl was just as unsightly as the zit on the face of a girl from the projects.

Where then do we get the idea that money equals success? What is it that allows us to believe that our self-worth is somehow equated to our net worth? Why do we allow ourselves to believe that having things somehow makes us better people? An angry or frightened wealthy Black woman is in just as much spiritual trouble as an ashamed or dishonest poor one. An insecure or envious poor Black woman has just as much to learn as an insecure, irresponsible wealthy one. The keys to the riddles are in two words, *spiritual* and *learning*. We have not been taught that success is an outgrowth of our *spiritual learning*. What we do and how we do it, the way we move through life, is a reflection of our ability to learn from our experiences and grow spiritually. The ability to love, give, do, have, is a direct reflection of what we know and how we feel about it. Knowing and feeling are spiritual functions which you cannot buy, no matter how much money your grandfather left you.

It's Not What You Do, It's How You Feel About What You Do

As Black women, our success is very often defined by the world and its standards. If we get a good job, a good husband, a nice house, and nice clothes, we are told to consider ourselves lucky and successful. Once again, appearances can fool people. No one cares if you are miserable on the job, cannot stand your husband, really want to live in a condo, and buy all your clothes at the Salvation Army. The even sadder part of the appearance-of-success scenario is that when we have the things, we too think we have found success. We have all the "things" that represent success, but we are miserable inside. Or we have everything, but we still feel like a failure. That is the real killer.

When I graduated from college, I was thirty-three years old. I graduated summa cum laude, with a 4.0 grade point average. I was president of the student government. I had completed my undergraduate degree in three and a half years. I had started school while I was receiving public assistance, and by the time I completed it, I was working full-time and raising my three children. Anyone in her right mind would have been pounding on her chest and strutting around like a peacock. I was miserable! First of all, after growing up in an environment where I was always told how stupid I was, I did not understand the magnitude of my accomplishment. Secondly, with the exception of my children, who had no choice, none of my family showed up at my graduation. Not my father, my brother, my grandmother—my mom was excused because she was critically ill—none of the people I thought should be proud of me bothered to show their face. I was crushed.

By the time I graduated from law school four years later, my mom and dad had passed, I had lost track of my brother, and I had just ended a four-year relationship. It was a disaster. I moped around, feeling sorry for myself, refusing to celebrate my success or myself. My close friends were happy for me and proud of me. They saw the pain in my eyes and really tried to make me feel better. Of course it was one of my sassy-mouthed friends who said just what I needed to hear to snap me back to reality: "If you let other people steal the joy from your success, you are going to get ripped off all your life!" That's when it hit me: I had not done any of it for myself; I had done it to make a better life for my children, to prove myself to my family, to prove myself to the world. When none of the folks who mattered to me responded the way I thought they should, I felt like a failure. In the middle of my success, I still felt like a failure!

When we do things for the sake of other people, we usually end up not feeling good about ourselves. When your success is measured by how someone else will respond, you never know what to expect. Remember, expectations equal results! When we do things to prove ourselves to others, we will never be able to produce enough evidence to successfully prove our case—the case that we are good, worthy, deserving of their love and recognition. If we have to prove ourselves to them, we probably do not need what they have to give. When we measure ourselves by the standards the world sets for us, there is a good chance we will never measure up. Success is relative. It means different things to different people. For my family, whose daily struggle was to find a meal and pay the rent, a college degree meant nothing. As far as they could see, I had wasted a lot of money to go to school and probably would still never be rich. When you only know lack, money equals success. I did not know it at the time, but money cannot buy success, nor will it make you feel successful.

We must begin from a position of success. We must know what it is we want, why it is important to us, and what we are willing to do to get it. We must set our own standards and live up to them. We must realize that whatever we do in this life is icing on the cake because we are born in a position of success. The motivational speaker Les Brown reminded me of this when he said, "You beat fourteen million other sperm to get here. What makes you think you are not a success?" Yet there are a large number of Black women who really do believe they are failures.

Don't Owe Your Success to Anyone

Barbara, like many of us, grew up among lack and restriction. In other words, she was poor. Her family had always been poor. Of course her parents wanted the best for her, but they never seemed quite able to make ends meet. They were always being put out, living with relatives, sleeping three and four to a bed and sometimes on the floor in somebody's house. There was always some crisis around money and the lack of it. Barbara grew up in an environment in which people believed that money would solve all your problems. They were never quite specific about whose money would solve the problem. They just assumed somebody's would.

Out of four children, Barbara was the only one who made it through high school and college. When she was promoted to a middle-management position at the age of twenty-three, she moved out on her own, away from her family. It didn't matter.

Two or three times a week, Barbara would get a call from a parent or a sibling in financial crisis. They always expected her to bail them out of their trouble, and she usually did. On those rare occasions when she had the courage to make an excuse not to, she would be berated about being "uppity and too good" for her family. Eventually she began to believe that she could not be successful if her family was still suffering. She felt guilty and kept asking herself, "Why me? Why should I have all this good?" The harder she worked, the more she earned, and the more they needed and wanted. It continued for years, even after she got married and had children of her own. Somebody always needed something and expected Barbara to provide it. Because she had internalized what her family told her and felt guilty about her own good fortune, Barbara could not feel good about what she had made of her own life. She was definitely in the valley.

We do not owe what we make of our lives to anyone. Nor do we owe what we make in life to anyone. Of course we want to help our family and friends, who supported, nurtured, and loved us through our ups and downs. However, we must realize, we do not owe them! We get confused because we all have a need to belong and be loved. If it appears that the loving acceptance we need and want is being denied, we are ready and willing to do whatever is necessary to obtain it. For some of us, this means trying to buy our place in the hearts of people who matter to us. We give because we are afraid people will stop loving us if we do not.

We must share and give because we want to, not because we have to. It was an honor for me to bring my first paycheck home and give my mother money. It was as though I were saying to her, "Look, all your hard work paid off!" She never asked me for anything. I gave willingly when I had it to give. On the other hand, I am aware of mothers, fathers, brothers, third cousins, and their neighbors who actually believe they have a right to what you have because they know you. Maybe they changed your diaper once or twice. These people have no shame about reminding you what they have done for you. If you have bought into the guilt they lay on you or if you have an unresolved need to be needed, you will turn over your entire paycheck in the bat of an eye.

Like Barbara, many Black women lose sight of the success in their lives because of false obligations to other people. Because our situation is a little better, we are led to believe that it is our obligation to pick up, pull up, and lift up others. In today's world, most of us are two paychecks away from homeless. We can only do so much and whatever we do must be done with a clear conscience. What we owe our family is to be happy. In our happiness we teach them there is another way of living. Particularly in the case of multigenerational poverty, who is going to lead the way out? Supporting someone to stay in a position of lack and limitation may not be the best way. Someone has to say, "Enough already! There is a better way!"

You can best show people how happy you are by what you do, enjoying your life and all in it! It is up to each individual to find his own way out of whatever is holding him back. You can assist and support. You cannot do the work for him because you have the means. People must make their own choices. If your family lives in the projects and you are fortunate enough to move to the other side of town, it is not your obligation to pay their rent. On the other hand, if you are a millionaire and your family lives in a rat-infested tenement, you may want to buy the building and renovate it. Whatever you do, make sure there is a commitment in your heart. Never do anything simply because someone says you must.

Set Your Own Standards and Live Up to Them

Carol's parents were both doctors. Yes, they were both Black doctors. They both taught on the university level. Carol knew at the age of seven that she would be a doctor and teach at some prestigious university. That is not what she wanted to do, but she knew better than to say anything about it. Carol went to the best schools and colleges. At age twenty-nine she was a full-fledged doctor, but working in a community health center on the poorest side of town. She loved her work and her patients. She felt that she was making a valuable contribution to life. Her parents went crazy!

Carol's idea of medicine was to provide quality service at a minimum cost for those least likely to have access to quality care. Her parents, on the other hand, thought medicine was a science, controlled by the elite, whose responsibility it was to give the best possible care to those who could afford the best. They taught because they were scientists who wanted to continue the tradition of class-based health care. They were outraged that Carol would allow them to spend all of *their money* to educate her so she could throw her life away never getting the recognition she deserved. At least twice a week Carol heard the "Why are you doing this to us" speech. Although she was doing great work at the clinic, she did begin to feel very unappreciated, unworthy, and unsuccessful. Carol was in a ditch.

One of Carol's patients was a young boy from a Latin country. When his mother brought him into the clinic, he was on the verge of death. Carol discovered he had a rare blood infection. As a result of her conscientious treatment, the boy made a full recovery, spending only a minimum amount of time in the hospital. Carol's parents were very proud of her, but their pride was overshadowed by their desire to have Carol report the case and her findings to the appropriate journals so she could get the recognition and respect due her. Carol was quite satisfied that her patient had recovered and was doing well. Her father told her she was robbing him of the opportunity to have his daughter recognized. Her mother simply said she was a fool. Carol held on to her position, refused to contact the professional journals, and eventually cut off all contact with her parents. They did not speak for two and a half years. Carol's mother broke down first. Her father followed suit. On the sixth anniversary of Carol's tenure at the community health center, her parents donated enough money to have the entire building painted.

There is a principle of the Kwanzaa, an African-American holiday called *Kujichugalia,* self-determination. This is a critical element of success which no one can determine for you. There will be times when people think they know what you should do to

278

make your success. At other times they will want you to do things which will bolster their success. At all times you must do what you can do to live up to the standards of success you have set for yourself. What is important to you? Success is not always fame and fortune. For some of us, it may simply be the knowledge that we did our best. When we do our best, when we give what we have, we feel good. For some of us, that good feeling can be enough.

We do not always need other people heaping accolades upon us to make what we do meaningful. Sarah Vaughan said, "I am not a special person. I am a regular person who does special things." If, according to your standards, there is more you can do to make yourself feel good, then by all means do it. If, however, you have done the best you can do, in the best way possible, accept the success you feel in your heart and let it be enough. No amount of money in the world would have saved that little boy. Carol being there, being used as a tool, was divine order. She could have listened to her parents, taken a teaching position at the university, and moved her office to a better part of town. My guess is that not only would she have been miserable, but eventually she would have wound up in a place she did not want to be, a valley.

Don't Be Fooled by Appearances

Lydia's mother was a praying, churchgoing woman. Her father, a strict disciplinarian, thought church was someplace you went when there was nothing good on television, but he supported his wife in going and taking their children.

Lydia, along with her five brothers and sisters, grew up in the church. At the earliest possible opportunity, they all ran to escape their father's sternness, Sunday school, and all that went along with being the child of a church mother. Most of them made out pretty well. They all married. Had children. And eventually, took their families back to the church. Lydia was the only one who went astray. At the age of nineteen, she became involved in the drug culture. She stayed that way for more than twelve years.

Lydia's father told her she was the scum of the earth. It got to the point where he would not allow her in or near the family home. Her mother, being a dutiful wife, obeyed his wishes. She would meet Lydia on the corner, give her a few dollars, and remind her to pray. If Lydia's father saw her in the street or around the house, he would either mercilessly berate her or totally ignore her. The situation was tearing the family apart. Her sisters pleaded with Lydia to get herself together, her brothers argued with her father about the way he treated her, and her mother kept praying, trying to hold it all together.

Lydia developed a critical illness and was not given long to live. All of the family rallied around her. All except her father. Lydia spent what she thought were her last days asking for forgiveness, beating up on herself for being a failure, apologizing to her mother, and begging to see her father. Her mother kept praying and making excuses for her husband. One of the church mothers suggested that they hold a special prayer service for Lydia. They called on pastors and mothers from the neighboring churches to come in and hold the vigil. Lydia's mother had just taken her seat in the first pew, with her children seated dutifully at her side, and the service was just about to start, when spirit urged her to turn around. When she did, she saw her husband of thirty-three years walking up the aisle. He sat down next to her and held her hand. Lydia is still alive, actually doing very well. She and her parents go to church together every Sunday.

Who is to say that Lydia failed in her life? Who is to say that she was not where she was divinely ordained to be, doing what she came to life to do? Success is a process of evolutionary unfolding. There are many levels to the process, some of which make absolutely no sense to us. Little by little we become that which we are meant to be. Step by step, we move through the divine process of our spiritual mission. Don't forget we have lessons to learn along the way. Life is a learning process in which we teach, learn, and sometimes serve as the object by which something else is taught. In all cases, under all situations, we must be patient with our learning process, patient as we learn our lessons, remembering success has many faces but no age limit.

It is such a rip-off when we choose looking successful over the key to real success, learning spiritual lessons. We rip ourselves off when we get caught up in what we think things should look like and what we should be doing or having. Some of us take the high road, others cannot find a road to take. The key is knowing that as long as you are alive, you are on the road to becoming that which you choose to be. If you truly want to find success in your life, give up every idea of what you think the outcome will be. We cannot see everything! We may be looking in one direction while our blessings are coming from another. When we give up our ideas of what success should be, we open our hearts and minds to greater possibilities. When we do the best we can, where we are, with what we have, taking our lessons in stride, the universe promises us that it will pay off. Lydia wanted her father's love and attention. She took herself through the valley to get it. In the end, Lydia got exactly what she wanted and succeeded in doing what her mother had not been able to do for thirty-three years. She brought her father to God. Is that success or what?

Don't Question the Value of What You Are Doing

When Rebecca got laid off, she thought her world had come to an end. She had put all of her time and energy into moving up the corporate ladder. Hard economic times and bad timing let her know her efforts had not paid off. Having been on her own since the age of thirteen, Rebecca thought that to be without a job was to have no meaning. She felt worthless and useless. She forced herself to go to the unemployment office. She hated herself each time she cashed her check. She desperately looked for a job everywhere, every day. She was just about to give up on herself when she saw a way out of her darkness.

She answered an advertisement requesting a telephone counselor for a local hotline. By the time she got there, the position had been filled. The woman who interviewed her asked if she would be willing to volunteer a few hours a day. The woman told her it was a sure bet that she would be offered a position as soon as it opened up if she were a volunteer. Besides that, volunteering would give her something to do with her time other than feeling bad about not working. Rebecca listened and accepted the woman's offer.

By her third month as a volunteer, Rebecca was about to give up hope when one of the staff members announced she would be moving to another city in a few weeks. Rebecca decided to try to stick it out. The work wasn't really that bad. She actually got three or four real crisis calls a day. The rest were lonely people who needed someone to talk to. In the interim, Rebecca beat up on herself, reinforcing her feelings of worthlessness for being unemployed. She was having a particularly bad day when she got the call that turned her mind and her life around.

A woman in the hospital had just been told by a team of ten doctors that the cancer which had invaded her body was fatal. They wanted her to know there was very little hope for her survival. In the middle of their medical report, she had picked up the telephone and called the hotline. Rebecca answered. As the doctors talked to the woman, she talked to Rebecca. Rebecca was able to keep her calm and give her hope. After the doctors left the room, she and Rebecca stayed on the telephone for four hours. The woman was a widow whose only son had died in a car accident. In addition to being ill, she was very lonely. Rebecca and her caller talked, laughed, and cried together. At various intervals, they prayed together. Rebecca finally asked the woman if she wanted to live. Of course! She was only fifty-six years old. There were still a few things she wanted to do. Rebecca told her that if she wanted to live, she would—no matter what the doctors had told her.

Against all policies, they exchanged numbers. They continued to talk for the next several weeks. When the woman went home, she called Rebecca. When she was able to hold solid food on her stomach, they went to lunch together. Eventually, she and Rebecca joined the same church. Rebecca did get the job. The woman did live. At every opportunity she tells Rebecca what a blessing it was for her that she answered the telephone. Rebecca tries to convince the woman that she is wrong. Explaining that she never wanted to be there and stayed only because she was unemployed, Rebecca refuses to take the credit for the woman's own will to live. Still, the woman has tried for years to convince Rebecca of the value in what she did. It is a value Rebecca still cannot see.

If you are in the valley, it is hard to see the good in what you do. If you measure your success by what you have, you will never see the good in what you do. Almost every Black woman I know thinks she should be someplace other than where she is. When things are not going according to our plans, we throw ourselves into the dungeon of despair and self-abasement. On the road to successful living and learning, we must realize, we are always exactly where we are supposed to be! When we hold on to desired outcomes and limited expectations, we lose sight of the value we have to offer just being alive. Rebecca's situation is a clear-cut case of how being on purpose brings you to the realization of success.

We must be clear about why we are here on the planet and about our mission in life. When we are clear and on purpose, we are more willing to take the ups and downs as we move toward our ultimate destination, which is not always a good job with a good salary. From a spiritual perspective, our ultimate destination in this life is peace of mind and the realization that we are on a spiritual mission. That mission is our purpose. When we have no idea what our purpose is, or whether or not we are living it, we tend to get mad, feel worthless, judge ourselves, and hold resentments about whatever experience we are having at any given time. However, when we are open and always prepared to receive the best, when we least expect it, our purpose will become clear as it emerges from the most unlikely situations.

Do what you can do. Do it to the best of your ability. Never doubt that what you are doing is right for you at the time you are doing it. Do not judge yourself. Always look for the blessing in every experience, even if that blessing falls on someone else. So many of us fall into the valley because we give up just before we make it. Always remember, don't give up five minutes before the miracle occurs. There is always something that will make everything worthwhile.

Ask For What You Want

The meaning of the name Dolores is, "to suffer." That is exactly what she did. Dolores suffered most of her life because she believed she could not have what she wanted. She had been on her job for twelve years, never being promoted. She talked to friends about it but she never asked her employer why. She realized that with her experience, she could probably get a better-paying position with another firm. Every now and then, she would go on an interview. When she was not hired, she would say, "That's okay. I didn't really want the job anyway." When she went to lunch with her friends from work, she would always give up the last salad or the last piece of pie: "No, that's okay, you take it, I'll have something else." It may all sound perfectly normal, but Dolores, she was suffering inside.

Dolores knew her husband was running around and she never said a word. She wanted her younger brother to move out of her house, but she felt bad about putting him out. Whenever her mother, sister, or friends called with a personal request to be driven somewhere or have something picked up, Dolores would stop whatever she was doing to accommodate them. "Sure, I'll do it. That is much more important than what I'm doing." Then she would complain about people using her and taking advantage of her kind nature.

Dolores was also an excellent seamstress. Sewing was her personal form of therapy which she used to make extra money. She would accept orders from people. Spend days, sometimes weeks, preparing a garment. When the person came to pick it up and pay for her work, Dolores would say, "Oh, just give me what you think it's worth." If you make someone a satin gown and hand-sew over a thousand beads onto it, it is worth more than a hundred dollars. But because she didn't ask for more, she didn't get more. When the woman left with the gown, Dolores cried. She felt totally ripped off. When the woman referred several of her friends to have clothing made, Dolores repeated the process of not asking, crying, and feeling as if her work was not being valued.

Dolores was a Special Ed student. She was stuck in a pattern and could not see her way out. No matter what anyone did or said to her, she would not open her mouth. She accepted her husband's infidelity, her brother's loafing, her family and friends' constant encroachment of her time and resources, and minimum wages for her expert work. She was on a collision course long before she had the accident. The day she actually ran her car into a tree in blinding rain, all of her issues came to a head.

She was blinded in one eye and nearly crippled. She literally had to fight her way back to life and to regain use of almost every part of her body. The same people she had gone out of the way for offered little support and assistance. They were all too busy, and whenever they asked her if she needed or wanted anything, she would respond, "Oh that's okay. I'm fine." Why you would ask a blinded, near-crippled person what she needs is beyond me! Her husband did wait until she got home from the hospital before he resumed his relationship with his mistress. Her brother turned out to be the most help.

While Dolores was recovering and adjusting to a visual handicap, her brother kept the house together, did the shopping, and drove her to and from therapy sessions. She had been walking on a cane for only two weeks when he resumed his position on his perch in front of the television and asked her, "What you gonna cook today?" That did it! She went off on him for all the years she had remained silent. Her mother and sister were next. And finally, her husband. When all was said, Dolores locked herself in her room, where she stayed for four days because she was "embarrassed" about the way she had behaved. When she came out of her room, she apologized to everyone and went back to working her way toward health and business as usual.

The most critical error Black women make in our lives and on our quest to find success is not asking for what we need or want.

We have allowed our environment and the people in it to convince us that we can have no more than we already have. We do not know how to ask for support or assistance. When we get it, we feel uncomfortable. When people try to assist us, we become fearful, thinking they are trying to "take over." In response to this fear, we try to do everything ourselves, then complain about being tired and feeling used or manipulated. We allow people to do their number all over us because we do not know how to say, "This is not what I want and I am not accepting it!" Most important of all, the overwhelming majority of Black women do not believe we deserve to be healthy, joyful, peaceful, abundantly wealthy, or loved just because we are who we are.

One of my spiritual teachers once told me, "If you don't ask for what you need, the need gets bigger." It is so true! When I need money and I don't ask for it, the bills become delinquent and the bill collectors become more aggressive. When I don't ask people to stop encroaching on my time and space, they find more things for me to do with the time I have. When I don't let people know that what they are doing makes me uncomfortable, unhappy, or insecure, they keep doing it and I feel worse. When I do not let people know I feel upset because of something they have said or done, even when it was innocently done, I feel worse about them and myself. This more than anything else damages our self-esteem and self-worth.

As Black women, we do little things, things we think have no meaning, that actually erode our self-value, self-worth, and self-esteem. We talk down about ourselves. Most Black women are quick to say what they have or have not done, to their own detriment. We hold on to old mistakes and judge ourselves mentally and emotionally unfit. We deny ourselves what we need and want in order to supply others with what they want. Almost every mother I know has walked around in run-over shoes or old clothes because "the children need" something. Then we wonder why we don't feel pretty, attractive, or lovable. If you do not take care of yourself, treat yourself well, shower yourself with good thoughts and feelings, you will develop the belief that no one else will do it either. Love you first! Nobody does it better! If you want to *have* success, you must *be* success. You cannot do either if you do not feel good about the instrument of success: yourself!

Ask for what you want. If you are denied the first time, ask again. There are times when we must ask others. There are times we must ask the universe. I prefer asking in prayer for what I want, and I always ask to be shown the way. More often than not, exactly what I ask for will be brought to me. Someone will give me information, make a suggestion, or offer me the very thing I requested. We do not have to suffer and struggle! We do because we are afraid to ask. When you believe you have a right to the best there is, it comes right to you. When you open yourself to receive, you do receive. Success not only means getting. For some of us, it also means knowing or feeling. For others, it is accomplishing or completing. Whatever success is for you, celebrate your victory every step of the way. Do not ignore the little things you do, accomplish, or complete. Give praise and thanks for everything you receive. Be willing to learn and grow, accepting the lessons and the blessings along the way. Above all else, when you need help, support, information, or guidance, ask for it!

The Law of Attraction

Any experience we have is ultimately for our own good. If we attract unpleasant experiences, it is in response to our most dominant thoughts and habitual behavior patterns. We cannot live beyond our level of thinking and feeling. Wherever we are is a reflection of where we think and feel we should be. This is the Law of Attraction. The basic premise of the law is:

What you give, you get.

We are not talking about what you give someone for her birthday or Christmas. This law deals with what you give the world in thought, word, deed, and most important of all, expectation.

To state this law another way: Whatever we attract, we need to attract, and whatever we attract is for our own good. We must attract what we think in order to be able to see it and do something about it. The state of your life, your home, your car, is a reflection of your mental state. If your thoughts are scattered and confused, your environment will reflect the same. Most of us think homes are messy because people do not pick up after themselves or because they don't have time to straighten up. This is not true in many cases. The law says, wherever you are, mentally and emotionally, you will be physically. This law, along with the Law of Cause and Effect, has the greatest impact on the realization of success.

Whatever we possess in this life is our reward for what we give to life. If we are not happy with what we have, if what we have is not sufficient to meet our needs, we must find what it is that we are thinking and doing to create the scarcity. If we are thinking we cannot, we will not. If we are speaking of lack, limitation, and obstacles, we will find them at every turn. These things are not imaginary. They are real. They are born in response to the energy we are putting out in life. How many times have you said, "I am broke! I can't afford it! I don't have the money!" Most of us speak in these terms. We are so busy being fooled by the physical appearances, what we see and hear, that we do not realize the supply of spiritual goods never runs out! Spirit is abundant and unlimited! If you realize you are spirit, then you know you too are unlimited, no matter what your situation looks like.

I like the Law of Attraction because it forces us to work. It makes us responsible. This law yields us returns in response to our demands upon it. If we don't ask, we don't get. If we ask for a little, the law will respond. This law moves us beyond restrictive thinking and dependency on others. It requires that we think plenty, speak plenty and expect plenty. It requires that we give openly, lovingly, and willingly to ourselves and others. It demands that we be specific in our thoughts and that we clearly define our goals and intentions. If we do not have a plan, a goal, a specific request from life, how can life provide us with that which we desire? This law fosters a greater understanding of all the laws and how to apply them to our lives. I believe the Law of Attraction will heal the relationship among Black women by making us conscious that what we do and say to one another will eventually become a reward, a reality in our own individual lives. This law will also cure us of our attachment to mediocrity.

The Law of Attraction is like the hall monitor. It watches what we do and reports it throughout the universe. This is an important issue because the law gives us what we deserve. It rewards us based on our readiness and willingness to have more. The key is in knowing that we cannot have what we want until we want what we have! We cannot receive more until we are ready for more. If we are angry, bitter, or ungrateful about where we are in life, that is the energy we will give off in the world. When we are complaining, whining, or neglectful of ourselves and our possessions, the law will report it. In response, we receive more to be angry, bitter, or upset over.

If you want a new or better job, give one hundred percent to the job you have, keeping in mind that you will be rewarded. If you are late, absent, or neglectful in your duties, why would the universe reward you with a better, higher-paying position? Love what you have, to get what you love! If you want a new home, a bigger or better one, take care of the home you have. Do not neglect to keep your home clean, neat, and orderly because you lack money. Stop saying, "I hate this house. I don't want to be here!" Talk like that will get you reported to the house monitor! If you want nice clothes, better friends, a more loving relationship, take care of the ones you already have. Do not complain and whine about what is not right or good. Take care of it! Fix what is not working with honesty, determination, and honor. If you cannot fix it, get rid of it!

If we want success, no matter how we define it as individuals, we must prepare ourselves to receive it by developing a success-filled mind and heart. Peace, love, joy, and gratitude will attract things like themselves to make us more peaceful, loving, joyful, and grateful. We must not accept less than we want, by developing the consciousness that we deserve the best. We must stop squeezing ourselves into uncomfortable and unproductive places and situations because we believe there is nothing else available. As we open new space in our hearts and minds to receive better and have more, we will. Above all else, we must not limit ourselves by defining how our good or success must come. Be open. Be clear. Be ready. And you will be rewarded accordingly.

The Way Out

Why does this chapter look different from all the other chapters? Because success means something different to everyone. There is no one way, process, or method of defining or finding what success is for you. Each of us, as we learn our lessons, in our own way, must define for ourselves what it is we want or need to realize what we define as success. There is, however, one universal aspect of being successful. That is, we must be patient.

I want it now! I want it this way! I want it when I want it! This does not work when you are in search of that thing, that condition, you define as success. Everything takes time. We must learn how to eat the mountain one bite at a time, realizing that bite by bite, we are getting to the core. There will be times when we are on our way, moving with a full head of steam, when all of a sudden—BAM!—we are hit with a setback. It may be devastating. It may just be annoying. Whatever it is, remember: it is good! You need the experience to foster maximum growth and development. Be patient! Do not give up or give in to difficulties.

Be patient with yourself. You do not have to know everything, be everything, do everything, all at once. If your brain is racing, telling you all the things you don't know, can't do, should know and be doing, tell your brain to shut up! You are in control! It is up to you to gently and lovingly honor yourself and your progress. A delay is not a denial! Be patient. Be willing to wait until the final outcome before you throw your hands up in despair. Nothing that is yours can be held from you or taken from you. STOP! Breathe! Ask to know the lesson. Move forward with a quiet brain and a trusting heart.

Here it is! This is the killer! The one thing Black women do to derail their success train faster than anything else. We talk too much! Go back to the Valley of Light. Silence is the key to success. Keep your mouth shut about what you want, what you are doing, what you plan to do. We talk so much, spilling the seeds of our success on unfertile ground, and then wondering why nothing is growing in our lives. Success is a birth process. The idea, thought, dream, or goal you have is like an embryo in the womb. That embryo must be nurtured. You must feed it good thoughts. Surround it with a good environment. Nurture and love it.

Keep your ideas in your mind until they are ready to be born. Of course there will be people you will speak to regarding the groundwork you must lay. There will be others you may call upon for assistance and guidance. This is fine. The talking you must avoid is the bragging. I mean getting on the telephone and telling your girlfriend about the dream you have, what you think, how you are going to be rich and famous. This kind of talk aborts the baby in your brain. I am also referring to the "I can't!," "I don't know how!," "They won't let me!" kind of talk that poisons the baby in your spiritual body. Everything happens first on the inside before it is revealed on the outside. If you simply must have someone to talk to about what you are doing, talk to yourself! If that doesn't satisfy your mouth, talk to God.

What is the Valley of Success? It is the experience of realizing what it is that we do that keeps us from getting what we want. How do we fall into the valley? By our thoughts, words, limited expectations, and actions. How do we get out of the valley? If you must have a formula, here it is:

> Be willing to start at the bottom!
> Feel good about whatever you are doing!
> Do not owe your good fortune to anyone!
> Set your own standards and live up to them!
> Never question the value of what you are doing!
> Ask for what you want!
> Want what you have!
> Expect the best!
> Be patient!
> Keep your mouth shut!

Now that you have the formula, we can rent out your space in the valley.

MEDITATION
WITH THE
MOTHER

*Love doesn't make the world go round, it makes
the trip worthwhile!*

—ANONYMOUS

*Dearest daughters, you have come full circle: From being blind, to
seeing the light, to being blinded by the light. From being lifeless, to
being alive, to giving your life away to things which make you lifeless. From being born of love, to being love, to giving your love to
that which cannot return your most precious gift. The circle has
become warped. Still you spin, searching to find your place, that
place that can make the load lighter on your journey.*

*My daughters, as long as I am in your heart, you are love! Stop
looking! Be! Love is the gift of life. The ease of breath. The unhin-
dered movement of all that supports your life. Love is what you are
when you have no material thing to give. Love is what you are
when all illusions have faded away. Love is what the Father and I
call you in your sleep, even when your spinning leaves you ex-
hausted and deafens you to our call. We will always love you, lift
you, hold you up in the light and surround you in the never-ending
glow of love.*

*Take time, daughters. Take time to listen, to hear, and to receive
the voice of love. It is the voice waiting to guide you, to nurture
you, to bring you to that place of peaceful recognition of the loving
light you are in the world. Without love, you will continue to spin
and fall, to be blind, deaf, and unaware that life is for loving and
loving is for life.*

*Nothing can replace our divine love. There is no way to fill the
void created when you lose sight of the love light the Father and I*

have placed in your soul. To receive our love does not mean you lose all else. It means all else becomes worthwhile. To remember our love does not mean you forget all else. Our love, divine love, transforms that which you know into a brighter picture. To acknowledge our love does mean there is no need to love all. We love you through others. We love you within yourself. We are all love has to offer you when all else seems meaningless. When you allow the Father and I to love you, you find your way back to the fold, back to the eternal circumference of true living, because our love is the real you.

Give up your lofty and misguided notions. Love is simple. It is peace in the morning. The stillness at night. It is the fragrance of flowers. The strength of trees. The love the Father and I have for you is the endless flow of the river which spills into the richness of the ocean. It is the powerful tides of the ocean which then direct the tides of your life. Our love is the ease of breath. The circulation of all systems. It is the vision of unlimited splendor. Love is unspeakable joy, everlasting grace, total fulfillment, and the reflection of all that you really are in your hearts. Love is what the Father and I have given you, asking nothing in return except that you use your life, in the eternal circle of living, to remind others that we are love.

The Valley of Love

☙

☙

11

WE HAVE ALL BEEN IN THE VAL-
LEY OF LOVE AT ONE TIME OR ANOTHER. THIS IS WHEN THE BOTTOM DROPS
out. Your eyes are swollen. Your head is spinning. Your heart is
broken. And your lover is gone! You loved and got nothing in return. The other person took it, dabbed the corners of his or her
mouth with the napkin you had washed, starched, and ironed,
pushed back from the table of your life, belched, and walked
away. You gave your all! In return, you got high blood pressure, a
bent back, corns on your little toe, and a stack of unpaid bills.
You gave all your time, energy, money, and whatever else you
could borrow or beg. In the end, he or she looked you dead in
the eye and asked, "Is this all? Is this it?" You are left walking in a
daze, wondering if this is all you get for giving your love. No! But
this is exactly what you get when you give yourself to what you
think love looks like.

Rachel loved Mike from the moment she saw him. He said he
loved her. To demonstrate his love, he married her, fathered her
children, and allowed her to spend sixteen years of her life loving
him back. One day, he stopped coming home on time. Before
Rachel could figure out what questions to ask him, he stopped
coming home on the weekends. Rachel was still trying to figure
out what she had done to ruin their Sunday afternoons in the

park with the children when Mike announced he was leaving. Rachel decided that her love had not been right enough, or good enough for him. It was all her fault.

The Valley of Love is designed to teach us that the only relationship we can have in this life is the relationship we are having with ourselves. We cannot love anybody more than we love ourselves. We cannot treat anyone any better than we treat ourselves. When you forget you, give up on you, or devalue yourself, anyone coming into your life has a universal responsibility to follow your lead. Oh, but we think we can show our goodness to others. We think if we give them our all, they will give their all in return. It simply does not work that way. Remember, "To thine own self be true!" Many of us do not go into relationships because that is where we want to be, we go into them to get away from where we are! If we are lonely, miserable, confused, broke, desperate, why in the world do we inflict ourselves on other people and expect they will give us true love in return? It's absolutely crazy!

All her life, Robin had believed she was unattractive. When Stanley told her she was beautiful, she immediately fell in love. She stuck it out with him while he was going to school. She supported him while he was getting on his feet. She took care of the children, the house, the bills, while he was getting his business established. He got established all right. He established himself with his best friend's sister. Bought her a house. Took her and her children to Bermuda. When all was said and done, he had the nerve to tell Robin that she didn't fix herself up to be pretty and she was not independent enough for him. Robin is still trying to figure out what she did that was so wrong.

Most of us end up in the Valley of Love through our relationships, but there are other ways to get there. We love our jobs and still get fired. We love our parents and still cannot seem to please them. We love our children and, still, they go astray. In response to what seems like unrequited love, we get angry with other people. We feel bad about ourselves. That is exactly the point! These people and circumstances come into our lives to demonstrate how quickly we will turn on ourselves. It is a lesson. The lesson is, you are standing on a weak foundation. You have not developed yourself to the point of total acceptance and love no matter what is going on outside of you. It is not about your relationship with your supervisor, your mother, your son, or your brother, it is about your relationship with you! No one can make you feel bad about you if you don't already have some hint of self-hatred hidden in the crevices of your mind. Be it love, lust, family ties, whatever you like—in the end, when a loved one is gone, you are left with yourself. The issue is, how do you feel about being alone with you? If you don't know, the universe brings you an experience to demonstrate exactly where you are.

Love, as we think we know it, is an inescapable fact of life which often takes us to a place of darkness, blindness, and dumbness. It is this state of mind we call being in the valley. How dark has the valley been in your life? How dumb have you felt or acted in the name of love? How much have you given? Taken? Rest assured, there are stories stranger than yours. Tales more tragic. There are stories of remarkable comebacks, and memories of the millions who did not make it. There are warnings we can all give, as well as things we dare not repeat. In this valley are those experiences that make us question our reason for living. The Valley of Love is a deep, dark, desperate place that takes the breath from your body, the beat out of your heart, the strength out of your knees, and the color out of your face. Is it a valley or a dungeon? Is it a gift or a trap? Is love the spirit of life or a spirit of darkness on the way to buy a beer who decides to stop by and sit a spell?

For future reference, in the Valley of Love lie those experiences which bring the lessons of all the other valleys into clear view. In the Valley of Love, you can turn to the Valley of Understanding, which will remind you about all the warnings you didn't heed. You went on your merry way, doing what you do, ignoring warnings, turning a ditch into a valley, a valley into a dungeon, a dungeon into a cave. When you met the boy, your spirit said, "Oh no! He is not the one for you!" Did you listen? You thought, "But he's so cute and he really does have a lot of potential!" The Valley of Love teaches us that "potential" means the person is not doing anything now! Do not put your love in a bank that does not have insurance at the time you make the deposit! Live in the moment! Get your good now!

Next, the Valley of Knowledge and Wisdom kicks in, reminding you: You knew it! You knew he wasn't the one. You knew he wasn't enough. You knew he was not being completely honest. You knew it but you kept trying to fix him, change him, see the good in him, because you loved him. You know your mother is overly critical. You have watched her criticize people for years. Still you try to please her, hoping you will be the first one to get a compliment out of her. Get real! The woman loves to criticize people! It is not your issue and you know it. You know these things but you have not been obedient! Nor have you been wise enough to know what to do about what you know. The Valley of Love is now offering you a course in Wisdom 101.

What were you looking for? What was your intent? Did you really think someone could make you feel good about you? Did you really think someone would want to be alone with you when you did not want to be alone with yourself? What was your purpose, my sistah, in squeezing yourself into a place or situation you had no business being in? You missed the lesson, the easy little lessons back in the Valley of Purpose and Intent. Now you are being tested in the Valley of Love and you can't find your notes?

Nothing is working in your life. You hate your job. Your house is a zoo. Your family is falling apart. You don't have two quarters to rub together. You haven't been to the dentist in six years. You don't exercise and you eat fast food. In the midst of this mess, you go out looking for somebody to love! You want to be successful at opening up your own business! Get real! If you can't take care of your basics, why do you think anyone else will take care of your desires? If you cannot put yourself in order, how do you expect to have order in anything you do? Now you're in the Valley of Love. You know your basics were not in order, but you went out for love and attracted your own mess to yourself. Success equals wanting what you have. You did not want the mess in your life. You attracted someone or something you thought could help you clean up the mess. Now that is a mess too! You have been very successful at creating a real big mess because you missed the lesson of the Valley of Success.

The greatest lesson the Valley of Love teaches us is that we always get what we expect. It may not come the way we thought it would come. It will, however, come up as a condition or experience in our lives. Quite often, what we get does not look the way we thought it would look. This is because the universe does not care what we say or do, but obediently fulfills our expectations. Expectations are those secret, often unspoken things buried in our hearts and minds. We often say we want something, but secretly believe it is impossible. The Valley of Love reveals our true expectations. Through the development or lack of development in our relationships it shows us what we truly expect for and from ourselves. We do not stay in bad situations or toxic relationships because we want to, we stay because somewhere deep inside, we do not expect more for ourselves. We sacrifice ourselves believing we cannot do any better. We are dishonest with ourselves and accept less than we want or deserve. Our stuff comes up in a variety of ways at various intervals in our lives, but as usual, we ignore what we see and what we know. In the Valley of Love, our stuff not only comes up, it is crystallized.

You meet this very nice-looking, gentle, attentive brother. You spend a wonderful afternoon together, talking and walking in the park. You exchange numbers and he promises to call. Two days later, you call him. He is busy and promises to call back. A week later, with the memories of your moments together swimming in your mind, you call him again. He's not home. You leave a message. Three days later, you decide he didn't get the message. You call again. He's home. He's not busy. He wants to come over. You say sure. You hang up the telephone and run around the house throwing things in the closet, hiding dirty dishes, fixing the place to look nice and neat when he gets there. He comes, gives you a laundry list of excuses and explanations as to why he hasn't called. You buy it all, hook, line, and sinker. He spends the night. You figure out that heaven must be just like this. He leaves after breakfast, promising to call you later. You don't hear from him for three days and now you are pissed off! You call him a dog and put him in a category with all the other brothers who have followed this pattern. The Valley of Love is the place you must go to realize it is not his pattern or their pattern, but your pattern!

This is a classic case of resistance. You resisted what the brother demonstrated to you. You resisted spirit's voice telling you to let it go, surrender. You resisted your good common sense and everything Momma taught you, because you were afraid. You resisted because you missed the lesson in the Valley of Nonresistance. You brought your die-hard, unproductive patterns into your love life, and now you've been disappointed again. You know why you resisted? You resisted because that dark spirit in the back of your brain told you that this fine young man did not want you. It told you that there was something wrong with you. It told you that you were too fat, too thin, too old, too dark, too short, or that your nose was too flat. That frightened you. It made you think you were not good enough. You were convinced that someone else, someone better than you in some way, would get what you wanted. *They are trying to steal my man!* So you went for it and you got it, the lessons of surrender and cooperation. Next time you meet a man who is too busy to call when he says he will call, cooperate with him. Don't call!

Valley of Love experiences come to remind us it may be time to do away with what is not working, whether it is our issue or the issues of others being imposed on us. When your heart is burdened, you must do away with what is unnecessary. In order to do this, you must get clear. If you missed the lesson in the Valley of Purpose and Intent, a brief trip through the Valley of Love is life's way of providing you with another opportunity to get clear. This is the perfect time for you to examine yourself and the experiences which have brought you to this place. If you have been betrayed, ask yourself: "Who have I betrayed lately?" If you have been rejected, ask yourself: "What have I been doing good for me lately?" If your best, most sincere efforts have been responded to with inconsiderateness or ingratitude, ask yourself: "What is the matter with me that makes me think I do not deserve to have more than this?" The Valley of Love is merely a reflection of what you are thinking about yourself and doing to, with, and for yourself.

I hear those cries of protest. I see you shaking your head in disagreement. "I didn't do anything to make them treat me like that!" "I wasn't looking for this, it found me!" You missed another valuable lesson. People do what they do because of who they are. It has nothing to do with you. People cannot treat you badly unless you stay around to be treated badly. People cannot disappoint you, reject you, or use you unless you interpret their actions that way. And what if you have the unfortunate karma of attracting some ugliness into your life that you truly do not deserve—what should you do? You must find what virtue or principle can be applied to the situation to bring you back to peace. Is it forgiveness? Faith? Trust? Do you need to pray for someone? Do you need to speak your mind? In other words, what is the lesson? Get the lesson and get out of the mess.

One reason we fall into the Valley of Love is that we fall in love with the object of our lesson. The universe will send someone our way to provide us with the opportunity to demonstrate what we have learned. The person may have absolutely no intention of staying with us, but we become so attached, we hang on. When he threatens to go, we cry and lay a guilt trip on him. He is human, just like we are. Human beings do not feel good about hurting other human beings, particularly if they do not realize they are the object of a lesson. They just don't know how to go. We don't know how to let go. So if the food and sex are reasonably bearable, the parties convince themselves they are having a good time. When it becomes unbearable, somebody makes the first move, usually him. Now we are left with the first lesson, compounded by heartache.

A Valley Experience

Relationships made her absolutely crazy. She knew it. She admitted it to herself. She decided to stay in solitude until she was clear about what exactly it was that she wanted and why she was having such a difficult time finding it. She wasn't sad, angry, bitter, or resentful. She was aware that she had some issues to clean up in herself and with herself before she could expect to find a true mate. I think this sister was on the right track. She stayed on the track for three long years.

Three years is not a long time when you are having fun. When you are serious about the business at hand, the time whizzes by. When you are having a good relationship with you, you really don't mind spending three years with you. This sister was having a ball. Since no one was around, she was able to tell herself all of the things she had been afraid to admit to anyone else. She had never had a good nonsexual relationship with a man. She wondered why. Perhaps it was because her stepfather had raped her. Perhaps it was because he had told her that sex was the way you showed a man you loved him. Perhaps it was because she really didn't believe she had anything to offer a man outside of the bed. In the first year, she spent her time and energy seeking answers to these questions. She found the answers and put them into practice.

By the end of the first year, she had several loving, healthy, warm, supportive relationships with men she was not sleeping with. They talked about a variety of subjects. They exchanged ideas and information. They supported one another in whatever they were doing or going through at the time. Sex was never an issue. These men loved her for who she was and what she had to offer. For the first time in her life, she understood what it felt like to be loved, protected, and supported by a man. It was great.

Why then, she wondered, had she spent so many precious years in toxic, abusive, dysfunctional relationships? She figured out it was because that was all she knew. Her parents, her aunts and uncles, and even some of her friends came from homes where violence was the norm. Where visible, demonstrative love was invisible. Where women served and men reaped the benefits. She realized she had a very distorted view of what it meant to be a woman and how that distortion related to the men in her life.

In the second year, she went to work on herself. Workshops, seminars, lectures, books—she devoured anything and everything she could find that would help her understand what was going on inside of her. She saw some pretty ugly things. She had to forgive quite a few people. The men she had met were loving and open enough to discuss much of it with her. The women she had met were showing her a new kind of love and feminine energy. It was not easy. She had to be very patient with herself. Very aware of herself. She had to honor what she was feeling and thinking at all times. She remained open to know, learn, and grow. It did pay off.

With a new insight and attitude, she knew she had to figure out what it was she really wanted in life. What did she want to do? Why did she want to do it? Most of all, what was it that her Creator, the spirit inside of her, wanted of her? The old saying, "When the student is ready, the teacher will appear," proved to be true. A friend of a friend knew someone who wanted someone else to help her do something. It sparked her interest. She followed up on the lead and landed a wonderful position doing exactly what she was good at, creating. She knew she was a creative person, but she had given up her craft in order to work and pay the rent. Now it was like a dream come true. She was doing what she loved, and getting paid to do it. She felt good about herself. She understood many of her experiences on a deeper level. She was flying high. That is when she met the buzzard.

She was minding her own business, creating, studying, loving herself. She was out walking, when he approached and asked her name. She told him, to which he responded, "I am your husband." She looked startled. He explained, "I was praying this morning when spirit said to me, 'You are going to meet your wife today.' Now she smiled—how had he known she was a spiritual student? He responded to her silent question: "When you passed me, I saw your light. I knew who you were. You are my wife." She was caught totally off guard. Never in her life had a man approached her from a spiritual base. This was it. Her prayers were being answered. They were off to the races.

He was nice, very nice. He liked all the things she liked. He could carry on a lively, entertaining conversation. He was interested in her work. He was a hold-the-door, pull-your-chair-out-for-you gentleman. She was beginning to believe that all of her work and study and past suffering was about to pay off. She had found a man, a real man, or at least that's what he appeared to be. They lived two towns apart, but you know what they say, "Love conquers all." The first couple of times they met, she felt really comfortable. It was not until they had been talking for at least a month that the alarms started to go off in her head. She tried to ignore them but she could not. When she lay down at night, the voices were too loud, too clear: "Slow down! Move slow!"

Her pattern had been to jump into relationships with both feet without testing the waters. In the past, it had gotten her into trouble. It had made her crazy! She didn't want to make the same old mistake again, but if the truth be told, she was tiring of sleeping alone. This spiritual stuff was fine, but it does not keep your feet warm in the winter. Besides that, she was so sure of herself, she was so grounded, that she thought she could never be hurt like that again. "But am I ready? Do I really want to give up my freedom, my space and time, to be with another person? Hell yes! What could this guy do to me? He can't do any more than I let him." She was getting really flip, tempting fate. We do that when we think we've got it together. We take foolish chances. Put ourselves in perilous situations. She was contemplating a dance with the devil, but the voices were just too loud: "Slow down!" She decided to be obedient.

It wasn't really anything he did, it was what he said. He was a little pushy. He took for granted that whatever he said, she would agree with. However, she had just spent three years in solitary *refinement*. She was clear and could hear what he did not say as well as what he did say. She detected a little chauvinism. She also detected a possessiveness that made her uneasy. When they did get together again, he made the move that confirmed her suspicions. He became sexually aggressive. At first he wanted a kiss. She declined to partake of his offer. He got a wee bit annoyed and demanded to know why. She told him she was not ready and not sure. He ran the you-are-my-wife line again. She wanted to tell him to shove it. She was not ready to marry anyone. She simply told him she needed more time. He wasn't pleased, but he let it go, for the moment.

When you have been in solitude for a while, and when you begin to like yourself, you become very protective of your space. You have not been moving the lower portion of your body, so the upper portion is in no rush. You really want to take your time, remain clear, and remain focused. When someone tries to push his way into your space, you become suspicious. And rightly so. In subsequent conversations, he began to ask very personal and probing questions. When she asked him why he wanted to know, he would respond with lines like, "Look! Just answer me!" Or, "Why do you have to be so secretive? What do you have to hide?" It was a clue that he was possessive and domineering. Her protectiveness of her privacy was also a clue that she was becoming frightened.

This sister had really learned and grown a lot in three years and still she was confused. Confusion is like a valley. You know what to do but you are not sure if it is the right thing. You know what you want but you are not sure what it will look like. When you are confused, you must breathe—breathing clears the brain. She had bit her tongue once, but now it was time to speak. She told him she was uncomfortable with his approach. He didn't like that and his annoyance frightened her. *Oh God, he's going to leave me!* So what! She told him that she was not interested in a sexual relationship. He asked her why not. She couldn't think of an answer offhand. She told him that she was willing to let him go unless they were able to come to a common understanding of what they were doing and what they wanted. He backed right up! The next few weeks were smooth sailing.

They talked about marriage once or twice but concentrated their efforts on learning about and understanding one another. She was completely honest and open about who she was, where she had been, and what she had done. It was new to her. She had no pretenses. She wore no false faces. She was very clear that the next man in her life would know all about her and love all of her. He would do that before he saw the labels on the sheets. He talked some about himself but seemed more interested in probing her. Fine. She wasn't going to move until she was absolutely comfortable, no matter what he said or didn't say.

In the quiet time she had alone, she began to get excited about the prospects of a new love, a real love. She thought about getting married again. She thought about having someone to cook for, to sleep with, to be there with on those cold winter nights. She thought about all her single girlfriends and how envious they would be. She would run out tomorrow and get some bride magazines. Oh, she was in the drama hot and heavy. Her mind was racing and her heart was fluttering. Since he was available, she focused her energy and attention on him. It made her softer. More open. He immediately recognized the change.

They had known each other for three months. He was about to start a new job and needed to buy a few things. Could she lend him some money. The wisewoman stood up. The martyr knocked her down. Of course, how much did he need. She would drop it in the mail. He would give it back in about two weeks. The wisewoman stood up again. The virgin knocked her down. Give it back whenever you can. We have to support one another. I'm not worried about it. Her vision had become blurred by the dreams in her head. She was confused. She was headed for the big-time valley.

A leopard never changes its spots. It cannot be a lion, tiger, or bear. The leopard may want to convince you it is something else. You may even want to believe it is something else. However, if you are lucky, you will see the true nature of the leopard poking through its fur. The next few conversations they had were a disaster. They were arguing over stupid things. He didn't like the way she said this or that. She didn't like his constant sexual innuendos. He didn't want a woman who wore pants. She made her own money and bought her own clothes. He wanted more children. She did not. It was getting really ugly. She was beginning to feel the stress. Her life and mind had been so peaceful for the past three years that she did not know how to handle this change. She knew all relationships took work. She knew there would be some give-and-take. She knew she was rather set in her ways. All of that she understood. What she did not understand was this growing fear and anxiety in the pit of her stomach. She finally recognized it as the craziness she had experienced in her past relationships. It was back! How? Why? She needed an answer. She prayed.

This wasn't fair. She had been doing her work. She had been obeying the laws. Why would the universe send her someone to disrupt her peace and joy? Who was this man and what did he want? Why had he approached her in such a spiritual way and then demonstrated such unspiritual characteristics? Maybe she was wrong! Maybe none of the work she had done would ever pay off. Maybe there really weren't any good men out there. Or maybe, just maybe, she wasn't good enough to attract a good man. She talked to one of her male friends. He told her to trust the process. She talked to one of her dearest, closest female friends, who told her time would tell. She spoke to herself. There was no answer at all. Every time she spoke to him, there was more stress and tension. When she stopped speaking to him, he demanded to know what was wrong. She told him she was praying for clarity. He laughed and told her that if she went to bed with him, she would get real clear.

If you do not get an answer to your prayer right away, hang up and dial again! Perhaps you have not stated the question appropriately. Perhaps you are not clear what the issues are. Perhaps it is simply not time. In that case, you must wait, stay on hold. However, when you truly want to know, your spirit will guide you as to how to frame the question to elicit an immediate response. She was obedient to spirit's inspiration and restated her prayer: "God, I know you know what is going on between me and this man. Let there be light in my heart and mind so that I will also realize what I already know! Amen." Within moments she reports that she got the following information: *"Wherever God is, there is peace. Wherever God is, there is joy. God's love for you is not aggressive, loud, or boastful. It is gentle and peaceful. It does not make you beg or wonder. You cannot fear losing it or being hurt by it. It settles in your heart with such blessed grace, you have no doubt as to what you are experiencing. If there is no peace, no joy, no grace, it is not God! Will you choose what is presenting it-self or will you choose God?"*

She had known it all the time! He was a fake! A phony trying to impose himself on her life. She would not have it! She would dump this guy immediately. But how? What would she say? How would she do it? Now all of her stuff came to the surface. The voices were warring in her head. She had to fight to stay focused. *But you can't disappoint Daddy.* This is not my daddy! *No, but he is a man just like your daddy. And if you give him up, what will you have? You've been alone for three years. Do you want to stay alone forever?* No. *What if you're wrong? What if you are making a mistake?* Well, then I'll suffer the consequences. *Suppose you never find anyone to love you. You're thirty-six, you know. You have two children. You've already blown it four times.* So what! I am not giving up on me. I am going to hold out until it is right. *Do you want to be right or do you want to get laid?* I want them both! *This guy looks like he would be great in the bed. Face it, girl, you know you want some! Who are you trying to fool?* Finally, as if there were someone else in the room, she screamed at the top of her lungs, "Shut up! Shut the hell up!" That's when the telephone rang.

They had not spoken for three days. She could tell by his voice that he knew he was in trouble. He tried to play it off. "I miss you when you don't call. Do you miss me?" Yes, sometimes. *Girl, you are getting ready to blow a good thing.* "Are you mad at me about something?" No, not really. *Why don't you invite him over for the weekend? Try him out. Then you will know for sure.* "Have you thought anymore about getting married?" No. "Why not?" Well, I told you I am praying for clarity. *Girl, you better stop praying and listen to him! Listen, he sounds so sweet.* "Look, you know I love you and I would never hurt you!" (This isn't fair. A man telling me he loves me. Now he's playing dirty!) *Look, he loves you. He's got a job. He's probably a great lover and you know your son needs a man in his life. What more do you want?*

It was the moment of truth. She did not want to play games with this guy. She knew, and she wanted him to know she knew. She could not figure out how to say it. She took a deep breath, surrendered, and let the words spill forth from her mouth. "Wherever God is, there is peace. There is no peace between us. That tells me that there is no spirit, no God in this relationship, and I don't want it." *Damn! You really blew it this time! You're crazy, you know that? You are really crazy!*

She had hung up and was getting ready for bed when she realized she had not heard his response. She had no idea of what he had said or how they had ended the conversation. She only knew that she was not in a valley. She knew her heart was not broken. She was not in a relationship she did not want to be in. She knew she felt peaceful, almost relieved. She also knew that if she had been wrong, she would remember what he had said. Later on, she wondered why he never called back. But then again, she was so busy being in love with her new love that those thoughts just floated right out of her mind. She had gotten the lesson. She had broken the pattern. She was not wrong. When I asked her if it was all worth it, she said, "Absolutely! If I had not trusted spirit when I did not know what else to do, I would have been in that relationship and would have never found this one."

The Way Out

Even those of us who are spiritually attuned and evolved cannot escape the valley. Be still! Tell the truth! Challenge your fear! Get clear! Integrate! Evolve! You know the process. If you are alive, if you are a woman, you must demonstrate that you have mastered the process and are willing to put it to use. The mere fact that the woman discussed above ever considered letting this man in her life once spirit had warned her demonstrated her willingness to be in the valley. The conflict inside her own head, her own heart, was the real test. In essence she is no different from the rest of us; those who have studied and those who have not, always have the opportunity to choose. If we choose in fear, guilt, or shame, we usually end up in the valley. If we follow the process, or some process that will help us stay clear and focused, we will escape. All too often we jump in and before we know it, we are trapped.

The Valley of Love reminds us that nothing that is divinely ordained for you will hurt you, nor can it ever leave you. If it is for you, you will know it and peace will reside in your heart. If you are worrying about the man you love leaving you or losing him to someone else, you are not in love. You are in fear and your issue is coming to the surface. You have to silence the voice of fear in your mind. You must be willing to confront your issues and face your fears. Don't be in such a hurry to jump into your destiny. Take your time. Move slowly. You cannot lose what is yours!

What are your expectations for yourself? Do you believe you can have the best? You may say you believe it, but the Valley of Love will let you know how willing you are to submit yourself to another person, even when it is detrimental to you. If you are willing to do that, you have missed some lessons and the Valley of Love experience is a makeup test. This is still about your relationship with you. Everyone comes along to show you what that relationship looks like. Are you loving you? Supporting you? Honoring you? Or are you criticizing you? Beating up on you? When you really love and take care of yourself, no one can come into your life and treat you badly. When you are honest with yourself, when you are taking care of yourself, everyone who comes into your life must live up to the standards you have set.

You must be tested and strengthened to determine just how ready you are. The universe will send you a lesson. You could be doing all the right things and still you will be tested. We are usually tested through the Valley of Love because, as women, we allow our emotions to rule us. It is a natural outgrowth of our nature. Hopefully, we will learn through our experiences that there must be a balance, an integration of the mind, heart, and spirit. If you have done all that you know to do, and still, someone or something you love leaves, know it was not yours! The lesson may be trust or faith or surrender. Give up your wild dreams and drama. Give up feeling sorry for yourself. Get busy doing the work of taking care of yourself, healing your wounds, mending your heart. Understand that the universe abhors a void. Your life must be filled with the substance of spirit. Because this is truth and not fact, anything that leaves you is only making room for something better. Be patient! It will come along in the divine time and the divine way.

When I think back to some of the love disasters I have experienced, it makes the following statement even more difficult to make: "Your mate is your mirror." When you look at that person, as well as the other people in your life, they are a reflection of the relationship you are having with yourself. Some of us cannot see the detrimental, unflattering things we do to ourselves. Many of us believe that the problems in our lives, the problems in our relationships, are the fault of the men in our lives. That man in your life is you. He is your mirror image. Just as when you look at your reflection in the mirror, your right side becomes your left side, spirit reflects our complementary image to us in the body of a man. If we are able to recognize what we do then by watching what the other person is doing, we can make the necessary adjustments. If we start blaming, we are lost. We have not learned the lesson. It is not a matter of fixing the other person, it is a matter of getting clear with ourselves. Take care of you! When you bring yourself into order, everyone in your environment will follow suit, or they will leave you. If they leave you, resist the urge to run after them and drag them back.

The Valley of Love is a cleansing process. When you are in this valley, you cry. Crying is the ultimate cleansing and purification process. Each tear of sorrow we shed contains no less than thirty-eight toxic chemicals. These are the toxic emotions and beliefs we hold—the same beliefs which have taken us into the valley. Crying is exactly what you should do when you are in this valley. This should not be just a normal crying session. This must be the kind of deep crying that rattles your soul and loosens all of the waste particles. Here the intensity of your experience calls for crying with an agenda. Get a pencil, a piece of paper, and a big box of tissues and write out an agenda for yourself. Cry away your fear. Cry away your false beliefs and negative emotions. Cry away every negative thought you have ever had about yourself, every unkind word you have ever said to yourself, every foolish thing you have ever done because you thought you were unloved and unlovable.

Forget him! He is not the issue here. Forget the job, the kids, your girlfriends. If anyone calls you while you are crying, do not give them your sob story about a lost love. When they ask why you are crying, tell them, "I am cleansing! I am healing! I am rising up out of the valley!" Cry out for help. Tell the Divine Mother, the angels, and the ancestors to come and nurture you. Ask the universal powers that be to bring you the lesson, lovingly and gently. Rock if you have to. Moan if you want to. If you cry long enough and loud enough, releasing the toxins which have invaded your mind and spirit, things will become very clear. By all means let out a couple of real loud screams. When you feel your entire being engrossed in what you think is the pain of the experience, call out, "Let there be light!" Then settle down and wait for the Mother to come and enlighten you.

You can do this! You can fall into the valley, learn your lesson, and grow. You can do whatever is needed to bring you to the level of self-love and understanding that will be required to break your pattern, resolve your issue. You can feel bad and recover. You can fall down and get up. You can learn your lesson and put the information to use to get on purpose. You can heal. You can know. You can do better if you really want to. There is so much value in this valley. This valley teaches us that the law is on our side. It is up to us to obey. It teaches us that we are not as smart, cute, or "on it," as we may think we are. This valley teaches us humility. Humble yourself to the spirit within and all you desire will come. Most important of all, the Valley of Love teaches us that love is not something out there that we must search for. Love is always present as who and what we are. Our job, our mission, is to recognize ourselves as love and then open ourselves to receive more of it.

MEDITATION WITH THE MOTHER

You may shoot me with your arrows . . . and still,
I rise!

—MAYA ANGELOU

My dear daughters, I have come to you in this way, at this time, to tell you I love you. Remember this, during your dark days, in the midst of your trying times, in moments of confusion and desperation, I love you. Never bow your head or apologize for the gift of life, love, and beauty the Father and I have bestowed upon you. As you have come, as you are, for all that you are becoming, I love you. Remember what a wonderful gift it is to be a woman, to share in creation with the Master. To bring forth life and nurture it at your breasts, no matter how placid or limp the breasts may be. You are the bearers, the bringers, the keepers of life, and for this, your willingness to serve, I love you.

All I ask in return for my love, dear daughters, is that you love yourselves as I love you. Love yourselves enough to say no to the things which diminish you. Love yourselves enough to be strong for you when you need you. Love yourselves enough to know that there is a light within you that is never diminished by what you look like or what you own. Love yourselves, my dearest ones, as though you were loving me. Because you are! When you love and honor yourself, you are loving me in the flesh. You are taking the gift of life, of womanhood, I have bestowed upon you and you are treasuring it. When I am treasured, I glow. I glow in your eyes. I glow in your heart. I glow in your life! When I am truly remembered and treasured, I have no choice but to give back what I receive—the riches of my life!

All the Way Out

12

*D*O YOU REMEMBER ANN? SHE WAS THE FRIEND WE MET IN "THE ANATOMY OF THE VALLEY." ANN IS A CLASSIC example of how the Valley of Love places us in all the valleys at once. These are, without a doubt, the most difficult situations to deal with. When we are like Ann, willing to learn, to grow and let go, we can and do survive. Yes, you can be in more than one valley at a time! The key to this type of experience is to talk yourself through it, which is exactly what Ann did. When your back is up against the wall, don't start swinging! Hopefully, you now realize that swinging from the wall can cause many bumps and bruises. Stop! Breathe! Do not abandon yourself! Be willing to tell the truth and look for the lesson. This is exactly what Ann did and she made it through.

For Ann, it was not the first time she had been in a relationship with a man who had other women. Repeatedly she had promised herself it would never happen again. Each time it did, Ann would accept the stories and promises that it was over. It would be over, for a while. Eventually, however, the same or another woman would surface in the shadows of Ann's relationship. Ann's usual response would be to doubt and question herself. She would ask why. Why can't I satisfy a man? Why can't I keep a man happy? Why do I always attract men who break my heart? Before she could get the appropriate response, she would move into another, more promising relationship.

Remember the process of enlightenment: detach, discern, enlighten yourself, integrate what you know, evolve to a new level of being. Finally, Ann followed the process. She knew she had to get to the core of the issue. Rather than beat up on herself by asking why, Ann decided she didn't care why! She was clear that this was not all her stuff. This guy had lied; it was as simple as that! Ann had been completely open and honest with him. Dishonesty was not her issue, it was his. "What is the lesson here?" In order to get a response to that question, Ann had to detach. Her normal pattern would have been to cry, fall apart, and have a long argument, debate, or discussion with the man which probably would have culminated with lovemaking. Then she would have to call all her friends and tell them what had happened (all except the lovemaking part) to elicit support and sympathy for her plight. Not this time! Ann was willing to be alone, to listen and to hear the quiet voice in her own soul. In order to do so, she unplugged the telephone, ran a nice warm bath, and stepped willingly into the Valley of Light.

For the first time, Ann was ready to figure out what had happened. She did not want drama or hysteria. She made a decision to know and accept what she knew. In order to know and fully understand, she had to step back and witness what had gone on in the relationship. Avoiding the need to be right, the fear of being wrong, and the tendency to blame anyone for anything, Ann took a long, hard, honest look at the relationship.

Honestly, she had seen the signs, but she had wanted so much to trust and believe in this man that she ignored what she had seen. Furthermore, when her own instincts challenged her to challenge him, she copped out. She did not want to pressure him. The truth was, she thought she might lose him. Besides that, he lied. When a person lies to you, you are at a disadvantage until the lie is revealed. At that time you must act.

Ann also did something many of us forget to do. She took the time to celebrate her successes along the way. She had taken some bold new steps in this relationship. She had made sure to let her mate know exactly what she expected from the relationship. Her purpose was a serious, committed, long-term relationship. Her intent was marriage. She had also taken great pains not to give him top priority in her life. He had his business to attend to, she had hers. When he broke his word, failed to honor a commitment, or took Ann's patient nature for granted, she let him know what she was feeling. She did not "hold her tongue" or suffer in silence. She never threatened him or gave him ultimatums, but Ann had let him know what she needed to be comfortable and happy in the relationship. She had, on several occasions, threatened to leave and changed her mind. But that she recognized as fear of failure, of bailing out before the ship goes down. So what is the lesson? Where is the lesson?

In her solitude Ann took the next, most frightening step of all, the step toward enlightenment. She looked at her behavior pattern. What was it that she had done this time that she had done before? What was it that she felt this time that was familiar to her? She knew she had not run to this relationship to get away from another. She also knew she had taken her time, establishing good communication and some degree of trust before there was any intimacy. She had asked and gotten answers to many of the questions she always had. She had also done and continued to do her work on her personal and spiritual growth throughout the relationship. She prayed and the answer came. She had not been obedient to the instructions from her spirit. She had not accepted the "truth" her mate had shown her by his behavior. She had accepted less from him than she wanted and needed. And despite all of her verbal pronouncements to the contrary, somewhere deep in her heart Ann knew she was afraid that *this* man was not *the* man life intended for her.

Ann knew he loved her. Not because he told her, but because she could feel it in her soul. This love was not sexual. It was not a mental construct. When she would think about this man, her soul felt at peace. Also, she was not the least bit worried about *losing* him to another woman. Ann was not willing to say that she did not want him because she did want to build a life with him. She was, however, willing to admit that she accepted him, knowing he was not "quite" on her spiritual level. She thought she could teach him what he needed to know. Ann knew that wasn't her job. She understood you cannot want for someone that which they do not want for themselves. Ann was positive that this was not about value or worth. She knew she deserved the best in life and was willing to receive it. This was about patience, obedience, courage, wisdom, and surrender, all laced with a little touch of fear. Ann realized that she had one foot in the Valley of Understanding, the other in the Valley of Nonresistance, and her heart in the Valley of Fear. Yes, you can be in more than one valley at the same time.

Without blame, shame, or question, Ann knew she would have to integrate this information into her heart and mind. She began with forgiveness. She had to forgive herself for being disobedient, her mate for being dishonest, and *her,* the woman who had revealed the truth in such a harsh manner. She also had to surrender. Ann had to surrender the relationship, all of her dreams and desires for it. She had to surrender the man, realizing she might never see him again. She had to surrender her anger toward the woman, her fear of being alone, and the overwhelming urge to find an answer that was easier to live with. All of this meant Ann would have to trust in the process of life by having faith that the final outcome of this situation would be the best for all concerned.

Did she feel bad? Yes. Did she cry? Yes. What she did not do was shut down her heart and mind to the truth. Did she call him? Yes. Did she accept his apology? Yes. What she did not do was deny what she knew to be true for herself by trying to convince him that he should give up the other woman for her. Ann had plans, so she carried on with them. She accepted the situation as it was and decided it had no place in her life. At the writing of this book, Ann and her male friend were still speaking. They had seen each other twice; once sexually, once not. He had not moved his clothes out of the other woman's apartment and she still worked for him. Ann was waiting for further instructions from her own spirit.

We can do this! Each of us has the power to do whatever it takes to make it through our challenges in life. People neglect to tell us we can do this, and we panic before we get the chance to tell ourselves, "I CAN DO THIS!" The valleys were not designed to hurt us. They are in fact a blessing in disguise! They stop us from making deadly mistakes. They force us to look at ourselves at the most opportune moments, the moments when we really don't know what else to do. I guarantee you that if you follow the road map in and out of the valleys, if you practice and have faith in the learning process of life, you will find yourself growing stronger, clearer, more willing to grow with each valley experience you encounter.

The examples which have been presented here are to help you understand there will always be valleys in our lives! No one is out to get you. No one is picking on you. Above all else, you must know by now that there is absolutely nothing wrong with you. As we live, we must grow. As we grow, the valleys become harder to recognize. They require a bit more work to get out of. Your way out is to know what it is you need to work on—what is your issue? You must also be able to practice whatever virtue you know you are lacking at the time of the experience. The lessons and virtues are your tools. You must also know the life lessons like the back of your hand. Know when you need to exercise your freedom, speak your truth, challenge a fear, or be patient. When you know what you need, you will recognize the valley for what it is, a lesson designed for your own good and growth.

There will be times when you are faced with a situation and you will not be sure it is a valley. When in doubt, pray. Act as if it is a valley. Follow the process and look for the lesson. Don't make the fatal mistake of always trying to identify your valley exactly. If you think you are in one, take the first name that comes to mind and practice the corresponding virtue, look for the corresponding lesson. Anything at all will help if you don't know what to do. Don't let yourself get tripped out about trying to do this process right. Do what your heart tells you to do and trust that you will be fine. If you trust yourself enough to know you can feel bad and recover, you will do just that. If you remember to laugh in the bad times knowing that some good must come out of them, you will see the good. Most of all, you must remember that you have the strength, courage, power, and divine right to change the course of your life to any direction you choose. As my dear friend Patricia Russell-McCloud always asks, If not you, who? If not now, when? YOU CAN DO IT!

You will
seek Me and find Me
when you search for Me with
all your heart.

JEREMIAH 29:13

We invite you to become a member of

Inner Visions Spiritual Life Maintenance Network:

As a member you will be entitled to:

🞄 Receive Bi-Monthly Newsletter

🞄 Attend Empowerment Workshops in Your Community

🞄 Have Access to Spiritual Teachers, Products and Services

🞄 Receive Discounts on Inner Vision Products and Services

🞄 Find Out What Is Going On in the African-American Spiritual Community

🞄 Fellowship and Communicate With Like Minded People

🞄 Fill out and mail in your subscription form today!

Receive a complimentary newsletter . . .

I would like to become a member of the Inner Visions Spiritual Life Maintenance Network:

Name _____

Mailing Address _____

City _____ State _____ Zip _____

Please send a copy of your Newsletter to my friend:

Name _____

Mailing Address _____

City _____ State _____ Zip _____

Send your completed form to:

Inner Visions Spiritual Life Maintenance Network

P.O. Box 3231

Silver Springs, MD 20918-0231